INTERNATIONAL STUDIES

The politics of the Soviet cinema 1917–1929

INTERNATIONAL STUDIES

PUBLISHED FOR THE CENTRE FOR INTERNATIONAL STUDIES, LONDON SCHOOL OF ECONOMICS AND POLITICAL SCIENCE

The Centre for International Studies at the London School of Economics and Political Science was established in 1967 with the aid of a grant from the Ford Foundation. Its aim is to promote research and advanced training on a multi-disciplinary basis in the general field of international studies.

To this end the Centre sponsors research projects and seminars and endeavours to secure the publication of manuscripts arising out of them.

Whilst the Editorial Board accepts responsibility for recommending the inclusion of a volume in the series, the author is alone responsible for the views and opinions expressed.

ALSO IN THIS SERIES

The Origins of Polish Socialism – Lucjan Blit
The Slovak Dilemma – Eugen Steiner
China's Policy in Africa, 1958–1971 – Alaba Ogunsanwo
Hitler's Strategy 1940–1941: The Balkan Clue – Martin van Creveld
The Totalitarian Party: Party and People in Nazi Germany and Soviet Russia – Aryeh L. Unger
Britain and East Asia, 1933–1937 – Ann Trotter
The Pattern of Sino-American Crisis: Political Military Interactions in the 1950s – J. H. Kalicki
Britain and the Origins of the New Europe, 1914–1918 – Kenneth J. Calder
The Marxist Conception of Ideology: A Critical Essay – Martin Seliger
The Middle East in China's Foreign Policy, 1949–1977 – Yitzhak Shichor

THE POLITICS OF THE SOVIET CINEMA 1917-1929

RICHARD TAYLOR

Lecturer in Politics and Russian Studies
University College of Swansea

CAMBRIDGE UNIVERSITY PRESS

Cambridge
London New York Melbourne

Published by the Syndics of the Cambridge University Press
The Pitt Building, Trumpington Street, Cambridge CB2 1RP
Bentley House, 200 Euston Road, London NW1 2DB
32 East 57th Street, New York, NY 10022, USA
296 Beaconsfield Parade, Middle Park, Melbourne 3206, Australia

First published 1979

Printed in Great Britain by
Western Printing Services Ltd, Bristol

Library of Congress Cataloguing in Publication Data

Taylor, Richard, 1946–

The politics of the Soviet cinema, 1917–1929.

(International studies)

A revision of the author's thesis, London School of Economics, 1977.

Bibliography: p.

Includes index.

1. Moving-pictures – Russia – History. 2. Moving-pictures – Political aspects. 3. Moving-pictures in propaganda. 4. Communism and moving-pictures. I. Title.

PN1993.5.R9T3 1979 791.43'0909'31 78–67809

ISBN 0 521 22290 7

CONTENTS

Preface *page* ix
Acknowledgements xi
Note on transliteration xiii
Abbreviations xiv
1 The pre-history of the Soviet cinema 1
2 The Bolsheviks, propaganda and the cinema 26
3 Revolution and Civil War 43
4 The disorganisation of organisation: the early twenties 64
5 The organisation of disorganisation: the later twenties 87
6 The Party takes control 102
7 Theory and film 124
8 Conclusions 152
Notes 158
Bibliography 184
Index 209

For my mother

PREFACE

Much has been written about Soviet literature and its political significance in the years immediately following the October Revolution, but little has been written about the political significance of the cinema. Jay Leyda's seminal history of the Russian and Soviet cinema and Marie Seton's biography of Eisenstein are concerned rather with the artistic development of the medium: they are not conceived as studies of its political organisation or its propaganda function. Yet the cinema is widely regarded as one of the most important media of mass communication and of political influence on public opinion in the twentieth century. Before the advent of radio and television the cinema was undoubtedly the most important such medium. This was the reason for Lenin's oft quoted (at least in Soviet sources) remark that 'Of all the arts... for us the cinema is the most important'. It was my intention, in undertaking this study, to examine the Soviet cinema in the 1920s from the perspective of its political function in the development of the new Soviet society, to investigate the attitude of the Soviet authorities towards the cinema, and the actual uses to which the cinema was put. I have looked at conflicting theories of film and its rôle only in so far as they seemed to me to have a more general political significance. An adequate study of Soviet film theory in the 1920s would be a separate, and very worthwhile, undertaking, for it is an area that still awaits its historian.

I have begun by outlining the history and development of the Russian cinema until 1917 and attempting to assess its position on the eve of the October Revolution. I have looked at the general significance of propaganda in the history of the Russian labour movement and discussed the rôle of the cinema in this context for the Bolsheviks in the early years of Soviet power. The major part of this work traces the development of the institutions for the organisation and control of the cinema from the disruption of the Civil War period, through the first attempt at centralisation in Goskino in 1922, to the establishment of Sovkino in 1925. I have looked at the difficulties encountered and tried to ascertain their causes. I have then examined the priorities within the cinema (newsreel production, the 'cinefication' of the countryside, and the need for educational films for children, peasants and workers) and the increasingly apparent discrepancy between promise and performance. This discrepancy, and the continued preference of Soviet audiences for Mary Pickford and Douglas Fairbanks rather than *Battleship Potemkin*, provoked a prolonged debate in the later 1920s that culminated in the Party Conference of March 1928. It was this conference that led to the final establishment of Party control over the cinema. The advent of this control coincided more or less with the resignation of Lunacharsky as People's Commissar for Enlightenment, the decline of the silent cinema, and the proclamation of the cultural revolution that was to accompany the collectivisation and industrialisation of the Five Year Plan. It thus marks the end of the period of experimentation and spontaneous revolutionary enthusiasm for which the Soviet cinema of the 1920s is justly famous. It marks the point at which Lenin's words have been realised in practice, and thus an appropriate point at which to conclude this study.

My conclusions are based on contemporary printed sources, as archive materials were not available. This is a problem with which students of Soviet history are well acquainted. The pursuit of historical truth is, to coin a phrase, an 'ongoing situation'. But, while all historical conclusions must remain tentative and be offered as part of the continuing process of academic debate, conclusions about Soviet history must remain more tentative than most. Confirmation or refutation can only approach finality when the Soviet authorities feel able to throw open their archives to scholarly research in the way that is taken for granted in liberal democracies. I would naturally hope that such a move would offer confirmation of my conclusions. If not, then clearly my judgement is at fault: *mea culpa, mea maxima culpa.*

Richard Taylor
Department of Politics
University College of Swansea

ACKNOWLEDGEMENTS

I am acutely aware that any piece of work that has taken over eight years to complete must owe a great deal to people – friends and colleagues included – too numerous to mention individually. I hope that those whose names have been omitted will forgive me.

This work began life as a London School of Economics Ph.D. thesis. I am grateful to the staffs of the British Museum Reading Room, the British Library of Political and Economic Science and the British Film Institute in London, the Lenin Library and the Institute for the History of the Arts in Moscow, and the University College of Swansea Library, for their assistance. I should like to thank the British Council and the Ministry for Higher Education of the U.S.S.R. for enabling me to spend two months at Moscow State University under the auspices of the Anglo-Soviet Cultural Agreement, and the Centre for Russian and East European Studies in Swansea for facilitating further research. I should also like to thank Mrs Pat Rees for her patience and good humour in typing the original manuscript.

I owe a very great debt to Dr Nikolay Andreyev, University of Cambridge, for stimulating and encouraging my interest in things Russian, and to Professor Leonard Schapiro, both for giving me the initial opportunity to pursue this research topic and for his subsequent advice, supervision and encouragement. I should also like to thank Professor W. H. Greenleaf for relieving me of some teaching so that this work could be completed.

I am grateful to the various friends who have shared and sustained my conviction that the cinema is a phenomenon worthy of serious study, and particularly to Jeffrey Richards and Tony Rayns: their differing interests in, and views on, the cinema have helped to broaden my own outlook. I should like to thank Antanas Andrijauskas for his generosity in supplying me with relevant books, Alan Bodger for his assistance with obscure points of translation, and George Boyce for his patience in dealing with numerous queries about the minutiae of bibliographical references and for many fruitful discussions. Finally I should like to express my profound personal gratitude to Neil and Deanna Harding, for being there, to Ifor W. Rowlands, who has painstakingly read the manuscript and whose friendship and criticisms have been invaluable, and to my mother and late grandmother, whose faith and encouragement have been generous and unfailing.

The strengths in this work are those that I have drawn from these and other people; the weaknesses are mine and mine alone.

R. T.

NOTE ON TRANSLITERATION

Transliteration from the Cyrillic into the Latin alphabet presents many problems. Perhaps the most important is the difficulty of reconciling the two principal requirements of any system adopted: on the one hand the need to convey to the non-Russian-speaking reader a reasonable approximation of the original Russian pronunciation, and on the other the necessity of rendering for the specialist an accurate representation of the original Russian spelling. There is a further complication in that some Russian names have a non-Russian origin or an accepted English spelling that takes little heed of the two requirements mentioned. I have therefore used two systems of transliteration in this book. In the main text and in the index I have used the generally accepted spellings of proper names (such as Lunacharsky, Trotsky, Eisenstein, Meyerhold, Mayakovsky, Gorky), whereas in the endnotes and in the bibliography I have attempted to cater for more specialist needs. Here the names listed above will be found as: Lunacharskii, Trotskii, Eizenshtein, Meierkhol'd, Mayakovskii, and Gor'kii. I hope that this dual standard will clarify rather than confuse the issue.

ABBREVIATIONS

The following abbreviations, acronyms and other terms have been used in this work and may require clarification.

A.R.K.	Assotsiyatsiya revolyutsionnoi kinematografii – Association of Revolutionary Cinematography.
A.R.R.K.	Assotsiyatsiya rabotnikov revolyutsionnoi kinematografii – Association of Workers of Revolutionary Cinematography.
FEKS	Fabrika ekstsentricheskogo aktëra – Factory of the Eccentric Actor.
Glavkomtrud	Glavnyi komitet truda – Chief Labour Committee.
Glavpolitprosvet	Glavnyi politiko-prosvetitel'nyi komitet – Chief Committee for Political Education.
Glavrepertkom	Glavnyi repertuarnyi komitet – Chief Repertoire Committee.
Gosbank	Gosudarstvennyi bank S.S.S.R. – State Bank of the U.S.S.R.
Gosizdat	Gosudarstvennoe izdatel'stvo – State Publishing House.
Goskino	Gosudarstvennoe kino – State Cinema enterprise, 1922–4.
Goskinprom Gruzii	Gosudarstvennaya kinopromyshlennost' Gruzii – State Cinema Industry of Georgia.
Gosplan	Gosudarstvennyi plan S.S.S.R. – State Plan of the U.S.S.R.
G.T.K.	Gosudarstvennyi tekhnikum kinematografii – State Technical School for Cinematography.
Komsomol	Vesesoyuznyi leninskii kommunisticheskii soyuz molodëzhi – All-Union Leninist Communist League of Youth.

Mezhrabpom	Mezhdunarodnaya rabochaya pomoshch' – International Workers' Aid.
M.Kh.A.T.	Moskovskii khudozhestvennyi akademicheskii teatr – Moscow Arts Theatre.
Narkomfin	Narodnyi komissariat finansov – People's Commissariat for Finance.
Narkomindel	Narodnyi komissariat inostrannykh del – People's Commissariat for Foreign Affairs.
Narkompros	Narodnyi komissariat po prosveshcheniyu – People's Commissariat for Enlightenment.
Narkomvneshtorg	Narodnyi komissariat vneshnei torgovli – People's Commissariat for Foreign Trade.
N.K.V.D.	Narodnyi komissariat vnutrennikh del – People's Commissariat for Internal Affairs.
O.D.S.K.	Obshchestvo druzei sovetskogo kino – Society of Friends of the Soviet Cinema.
O.K.O.	Ob"edinënnoe kinoizdatel'skoe obshchestvo – United Society of Film Producers.
P.O.F.K.O.	Petrogradskii oblastnoi fotokinokomitet – Petrograd Regional Photographic and Cinematographic Committee.
Proletkino	Proletarskoe kino – Proletarian Cinema organisation.
Proletkul't	Proletarskaya kul'tura – Proletarian Culture movement.
Rabkrin	Raboche-krest'yanskaya inspektsiya – Workers' and Peasants' Inspectorate.
R.A.P.P.	Rossiiskaya assotsiyatsiya proletarskikh pisatelei – Russian Association of Proletarian Writers.
R.K.P.(b).	Rossiiskaya kommunisticheskaya partiya (bol'shevikov) – Russian Communist Party (Bolsheviks), 1918–25.
ROSTA	Rossiiskoe telegrafnoe agentstvo – Russian Telegraph Agency.
R.S.F.S.R.	Rossiiskaya sovetskaya federativnaya sotsialisticheskaya respublika – Russian Soviet Federative Socialist Republic, applied to the whole country 1917–24, but to the Russian Republic alone since 1924.
Sevzapkino	Severo-Zapadnoe oblastnoe upravlenie po delam fotografii i kinematografii – North

	Western Directorate for Photographic and Cinematographic Affairs.
Sovkino	Sovetskoe kino – Soviet Cinema enterprise, 1924–30.
Sovnarkom	Sovet narodnykh komissarov – Council of People's Commissars.
Soyuzkino	Soyuznoe kino – Union Cinema enterprise replacing Sovkino in 1930.
S.R.Kh.K.	Soyuz rabotnikov khudozhestvennoi kinematografii – Union of Workers of the Fictional Cinema.
V.A.P.P.	Vsesoyuznaya assotsiyatsiya proletarskikh pisatelei – All-Union Association of Proletarian Writers.
Vesenkha	Vysshii sovet narodnogo khozyaistva – Supreme Council of the National Economy.
V.F.K.O.	Vserossiiskii fotokinematograficheskii otdel Narkomprosa – All-Russian Photographic and Cinematographic Section of Narkompros.
V.G.I.K.	Vsesoyuznyi gosudarstvennyi institut kinematografii – All-Union State Institute of Cinematography.
V.K.P.(b).	Vsesoyuznaya kommunisticheskaya partiya (bol′shevikov) – All-Union Communist Party (Bolsheviks), 1925–52.
V.O.K.S.	Vsesoyuznoe obshchestvo kul′turnykh svyazei s zarubezhnymi stranami – All-Union Society for Cultural Relations with Foreign Countries.
Vserabis	Vserossiiskii soyuz rabotnikov iskusstv – All-Russian Union of Workers in the Arts.
V.Ts.I.K.	Vserossiiskii (Vsesoyuznyi) Tsentral′nyi Ispolnitel′nyi Komitet – All-Russian (All-Union after 1924) Central Executive Committee.
V.Ts.S.P.S.	Vsesoyuznyi Tsentral′nyi Sovet Professional′nykh Soyuzov – All-Union Central Council of Trades Unions.
V.U.F.K.U.	Vseukrainskoe fotokinoupravlenie – All-Ukrainian Photographic and Cinematographic Directorate.

1. THE PRE-HISTORY OF THE SOVIET CINEMA

I consider that the cinema is an empty, totally useless, and even harmful form of entertainment. Only an abnormal person could place this farcical business on a par with art. It is complete rubbish and no importance whatsoever should be attached to such stupidities

Nicholas II, 1913[1]

1895–1916: CHILDHOOD AND ADOLESCENCE

When the October Revolution took place in 1917 the cinema was still less than a quarter of a century old. Man's centuries of effort to create a 'living picture' had culminated in the Lumière brothers' cinematograph machine. Previous inventions had required the spectator to look into a box to observe the image, but the cinematograph involved the projection of a moving image on to a screen; hence, with duplicated film prints, the same spectacle could, at least in theory, be enjoyed simultaneously by an infinite audience throughout the world. The age of the mass media had arrived.

Although the cinema's origins were more recent than those of the other media of the Revolution (posters, newspapers, political meetings, *inter alia*), its development was much more rapid. As a Soviet critic of the 1920s wrote:

Two paths.

One is long and stretches through the centuries: the other is short and triumphant, rushing from one victory to another in a quarter of a century.

The path of the cinematograph and the path of the cinema.

The path of a *technical invention* for the demonstration of living, moving photography.

And the path of a new art, different from all the others – the Art of the Cinema.[2]

The cinematograph was given its first public demonstration by the Lumière brothers in Paris on 28 December 1895[3] and the new invention soon spread to Russia. Louis Lumière firmly believed, and stated, that the cinema was an invention without a future[4]

and he therefore determined that its present should be as lucrative as possible. To this end representatives of his firm were despatched all over Europe and the first public demonstration in Russia was given on 4 May 1896 at the Aquarium variety theatre in St Petersburg, between the second and third acts of an operetta called *Alfred Pasha v Parizhe* (Alfred Pasha in Paris).[5] The cinematograph met with such tremendous success in both St Petersburg and Moscow that it became the principal attraction of Charles Aumont's *café chantant* at the Nizhny Novgorod Fair in the summer of 1896.[6] It was there that Maxim Gorky first saw a moving film, the famous *L'arrivée du train en gare*, which showed a train entering a station, disgorging its load of passengers, and leaving again. Gorky's impressions of this simple film are worth recalling for they indicate the profound initial impact of the film as a medium on new audiences, from Gorky in 1896 to the Soviet peasantry of the early 1920s, and underline the measure of the changes that the cinema underwent in the intervening years. In his newspaper column Gorky wrote:

> Yesterday I was in the kingdom of the shadows.
>
> If only you knew how strange it is to be there. There are no sounds, no colours. There, everything – the earth, the trees, the people, the water, the air – is tinted in the single tone of grey: in a grey sky there are grey rays of sunlight; in grey faces, grey eyes, and the leaves of the trees are grey like ashes. This is not life but the shadow of life, and this is not movement but the soundless shadow of movement.
>
> I must explain, lest I be suspected of symbolism or madness. I was at Aumont's café and saw the Lumières' cinematograph – moving photographs. The impression it produced was so unusual, so original and complex, that I can hardly convey it in all its nuances, but I can attempt to convey its essence. . .
>
> A railway train appears on the screen. It darts like an arrow straight towards you – look out! It seems as if it is about to rush into the darkness in which you are sitting and reduce you to a mangled sack of skin, full of crumpled flesh and shattered bones, and destroy this hall and this building, so full of wine, women, music and vice, and transform it into fragments and into dust.[7]

It was in May 1896 that the first actual filming in Russia also took place – of the Tsar's coronation – and the film proved an added attraction to new audiences, spreading the cinema's influence to the Ukraine and beyond.[8] For the first few years however almost all the films shown in the Russian Empire were imported from France. The Lumière patent monopoly restricted the growth of the new industry and imposed upon it a basically unstable pattern of organisation: the exhibitor had to purchase his equipment and supply of short films in Paris and travel around the country, moving on when his audience potential in one place was exhausted. Once his stock of films had become either worn or outdated, the exhibitor would either sell them for up to 40 per cent of their original price or lease them at around 20 per cent of their original price to poorer exhibitors.[9] With the profits made both in this way and from actual exhibition the exhibitor could return to Paris to purchase new equipment and new film 'sensations'. Some of these 'wandering' (*brodyachie*) or 'mobile cinematographs' (*podvizhnye kinematografy*) were ingenious: although most exhibitors travelled by road, as early as 1906 one used a barge with a mobile generator to show films along the banks of the river Volga.[10] This idea was later used with greater success by the Bolsheviks, but in 1906 it was a failure. Lack of electricity was a constant problem and hampered development, especially in the rural areas. As a result many projectors were powered by oxy-acetylene or ether, which created a considerable fire risk.[11] Félix Mesguich, one of Lumière's photographers sent to Russia to film scenes from Russian life, describes one such fire in Nizhny Novgorod in 1898 but attributes it to arson by ignorant peasants who thought the cinema to be the work of the devil.[12]

Film shows at this time consisted of a series of short 'scenes from life', each between ten and twenty minutes in length and similar to *L'arrivée du train en gare* in content, with the whole programme lasting about an hour; in the cinema's infancy audiences were content to marvel at the sheer technical achievement of a moving picture.[13] The cinema was still regarded as a fairground attraction and not to be taken seriously in its own right, as Viktor Shklovsky remembers:

> Using my advantage as a man of the last century I can recall the appearance of the cinema. It turned up in tiny narrow little theatres, fairground booths and tumbledown shops. The programme rarely changed! Bells, announcing the beginning of a performance, sounded all the time to attract people off the street; often the small room was completely empty. . .
>
> And so something new was born, unaware of its own immortality, or of the fact that it would last for several centuries.[14]

The artistic and technical standards of the cinema's offerings were of course primitive and it laboured for a long time under its origins in the market place – and not only in Russia.[15] Until shortly before the outbreak of the First World War the cinema was above all a form of entertainment for the semi-literate urban proletariat: their sole aim was to escape from the squalor of their everyday lives, an aim reflected in the fact that cinemas, initially known as *teatry zhivoi fotografii* (theatres of living photography) or *elektroteatry* (electro-theatres), became popularly known as *illyuziony* (illusions).[16]

The rapid growth of the touring cinematographs, despite all the obstacles, led to a conviction that permanent theatres (*postoyannye kinoteatry*) would be viable, at least in large centres of population. Two such cinemas were established in Moscow in 1903, after an earlier attempt in 1897 in Novorossiisk had proved a failure.[17] The mushroom growth of these cinemas, with names such as Illyuzion (Illusion), Chary (Marvels), Mirazh (Mirage), Fantaziya (Fantasia) and Mir Chudes (World of Wonders), led to a demand for more, and eventually for longer, films to fill their programmes. This in turn led to a replacement of the old system of outright sale to travelling exhibitors by a more complex system of distribution through exchange and rental.[18] To this end Pathé, which had by now bought the original Lumière patent, opened an office in Moscow in 1904; they were closely followed by Gaumont in 1905.[19] Films were now sold in Moscow rather than in Paris, and thus became available to a wider range of entrepreneurs. This became therefore a period of self-generating expansion, as the profits which accrued from Russian distribution offices later provided domestic capital for the first Russian productions.

By now the films themselves had begun to progress towards adaptations of simplified stage plays on the fiction (*khudozhestvennyi*) side, while the documentary film was boosted by the Russo-Japanese War and the 1905 Revolution; for the first time people were curious to *see* what was happening. Although the government confiscated and destroyed all copies of films of the events of 1905,[20] the events themselves were enough to provoke an interest in newsreels and documentaries, and that interest was skilfully exploited. One French company went as far as fabricating 'Russian' newsreels in Paris for its domestic audiences in order to overcome the problems posed by this tsarist censorship[21] and at the same time satisfy the curiosity of those to whom Russia was quite naturally still a distant, exotic and fascinating land.

At the same time the Russian audience was beginning to tire of mere 'illusions'; this was partly due to repetition, partly to the fact that the cinema was losing its novelty value as a technical achievement, and partly to the changing social composition of the audience which resulted from the establishment of the permanent cinemas in the cities. Interest grew for a time in regional newsreels, which were produced in Kiev, Odessa, Kharkov and Ekaterinoslav,[22] and in Kobtsev's travelogues of Siberia; most of these were produced and distributed by local cinema owners and thus had a ready-made market.[23] However, the high cost of production meant that such regional newsreels did not remain commercially viable for long, and they were soon replaced by those with a more national appeal. From this it was but a small step to the establishment of the first Russian film studio by Drankov in 1907.[24] Pathé realised the attraction of films on Russian themes for Russian audiences, and in 1908 they released *Donskie kazaki* (Don Cossacks). Its success was phenomenal: the film was printed in 219 copies, whereas no other film before the outbreak of the First World War was printed in more than twenty copies.[25] The following announcement, which shows the rationale behind the production, appeared in the press: 'Up till now the Russian public, sitting in Russian theatres, paying Russian money, has not seen subjects from Russian life.'[26] As we have seen, this was an exaggeration, if newsreel and documentary film is taken into account; but it is true that *Donskie kazaki* was the first feature film on a Russian theme. The next step was the first all-Russian production of a feature film on a Russian theme. This was Drankov's *Stenka Razin*, also known as *Ponizovaya volnitsa* (Brigands from the Lower Reaches), again made in 1908.[27]

With the start of domestic film production in Russia the competition between rival firms sharpened considerably. Khanzhonkov opened a special titling laboratory for the adaptation of imported films.[28] In the face of Pathé's powerful competition (until 1910–11 they controlled over 75 per cent of the market)[29] Drankov aimed at sensation: he made one film called *Pozhar v Peterburge* (Fire in Petersburg) and another called *Moskovskii Khitrov rynok* (The Khitrov Market in Moscow), but when this latter film met with no success he retitled it *Byvshie lyudi – Tipy M. Gor'kogo* (Former People – Types from Gorky).[30] He spared no expense to be first with pictures of the Messina earthquake and for similar commercial motives he managed, with the cooperation of the writer's wife, to film Lev Tolstoy. This piece of film, still extant, appeared to many to give the cinema the seal of respectability, while for others it demonstrated anew the possibilities of film:

Yesterday I saw Lev Tolstoy at the cinema. . .The pictures came one after the other – pictures which our children and our great-great-grandchildren will also see and which will perhaps be the only things from our whole epoch to preserve this name. . .In the small room there were about a hundred spectators and it was almost dark, but you could feel quite distinctly that all these people who had gathered there by chance were warmly and deeply excited by this unexpected gift from the cinema. They had seen Tolstoy – and something purifying had passed over them.[31]

A more colourful character from this confused period in the Russian cinema was the Yaroslavl sausage manufacturer, G. Libken, who converted a disused orangery into a studio in order to make films starring his mistress, the singer Maria Petini.[32] It is small wonder that in 1910 Kornei Chukovsky launched a blistering attack on the cinema for the predominance of trivial fantasy and for the degree of commercialisation in the dark depths of its subculture:

And there is the cinema, that collective creation of those very Kaffirs and Hottentots who live 'below'.

In quiet and in silence, as if dumb, these Kaffirs and Hottentots of the nineteenth and twentieth centuries have pottered about, giving birth and dying, having no opportunity to express their Hottentot soul.

They neither painted pictures nor wrote books and it was impossible to distinguish them from the intelligentsia. They only knew how to be born, to potter about and to die, and nothing, absolutely nothing, could prove their [separate] existence.

But suddenly the cinema appeared and immediately, for the first time in history, their ideology found its full spontaneous expression.

You will have noticed in the cinema that as soon as a film is finished, whether a comedy or a tragedy, the image of a cockerel appears on the screen.

This is the trade mark of a production firm which prepares the literature of the cinema.

As distinct from other tales and stories, the tales and stories of the cinema carry a trade mark, like our galoshes, our samovars, cigarettes, matches and knives. These ballads, legends and tales are a market product, an ordinary wholesale commodity sold by the block, and if, to some extent, they reflect our separate personalities or our social milieu, like every commodity on the contemporary market, it is only very rarely and to a very limited extent.[33]

Others were beginning to see the cinema as a rival to, and perhaps ultimately a substitute for, the theatre,[34] and it was the apparent threat to the theatre which finally forced the Russian government to attempt to impose some controls upon the growth of the new industry. In 1908 the government issued a regulation imposing limits on both the number and the location of cinemas:

electric theatres. . .in view of their abnormal development. . .should not be opened at a distance of less than 150 sazhni [approximately 320 metres] from one another (at the same time the same distance must be observed for the establishment of cinemas near *cafés chantants*, theatres and all other places of amusement). . .the total number of electric theatres in the city of Moscow must not exceed seventy-five.[35]

For a time, limits were placed on cinema opening hours, and in January 1909 the government, again to placate the owners of 'legitimate' theatres, banned the musical accompaniment of films.[36] The enemies of the cinema were having a field day or, as is soon transpired, a final fling. One scientist observed, 'The cinema appears without doubt to be harmful to the sight',[37] and others attacked it as 'the breeding ground of fire, blindness and moral perversion'.[38] Their triumph was however short-lived. Both the restriction on opening hours and that on the use of music were lifted by public demand,[39] and the cinema could by this time be seen to have achieved both popularity and respectability:

> If you walk in the evenings along the streets of the capital, of the large provincial towns, local towns, large settlements and villages, on every street you will see the same phenomenon with the solitary, flickering kerosene lights: an entrance illuminated by lamps, and by the entrance a crowd waiting in a queue – the cinema.
>
> If you look in the auditorium the composition of the audience will amaze you. Everyone is there – students and gendarmes, writers and prostitutes, officers and cadets, all kinds of intellectuals, bearded and with pince-nez, and workers, shop assistants, tradesmen, society ladies, fashionable women, officials – in a word, everyone.[40]

Nevertheless in early 1909 there had been a drastic decline in receipts at cinema box-offices; one film journal lamented:

> The cinemas are at present undergoing a crisis; we are witnessing some kind of illness from which we can see no escape. It could end either with the death of the patient or with his complete recovery. This illness started recently but immediately affected the entire organism. Its first, and most ominous, symptom is a fall in takings.[41]

This fall resulted partly from the government's restrictive measures and partly from the industry's failure to keep pace with changing public tastes. Despite this setback it must be remembered that by this time the audience for the cinema already vastly exceeded that for theatres, concerts, circuses and music halls combined.[42] Nevertheless to prevent a further slide in box office receipts film producers were compelled to expand their horizons; animated and trick films were introduced, melodramas, comedies and other fictional films made to cater for the new audience's requirements.[43] In 1909–10 the first so-called 'singing projectors' (*poyushchie apparaty*) appeared. They comprised a projector linked to a phonograph, and were given names like Photochromoscopograph, Grammophysioscopophone, Kinemerephone and Chronomegaphone.[44] But this invention, in all its forms, was short-lived.

The problem of censorship in the pre-Revolutionary cinema appears to have been exaggerated.[45] Although some films were confiscated and destroyed,[46] there was no organised central censorship body. Nor was any self-censorship organisation, such as the British Board of Film Censors set up in 1912,[47] established by the Russian film industry. On the other hand, some films were banned for quite arbitrary reasons: a farce about the dangers of alcohol was suppressed purely because of its title, *Zabastovka Zagulyaikina* (Zagulyaikin's Strike).[48] It must be remembered that the cinema in Russia offered little danger from a political standpoint because production was in the hands of men whose paramount interest was commercial. There was therefore little need, from the government's point of view, for the direct censorship of films from outside the industry. However, at the insistence of Church and Synod, the production of all biblical films was prohibited,[49] and in 1910 the renewed threat of the import of such films brought a stern reminder from the police to local Governors:

> In view of reports reaching the Department of Police that spectacles have recently been permitted showing, by means of living photography, the sacred images of Christ the Saviour, the Holy Mother of God and the Blessed Disciples of Christ, in defiance of the decree of the Holy Synod conveyed in the Ministry of the Interior's Circular No. 2094 of 2 May 1898, the Department of Police, on the orders of the Minister of the Interior, requests Your Excellency to take decisive steps to implement the above-mentioned Synodal decree.[50]

The other obvious area for censorship would appear to have lain in the field of pornography, but there is little evidence to suggest that any steps were taken to control this. Indeed a list of film titles would suggest the opposite.

At the other end of the spectrum initial efforts were already being made to employ the new invention for educational purposes. In December 1908 the Russian Technical Society in Odessa had started a very successful series of educational film programmes for children, using films imported from England in combination with explanatory lectures.[51] There is evidence that similar experiments were carried out on a smaller scale in Moscow and St Petersburg, Samara, Nizhny Novgorod and Ekaterinburg, Kiev, Riga and Smolensk.[52] Indeed, as early as 1902 the First Congress of Teachers of Natural History had called for the 'cinefication' (*kinofikatsiya*) of schools,[53] and in 1911 the First Zemstvo Congress on Education recommended that each district should have its own cinema equipment for educational purposes.[54] In 1912 the First All-Russian Conference on Education stressed the need for educational cinemas to combat the influence of commercial installations.[55] and similar resolutions were passed by other organisations ranging as far afield as the All-Russian Congress of Bee-Keepers![56] All of them were opposed to the elements in the cinema that 'pour poison into the soul of the rising generation' and showed 'pictures of all kinds of cruelties, murders, hunts and duels'.[57] In 1911 the Khanzhonkov firm had founded a Scientific Section and this soon produced a propaganda film on the perils of alcoholism called *Pyanstvo i ego posledstviya* (Drunkenness and its Consequences).[58] A host of similar 'educational' films followed.

The potential of the educational cinema was greatly enhanced when in 1912 Pathé perfected the KOK (COQ – the Pathé symbol) projector, specially designed for use in the Russian countryside. It cost 175 roubles and weighed fourteen kilograms, including a dynamo which produced the necessary power. It used a special film printed on non-inflammable acetate to satisfy the Ministry of the Interior's safety regulations, and could be used virtually anywhere. However, since these special films were manufactured only by Pathé, the net result was to strengthen their monopoly and weaken the educational cinema, particularly when the supply of films dried up completely with the advent of war.[59]

The arguments over the cinema's legitimacy as an art form continued throughout this period and indeed in some quarters they persisted into the 1920s and beyond.[60] Many leading figures in the cultural world viewed the cinema with disdain. In 1913 Mayakovsky wrote:

> Can the cinema be an independent art form? Obviously not. . .Only an artist can extract the images of art from real life and the cinema can only act as a successful or unsuccessful multiplier of his images. . .The cinema and art are phenomena of a different order. . .Art produces refined images, whilst the cinema, like the printer's press for a book, reproduces them and distributes them to the remotest and most distant parts of the world.[61]

But all this time the cinema was forging ahead. Recovering from the crisis of 1909, Russian domestic production expanded so rapidly that by 1913 the country was suffering from the first of many so-called 'screenplay crises' – too many film-makers chasing too few ideas. The number of film-producing firms had multiplied and one of the newcomers, Stern and Co., even attempted to resolve the crisis by offering prizes in a competition.[62]

Nevertheless, despite the vast and rapid expansion in home production, on the eve of the First World War about 90 per cent of the films shown in Russian cinemas had been imported, partly because the imported product was still more attractive to the audience than the home product, but mainly because imported films were almost always cheaper to hire.[63] Russian films were usually produced in only ten or twelve copies and so could not compete in price with mass-produced foreign films, which sold for only a few kopecks more than the unexposed negative film stock. The cinema, in the view of contemporary writers, had developed from a mere amusement into something approaching an art form: both documentary and fiction films had broadened their horizons. The home industry had grown rapidly, although production and distribution were still largely in the hands of Pathé, Khanzhonkov, and Thiemann and Reinhardt, and the overwhelming majority of films shown were still imported.[64] Finally, the potential of the cinema in the field of science and education, and by implication also in agitation and propaganda, had begun to be realised in theory, although very little had been achieved in practice. The Tsar himself had tended to regard the cinema as something of an amusing toy and since 1896 he had in this light allowed the imperial family to be filmed on frequent occasions.[65] From 1907 onwards some of these films had been seen in cinemas under the series title *Tsarskaya khronika* (The Tsar's Chronicle).[66] In the spring of 1914 the cinema received a greater accolade: Khanzhonkov was awarded the Order of Stanislav, Second Class, 'for his exceptionally useful activity in the field of our national cinema', and lesser awards were granted to other film workers.[67] It was however the First World War that finally put the Russian cinema on its feet; the war brought drastic changes in the film industry as in almost all other sectors of Russian life.

First and foremost, the outbreak of war affected the structure of the home market. It became increasingly difficult, and eventually impossible, to import films and film stock from France. The Pathé monopoly had relied entirely on imports, as the firm had always considered the construction of a production studio in Russia to be too risky an enterprise. In the changed wartime conditions the monopoly therefore collapsed. This hiatus in supply did not come about because the Russian government had imposed import controls or a monopoly of foreign trade; it had done neither. The difficulty lay above all in transportation across the war-torn European continent, and secondly in a gradual cessation of production in France and Italy.[68] In addition, the British government forbade the export of films and equipment beyond the frontiers of the British Empire, while the Swedish authorities included film in an order prohibiting trade in strategic materials.[69] Since Russia produced no film or equipment of her own, the resulting shortages led to a sevenfold rise in the price of film stock in five years.[70] Under more normal circumstances Germany would have provided an alternative source of supplies and the shortage might well explain the initial reluctance of the Russian government to take decisive measures to curb imports from what was now an enemy country. On the outbreak of war the authorities confined themselves to imposing a heavy tax on films imported from Germany, but in 1915, as a result of public pressure, such films were banned completely. It is interesting to note that, in deference to Russian national feeling, Persky, an entrepreneur who continued to import from Germany until the ban, advertised his films as being of Danish origin. For example, Paul Wegener's famous film of the Prague ghetto, *Der Golem*, made in 1914, was advertised as a 'legend of the Vilna ghetto' because Prague now lay in enemy territory.[71] Anti-German feeling ran so high that the firm of Thiemann and Reinhardt was ruined. In the autumn of 1914 their Moscow office was burned down and ransacked and Thiemann himself was sent into internal exile in Ufa. His wife attempted to maintain the business with ever diminishing success until it finally closed down in 1916.[72] Thus, two of the principal firms in the Russian film industry were undermined by the War, while the third, Khanzhonkov, continued in business but without any significant expansion in its activities. In their stead new firms like Ermolev, originally a subsidiary of Pathé, Kharitonov, and Vengerov and Gardin came to the fore.

Between 1913 and 1916 the number of Russian film-producing firms rose from eighteen to forty-seven,[73] while film production increased as follows:

1913 129 films, mostly short,
1914 232 films, mostly full-length features,
1915 370 films, mostly full-length features,
1916 499 films, mostly full-length features.[74]

By 1916 foreign films accounted for only 20 per cent of the new films shown in Russian cinemas.[75] Despite the loss of territory and the evacuation from Poland, the number of cinemas in the Russian Empire continued to grow. Estimates of the number in operation in 1916 vary from two thousand[76] to four thousand[77] but the real figure almost certainly lies somewhere in between.[78] Thus the growth in demand for Russian film production did not result entirely from the curtailment of imports. Added impetus was given by the accelerated movement of population from the countryside to the towns; this process was in turn stimulated by the increased labour force in the armaments factories, the influx of large numbers of refugees from the occupied, evacuated and threatened areas, and the stationing of soldiers, both on billet and in transit, in the cities. The sufferings of war and the social and psychological conflicts engendered by urban overcrowding led to a desire for escapism, while monetary instability, the prohibition of vodka, and aspects of the urbanisation process itself all helped to channel this desire into the cinema. The growth figures already cited to some extent underestimate the true growth of the cinema during these years because between 1913 and 1916 cinemas began to show their film programmes five or six times a day instead of two or three.[79]

In short the First World War finally established the Russian cinema. Almost unlimited demand and the absence of foreign competition meant that Russian producers were able to expand, hindered only by the limitations imposed by material shortages. As a contemporary wrote:

> But then the War came – the tragic, cruel and great decider of the fate of peoples – and immediately all the foundations were overthrown, all human relationships were rearranged.
>
> Everything that until then had seemed improbable, impossible and inconceivable, appeared both probable, possible and conceivable.
>
> From the beginning of the War the borders were closed and Russia left without foreign films. At first Russian cinematographers went to pieces.
>
> – The end! No films; the cinemas will have to close.
>
> But this only lasted for a very short time. And then we began to use our own means.
>
> And what happened?
>
> Such a short time has passed, yet look where the Russian cinema has got to now.
>
> Look at a Russian film and you will wonder: when did they attain such perfection? Where did they acquire such taste, such feeling, technique and artistry?
>
> And the explanation is quite simple: they did not acquire them from anywhere – they were already there.
>
> They were their own, native and Russian.[80]

The war also brought in its wake the first use of the film for the purposes of political propaganda. In March 1914 the Skobelev Committee, which had originally been established as a charitable institution to assist veterans of the Russo-Japanese War, set up a Military Film Section.[81] On the outbreak of war it was given the exclusive right to film at the front,[82] but the press complained about the quality and the sparsity of its films and its monopoly was eventually revoked. Private producers, on the other hand, were quick to take advantage of the war. In September 1914 the

Filmoteka firm released *Svyashchennaya voina* (Holy War), allegedly a First World War newsreel, but in fact a collection of pre-war newsreels with new, falsified subtitles.[83] A contemporary columnist observed of another such film: 'An excerpt from a Pathé newsreel of 1911 showing a forest fire near San Francisco was described here as *Fire in Argonnes.* We come across such deceptions every day.'[84] Other films were released with such luridly patriotic titles as *Slava nam, smert' vragam* (Glory to Us, Death to Our Enemies), *Doloi nemetskoe igo!* (Down with the German Yoke!) and *Za chest', slavu i schast'e slav'yanstva* (For the Honour, Glory and Happiness of Slavdom), but the majority of films produced still reflected the tendency towards escapism.

The shortage of materials tended to favour the larger producers, as they were in a stronger position to obtain the available supplies, and so the smaller producers often turned to pornography to make money. There was little control over this type of film[85] but it created a hostile reaction in the press, which began to demand that the government should intervene to ensure a healthier state of affairs. In 1914 a leading reactionary deputy to the Duma, Purishkevich, demanded the introduction of censorship and the establishment of a government film monopoly after he had been lampooned in a film. He proposed:

> the prevention of the spread of cinemas into the villages without film censorship through the establishment of a legally based special mixed commission with representatives of the Ministries of People's Education, Internal Affairs, War, the Navy and the Holy Synod. . .and the introduction of a government monopoly of cinemas.[86]

In the following year these ideas were developed in a closely argued pamphlet entitled *Kinematograf kak pravitel'stvennaya regaliya* (The cinematograph as government regalia), written and published by V. M. Dementev. Using a mixture of quasi-military arguments he proposed the establishment of a government cinema monopoly, on the lines of the spirit monopoly, which could be used as a weapon for education and propaganda. To this end he even suggested that a cinema should henceforth be known as a *tsarskaya palatka* (royal pavilion).[87] Newspapers like *Novoe vremya* were also attacking the cinema for its immorality and lack of patriotism, and the Holy Synod busied itself with a plan to close down all but educational cinemas.[88]

In 1916 the Minister of the Interior, Protopopov, proposed that a government commission should be established to investigate the possibility of a government film monopoly 'in order to utilise it for educational and moral ends'.[89] When the suggestion was rejected by Bark, the Minister of Finance, Protopopov established his own commission, and at the end of 1916 it produced a report.[90] A contemporary newspaper noted:

In the plan, which has been transmitted through the relevant government organs into the highest spheres, it is pointed out that the cinema, if it were established on a broader basis, could be used by the government to instil healthy political and social opinions among the populace. It could lessen the sharpened conflict between different classes and bring patriotic and monarchist ideas to the people. Government cinemas should be aimed largely at the lower classes of the nation.[91]

The Minister of Education, Ignatev, supported by Khanzhonkov (who, through an arrangement with the Ministry, produced most Russian educational films), proposed the creation of a Special Cinematographic Committee, including a film archive, but in December 1916 the Minister lost his job.[92] Both projects were in any case swept away by the events of 1917. Nevertheless one project did bear fruit: on 15 September 1916 a film school was opened by Vengerov and Gardin. This served as a foundation for the post-Revolutionary school, although it was largely ineffective before then.[93]

By 1917 the Russian cinema was already the principal form of entertainment for the urban masses of the population although, for both technical and economic reasons, it had as yet penetrated little into the countryside. The cinema was no longer a mere fairground attraction and in this sense, although still scorned by some intellectuals, particularly in theatrical circles,[94] it had achieved a certain respectability. At least people now took it seriously. Mayakovsky had now modified his attitude,[95] and in 1915 Meyerhold had made a film of Oscar Wilde's *The Portrait of Dorian Grey* (*Portret Doriana Greya*).[96] As far back as 1913 in his 'Pis'mo o teatre' (Letter on the theatre) Leonid Andreev had attacked his fellow intellectuals for ignoring the cinema as a passing form of amusement[97] and had predicted the future possibilities of the new medium:

The miraculous Kinemo!. . .If the highest and most sacred aim of art is to create contact between people and their separate souls, then an enormous unimaginable socio-psychological role is destined to be played by this artistic Apache of the present!. . .Having no language, being equally comprehensible to the savages of St Petersburg and those of Calcutta, it truly becomes the genius of international contact, brings nearer the ends of the earth and the spheres of the soul, and gathers into a single stream the whole of quivering humanity.[98]

By 1917 however these possibilities had not yet been realised. The content of films reflected the escapist desires of the audience (foreign serials like *Cabiria, Maciste* and *Fantômas* were popular) and even the number of patriotic war films had declined.[99] Despite protestations of intent very little had been done in the field of education, agitation and propaganda, and attempts at government control had met with little success. The solid foundations of a domestic film-producing industry had been laid, but it was still dependent on foreign capital investment and, even more significantly, on the importation of foreign film stock and projection equipment. This latter dependence was to prove disastrous in the coming years, and the cracks in the façade were already beginning to show by 1916. Nevertheless at the end of 1916 the Russian cinema showed all the outward signs of a flourishing economic concern. As a political force it was virtually non-existent, but intellectually and artistically it was beginning to gain recognition. As Kozintsev has observed, 'The monster had begun to transform itself into an art form'.[100]

1917: COMING OF AGE?

For the Russian cinema the year 1917 did not in itself bring any cataclysmic changes. Neither the February nor the October Revolution acted as a new broom sweeping clean, although the disappearance of the *ancien régime* was eventually to pave the way for the new Soviet cinema. However this process did not begin in earnest until the Civil War was already raging, and it was not completed for at least another decade. Instead the year 1917 marked the consolidation and development of existing trends, a further deterioration in the economic situation being accompanied by a decline into factional quarrels, a fall in production and, eventually, the first direct hints of forthcoming nationalisation.

By 1917 the cinema was already the principal form of entertainment for the urban masses and the industry was gathering strength all the time. By then there were over four thousand cinemas with annual takings of twenty million roubles,[101] an increase of one third over the previous year, but the situation was somewhat analogous to the South Sea Bubble and the fragmentation that had afflicted the organisation of film production since 1914 spread to the organisation of the labour force. We have seen that, of the three major pre-war producers, Pathé and Thiemann had collapsed because of the curtailment of imports, although

Thiemann had also been seriously affected by the arrest of the owner in the wave of popular sentiment against the Germans. By the time of his return from exile in the summer of 1917 it was already too late for him to save his firm. His two leading directors, Vladimir Gardin and Yakov Protazanov, had both departed to rival firms. Only Khanzhonkov maintained any significant degree of his former economic strength; in 1917 he managed to build and open a new studio in Yalta, where he hoped to continue production until the situation in Moscow had stabilised.[102] However Khanzhonkov's leading actor, Ivan Mosjoukine, had gone to work for the Ermolev studio, while the director, Pyotr Chardynin, and the actress, Vera Kholodnaya,[103] had been employed by the relative newcomer Kharitonov, whose studios were now the most important source of film production in Russia. The death of another director, Evgeny Bauer, in June 1917 was a further blow to Khanzhonkov. The situation was aggravated by the shortage of film stock and the lack of suitable subject matter for film scenarios. In an attempt to solve the latter difficulty Khanzhonkov resorted to the by now familiar device of offering prizes in a screenplay competition,[104] but for his production organisation this solution came too late. Both the Khanzhonkov and Pathé organisations did however have one considerable advantage over both Thiemann and the newcomers in that, although their own production had stagnated, they owned significant distribution networks which were essential to the financial viability of their rivals' product. Hence Khanzhonkov was saved from bankruptcy by the profits accruing from the distribution of the imported Italian spectacular serial *Maciste*.[105] The Pathé distribution network was likewise used to convey the products of the Ermolev studios. The distribution of films on a national basis was in the hands of five companies: Pathé, Khanzhonkov, Khapsaev, Transatlantic and Biofilm. The last two distributed only imported films. In addition, there were several absolute local monopolies in certain areas, for example, that of Khapsaev in Rostov-on-Don.[106]

It was partly in order to rationalise the organisational structure of the industry and partly to strengthen it against possible government interference that the cinema entrepreneurs expressed interest in the formation of a union, preferably a single union embracing all those active in the cinema, whether on the artistic, technical, service or managerial side. After the first attempt to create such a union had failed, the journal *Proektor*, which on the whole represented the entrepreneurial point of view, wrote in

June 1917 in an editorial entitled 'Cinema workers, organise yourselves!' ('Kinodeyateli, organizuites'!)

At this difficult moment of economic and political ruin, when it is hard to busy oneself with one's own affairs, every one of us, remaining at his post and performing his duty, should at the same time be helping his country to organise.

Every social group, every professional element should be organised at this terrible moment in Russian history.

We cinematographers must likewise organise ourselves to fulfil our duty as citizens.

Great and fertile Russia has until now suffered from a lack of order. But she will find it when separate groups, united by their common interests, are organised. Every battle is won by the force that is best organised.[107]

It is improbable that at this stage the last sentence was intended as a sinister warning; nonetheless it would have been an appropriate one.

Throughout the manoeuvrings to organise the cinema's labour force in the course of 1917 there remained in existence three principal groupings of those involved. Given the state of the cinema at the time it would have been reasonable to expect a division along what could be termed defensive lines reflecting the organisation of the industry into production, distribution and exhibition. Instead the labour force split into a different pattern of defence, one which defended self-interest rather than protecting the industry as a whole against external pressures; entrepreneurs, technical staff and those on the creative side all formed separate groups.

The organisational impetus came from the entrepreneurs, whose financial stake in the industry was greatest and most influential; their aim was to create a single all-embracing union which would best protect their investment and their interests. On 3 March the Moscow Society of Cinema–Theatre Owners (Moskovskoe Obshchestvo Kinoteatrovladel'tsev) called a meeting at the Ars cinema in Moscow, which was owned by its chairman, P. Antik, to discuss the project. A provisional committee of six people, including Antik, was elected; four of its members represented entrepreneurial interests. Three days later an expanded meeting discussed the feasibility of creating a single union covering everyone in the industry. Antik and his provisional committee resigned to make way for a more representative body, now that more of the interested parties had been gathered together. However the Provisional Government had just placed all Moscow's cinemas and theatres under the control of the All-Russian Theatre Society (Vserossiiskoe teatral'noe obshchestvo) which was known to be hostile to the interests of the cinema vis-à-vis the theatre. Although the establishment by the Moscow City Soviet of its own Cinema Section on 15 March created something of a counterweight, it did little to assuage fears of outside interference in the affairs of the industry. The motivation for active participation was therefore greatest amongst those who had most to lose, and the committee that was chosen to head the new organisation was heavily weighted in favour of the entrepreneurial side: of the twenty-two members, eleven were involved in management of some description, one published the journal *Cine-Fono*, and only three represented the technical staff.[108] The new union adopted the high-sounding title of the Union of Patriotic Cinematography (Soyuz otechestvennoi kinematografii).

Nevertheless the meeting did make suitably revolutionary gestures. It passed a resolution attacking counter-revolutionary activity and another, put forward by the director, I. Perestiani, condemning the crude profit motive and emphasising the educational functions of the cinema. Given the composition of the gathering, the tone of the resolution was remarkably strong:

> In view of the immense power of the screen, for which such a wide field of activity as a truly democratic theatre amongst the popular masses has been opened, we consider that the people, having opened the doors to knowledge and enlightenment for themselves, should see in the screen that cultural force which will convey these things to all four corners of our great fatherland. In addition, it is with great regret that the conference declares that people for whom the cinema is exclusively a source of profit and who have no scruples about their methods,[109] are striving to use the liberation of artistic expression for the demonstration of pornographic themes relating to the old order, the very titles of which are obscene, and are cynically connecting them with the sacred cause of the Russian Revolution.[110]

The meeting also resolved to pool all existing film of the February Revolution, distribute it and donate the profits towards a fund for political prisoners released from tsarist gaols. Little film of the Revolutionary events had actually been shot,[111] but what there was was edited into the film *Velikie dni rossiiskoi revolyutsii ot 28 fevralya po 4 marta 1917 goda* (The Great Days of the Russian Revolution from 28 February to 4 March 1917). The negative of this film was handed over to the Moscow City Soviet, acting on behalf of the Provisional Government, on 17 March.[112] This effort by the Union of Patriotic Cinematography eventually raised the sum of forty thousand roubles. However, for the future development of the cinema these events were of no more than passing significance. In the long term the most important consequence of the conference lay in its failure to establish a single, comprehensive and credible cinema union. What unity had been achieved existed only on paper, and the failure to achieve anything more substantial opened the way to the development of narrower professional unions representing different factional interests rather than the interests of the cinema as a whole. These divisions in turn facilitated the eventual subordination of the cinema to new organisations outside the existing framework of the industry.

The first, and most important, of these professional cinema unions had already emerged on the same day as the putative umbrella organisation, 6 March 1917. It was named the Union of Workers of the Fictional Cinema (Soyuz rabotnikov khudozhestvennoi kinematografii) and known as S.R.Kh.K. for short. The Union was intended to represent the interests of the creative workers in the film industry.[113] Its first heads were M. Bonch-Tomashevsky, who favoured the concept of a single union and was therefore suspected by the Bolsheviks of acting as a tool of the entrepreneurs,[114] and N. Turkin, then editor of the journal *Vestnik kinematografii*. The Union had its headquarters in the Tenth Muse café in Kamergersky Street and was also widely known by that name. Soviet sources often suggest that the café became a notoriously disreputable centre of gambling and drug-taking,[115] but this is not borne out by less obviously politically motivated sources. The accusation, ironically enough, would seem to have originated with Bonch-Tomashevsky himself. It is symptomatic of the fluidity and confusion of the situation that one of the first leaders of S.R.Kh.K. should, after only a few months, be writing in *Vestnik kinematografii*, owned by the other leader, in the following deprecating terms:

> It is true that the café is flourishing. It is bustling with life the whole day long. It is full of people who aren't even involved in the cinema and its budget grows from day to day...But the club? What is there in this club, this place for recreation?...Violence is rampant, lotto flourishes and... deserters are rounded up there.[116]

Bonch-Tomashevsky had disagreed with his colleagues on the committee of S.R.Kh.K. and this is a probable explanation for his allegations. In fact, while gambling was permitted in the club, the profits were used to subsidise the Union's other activities.[117]

The third group of cinema workers – the *sluzhashchie* or technical and service employees – were also the least influential both politically and economically. They might have gained a great deal from the creation of a single union able to protect the cinema industry effectively against outside interference, yet, while their own unions remained divided and relatively powerless, their leaders never espoused the cause of unification. This was in direct contrast to the leaders of both the Union of Patriotic Cinematography and the Union of Workers of the Fictional Cinema. Consequently the technical and service employees remained divided into organisations such as the Union of Cinema Mechanics (Soyuz kinomekhanikov) and the Union of Piano Accompanists (Soyuz pianistov-illyustratorov), the Union of Employees in Cinema Theatres, Offices and Studios (Soyuz sluzhashchikh v kinoteatrakh, kontorokh i atel′e) and the Union of Workers in Cinema Enterprises (Soyuz rabochikh kinematograficheskikh predpriyatii). There was a single attempt to establish a closer relationship with S.R.Kh.K. but the impetus for this came from the latter association.

Following the failure of the Union of Patriotic Cinematography to realise anything more than a unification on paper, it reverted to being a professional rather than an industrial union. At the meeting on 6 March Antik had perturbed his fellow delegates by demanding openly that their Union should represent the employers' side and abandon all pretence at representing the interests of either the creative or technical employees.[118] Although he was defeated at that meeting, it was his view that eventually prevailed. In July the constitution of the new employers' organisation, the United Society of Film Producers (Ob″edinënnoe kinoizdatel′skoe obshchestvo), was published.[119] The journal *Proektor* described O.K.O., as the organisation was known, in the following terms:

> O.K.O. is the organisation of film producers (manufacturers and distributors). Members of O.K.O. may be the owners of studios, laboratories, rental offices, representatives of Russian or foreign film companies, and also the managing directors of sections of the stated enterprises and publishers of the film press.
>
> The aim of O.K.O. is to create normal conditions for the development of artistic and general professional interests of its members. That is, O.K.O. is not a narrowly professional union.[120]

The foundation of O.K.O. did of course clarify the situation in that its members thus declared themselves as a specific interest group, but the effectiveness of the Society was somewhat hindered by the exodus of the leading producers to areas where they hoped to make their films, and perhaps their fortunes, in relative peace and quiet. The O.K.O. Presidium, which had been elected on 6 May, reflected this problem. Khanzhonkov, the producer, had been elected Chairman while his rival, Ermolev, had been chosen as his Deputy Chairman. Both of them soon left for the south, leaving the treasurer, S. Luré, editor of *Cine-Fono*, to run the organisation in their absence.[121] How O.K.O. would have fared had they remained in Moscow is of course impossible to say with any accuracy, but the departure of two such powerful figures at such a crucial moment can only have weakened the Society. Nevertheless O.K.O. still managed to exert some influence in the protection of its own interests and those of the cinema as a whole, although the two were not always synonymous. Against this background S.R.Kh.K. felt a need to strengthen its own position vis-à-vis the new employers' organisation. The motives of S.R.Kh.K. are nicely revealed in the memoirs of a contemporary:

> The size of the gulf between us is demonstrated by the following incident: when I went to a conference at the Tenth Muse with two members of our administration – the mechanic Gromov and Seleznev, a studio worker – the porters, seeing the remarkably undistinguished clothing of my comrades, refused to let them in.
>
> I entered alone, told Nikandr Turkin and demanded that my comrades should be admitted. Then Turkin went out to the porter's lodge and uttered the historic phrase, 'Let these people in. We need them.'[122]

The cinema then was in a state of confusion, although it would be misleading to attribute this confusion solely or directly to the political situation of the country. If anything it would seem that the cinema was too preoccupied with the problems of supply and internal organisation to concern itself with the possible long-term effects of the February Revolution, while the government was concerned with the immediate problems of its own survival.

The government's attitude to the cinema was characterised above all by a certain bewilderment. It is true that censorship was officially abolished on 10 May but this measure was probably aimed as much at relieving the government of an unnecessary administrative burden as at signifying any positive policy of cultural enlightenment.[123] The Provisional Government's treatment of the Skobelev Committee is more instructive. The Committee had been deprived of its exclusive right to film at the front in December 1916, a right that it had not fully exercised for reasons of profitability, yet it remained the only cinema organisation directly controlled by the government. On 30 March the government established a Commission of Enquiry into the Skobelev Committee and on 3 April the Committee was placed under the jurisdiction of the Ministry of Education. In June it produced the first of thirteen government newsreels which, under the series title

Svobodnaya Rossiya (Free Russia), became by force of circumstances little more than propaganda vehicles for the Provisional Government. At the end of the same month the Committee was transferred to the Ministry of Welfare and on 13 August it was finally passed back to the Ministry of War.[124] It is difficult to judge whether all these changes represent significant shifts in policy or whether they reflect nothing more than administrative convenience, although it is perhaps even more difficult to reject the latter interpretation.

The government did however encounter the hostility and active opposition of the cinema lobby in its efforts to cope with the energy crisis that developed during and after the winter of 1916–17. On 5 May 1917 restrictions on the use of electricity were announced.[125] The conflict over the closure of cinemas which resulted from these and similar restrictions was to become a leitmotiv in the film world during the Civil War, and this conflict was further embittered by the feeling that the practice of the Revolution had betrayed the hopes engendered by the overthrow of the tsarist autocracy. If, apart from its abolition of censorship, the government failed to live up to these hopes, the cinema could hardly claim to have lived up to them either. Caught unawares by the Revolution (or overcome by their enthusiasm for it?) Russian cameramen did not begin to film the revolutionary events until 1 March and their material was later edited into the film mentioned previously.[126] There is thus no filmed record for the historian of the most significant part of the February Revolution, the abdication of Nicholas II. In addition, the abolition of censorship was greeted, not by an upsurge of revolutionary enthusiasm in the shape of previously suppressed socio-political criticism on the screen, but by a flood of semi-pornographic films, often linked in their salacious content with the fallen dynasty of the Romanovs.[127] Titles in the following vein abounded: 'Dark Forces – Gregory Rasputin and His Associates' (*Tëmnye sily – Grigorii Rasputin i ego spodvizhniki*), 'In the Tenacious Clutches of the Double-Headed Eagle' (*V tsepkikh lapkakh dvuglavogo orla*) and 'The Trading House of Romanov, Sukhomlinov, Myasoedov, Protopopov and Co.' (*Torgovyi dom Romanov, Sukhomlinov, Myasoedov, Protopopov i kompaniya*).[128] Admittedly the shortage of basic materials hampered production and made more ambitious projects impossible but nevertheless the profit motive, or rather the quick profit motive, does seem to have reigned supreme. After July 1917 the first-run luxury cinemas of Moscow and Petrograd settled down to the profitable exhibition of popular foreign films such as the French *Judex.*

The Revolution and the establishment of unions had encouraged film workers to strike for their demands,[129] and the disruption that this added to an already uncertain situation led a number of important producers to leave the centre and transfer their activities to the south.[130] In the spring of 1917, as we have seen, Khanzhonkov had moved to Yalta, taking his entire staff with him, including the director, Evgeny Bauer, who died a few weeks later, and the designer Fyodor Komissarzhevsky. This did not prevent Khanzhonkov from remaining titular Chairman of O.K.O., although his active participation in the conduct of the Union was minimal.[131] His Deputy Chairman and rival in the field of film production, I. Ermolev, also established himself in Yalta with the director, Yakov Protazanov, and the actor, Ivan Mosjoukine. But by 1917 both Khanzhonkov and Ermolev had, as we have seen, been overtaken by Kharitonov who had already established a studio in Yalta. In the autumn of 1917 he was able to move into new studios which had been built for him in Odessa.[132] The majority of these people, among them the most experienced actors, directors, writers and designers of the pre-Revolutionary cinema, were eventually to go into exile. Although a few, notably Protazanov,[133] later returned, the Soviet cinema was deprived of a major source of talent in the years of its infancy. In this field at least the Bolsheviks were thus unable to follow Lenin's instruction that they should build the new order with 'old bricks'. This factor alone necessitated a new start, the adoption of emergency measures which were in turn to have a formative influence on the development of a distinctive post-Revolutionary cinema.

The position was not improved by the behaviour of some film workers in the face of the changing political situation. It became fairly common during the Civil War period for film to be hoarded or buried in anticipation of better things to come. Concealment ensured that film could not be confiscated and that the profits from its distribution or exhibition would not be lost to a rival. In 1917 it was often dangerous for newsreel cameramen to shoot film because anyone carrying a camera was liable to be suspected of espionage.[134] Newsreel film was therefore exceptionally valuable and for this reason much of it was hidden. The Polish cameraman, Modziełewski, went one step further. When he went into exile in 1917 he took with him much valuable footage, which has been subsequently lost, of the February Revolution and of the activities of Lenin.[135] Similarly an agreement between O.K.O. and the Cinema Committee of the Moscow City Soviet enabled film producers to remove a great deal of valuable equipment to the Crimea and then to spirit it abroad, thus impoverishing the nascent Soviet film industry still further.

When the Provisional Government took steps to restrict the consumption of electricity,[136] the effect of these restrictions on the cinema was severe; opening hours were drastically curtailed and a number of cinemas were forced to close altogether. The situation provoked a protest from the Moscow City Soviet, which was concerned with the day-to-day implementation of central government policies.[137] The Soviet Cinema Section was constrained to point out that the electricity consumption of individuals in separate households was significantly higher than that of a mass of people gathered together in the darkness to watch a film. (This argument also became a recurrent theme of the Civil War years.) Nevertheless electricity supplies for film production alone were cut initially by 60 per cent.[138]

The government's electricity restrictions were only one of the subjects discussed at the Second All-Russian Conference of Cinema Workers. This gathering, called by O.K.O., was originally intended as a full-scale congress (*s"ezd*), but it was held on the eve of the Kornilov troubles and of a threatened railway strike.[139] A large number of delegates, particularly those who were now working in the Crimea, were therefore unable to attend. In addition, the technical staff organisations refused to attend because they feared that their interests would be swamped by those of the entrepreneurs. In these circumstances the congress organisers feared that attendance would fail to reach a quorum and so they renamed the congress and demoted it not merely to a conference (*soveshchanie*) but to a preparatory one (*predvaritel'noe soveshchanie*). This opened on 22 August in the Ars cinema, which had earlier seen the formation of the Union of Patriotic Cinematography.[140] One of its first decisions was that the eventual congress should be summoned before 1 December. The Conference then went on to spend its first day discussing the material problems of the cinema, its lack of electricity supplies and the shortage of film stock in particular, and adopted a resolution calling for the restoration of normal working conditions as soon as possible. The position of the Russian cinema after the War was over was discussed on the third day and a tax on imported films, which would pay for the cost of domestic production, was proposed. All these discussions and decisions were however swept aside by subsequent events. Of more lasting significance are the events of the second day, when the delegate of the Skobelev Committee, G. Boltyansky, also a member of the Petrograd Soviet of Workers' and Soldiers' Deputies, read a report on 'The Revolution and the new tasks of the cinema' ('Revolyutsiya i novye zadachi v kinematografe'). He emphasised the need for the municipalisation of cinemas to ensure that the industry devoted itself to social and political tasks and, in particular, to the production and distribution of films aimed at spreading culture and enlightenment amongst the masses of the population. These terms were of course never defined so that even the entrepreneurs, while rejecting his Marxist analysis of the death throes of Russian imperialism, could accept his espousal of the educational rôle of the cinema. However a motion approving this part of his report was cleverly combined with an appeal to local soviets to restore electricity supplies so that the cinema could perform its new-found social and political tasks without hindrance. This addition was rejected by Boltyansky who issued a specific disclaimer both for himself and for the organisations that he represented.[141] In this state of disarray the Conference came to an end. Within two months the Provisional Government had increased its restrictions on electricity consumption so that cinemas were only allowed to open three days in every week. Here again, they were overtaken by events. The November issue of *Proektor*, after a long editorial denouncing the new moves, stated quite simply:

> The preceding lines had already been set up in type when events took place in Moscow which will radically alter the pattern of our lives. The City Duma, which was supposed to ratify the Commission's decision,[142] has ceased to exist. The attitude of the new authorities towards the cinema is not known.[143]

Events had indeed taken place that would in the long run radically alter the pattern of the Russian cinema, but the exact shape of the new pattern was to emerge only slowly in the ensuing months and years.

2. THE BOLSHEVIKS, PROPAGANDA AND THE CINEMA

Of all the arts for us the cinema is the most important.

Lenin, 1922.[1]

When the Bolsheviks seized power in October 1917 they took control only of the 'commanding heights' of a disintegrating administrative machine, a machine whose malfunctioning had largely contributed to the collapse of the previous system of political control. While the machine itself, and those who staffed it, were not necessarily anti-Bolshevik, neither were they inherently anti-tsarist. Their position may be appropriately compared with the ineffectual inertia of the now fallen Provisional Government, and for this reason the Bolsheviks could not rely on the existing machinery of government for the transmission and execution of their orders, let alone use it actively as an instrument for social and political change.[2] The situation was further complicated by the reaction of the non-Bolshevik forces to the October Revolution. The ravages of famine, disease and armed insurrection in the provinces that characterised the first three years of Soviet power effectively prevented the 'party of the masses' from establishing, let alone maintaining, contact with the masses in whose name it claimed to be acting, and thus exposed the fundamental weakness of the Bolsheviks' political position. Ruptured communications between the centre and the periphery brought difficulties in both the practical and theoretical fields; it was an emergency situation that demanded emergency measures.

The new government aimed to mobilise the masses into active involvement with the Bolshevik cause and to train them into appropriately new patterns of political, economic and social thought. In this way their future support could be relied on as an automatic reaction to predetermined stimuli transmitted from the nerve-centres of Bolshevik organisation. On the morrow of the Revolution, at the Second All-Russian Congress of Soviets, Lenin stated:

> In our view the state draws its strength from the consciousness of the masses. It is strong when the masses know everything, can make judgements on everything and approach everything consciously.[3]

Four years later he clarified his meaning:

While we have in our country a phenomenon such as illiteracy it is difficult for us to speak of political education. . .An illiterate person stands outside politics; he has first to be taught the alphabet. Without this there is only rumour, scandal, gossip and prejudice, but no politics.[4]

If then the masses were to be mobilised they must first of all be given the rudiments of literacy and education, for only then could they be fully integrated into the political and economic activity of the new Soviet state.

But in the immediate years after the Revolution the new Soviet state was in no position to integrate the masses into its activities. It did not have the necessary administrative machinery or competence, it did not have the conventional political power, and it did not have the military strength to reorganise the social and economic structure of the country. Apart from anything else, and despite subsequent assertions, the October Revolution was a revolution from above. Unable to rely upon administrative fiat and incapable of using force, the revolutionaries were compelled initially to shield themselves, but later were also able to strengthen their position, through the use of agitation and propaganda.

In the English language the concept of 'propaganda' covers many eventualities, but in Russian the distinction between 'agitation' and 'propaganda' is a commonplace of socialist parlance. The distinction was first developed by Plekhanov in 1892: 'A propagandist presents *many* ideas to one or a few persons; an agitator presents *only one or a few* ideas, but he presents them to a *whole* mass of people.'[5] This distinction was developed by Lenin in *Chto delat'?* (What is to be done?):

the propagandist, dealing with, say, the question of unemployment, must explain the capitalistic nature of crises, the cause of their inevitability in modern society, the necessity for the transformation of this society into a socialist society, etc. In a word, he must present 'many ideas', so many, indeed, that they will be widely understood as an integral whole only by a (comparatively) few persons. The agitator, however, speaking on the same subject, will take as an illustration a fact that is most glaring and widely known to his audience, say, the death of an unemployed worker's family from starvation, the growth of impoverishment, etc., and, utilising this fact, known to all, will direct his efforts to presenting *a single idea* to the 'masses', e.g., the senselessness of the contradiction between the increase of wealth and the increase of poverty; he will strive *to rouse* discontent and indignation among the masses against this crying injustice, leaving a more complete explanation of this contradiction to the propagandist.[6]

In the period when Lenin was writing this, in 1901–2, when the Party's activities were confined to the secret and the underground, 'the propagandist operates chiefly by means of the *printed* word; the agitator by means of the *spoken* word'.[7] Propaganda, then, is more of a long-term activity, a preparation of the background. Agitation, on the other hand, is more immediate, and more specifically directed. It was clearly agitation rather than propaganda, to use their own terminology, that the Bolsheviks required in the aftermath of the October Revolution and, indeed, for some years afterwards. However agitation and propaganda are obviously activities of a kind, even if they differ in detail; the *agitki* of the Civil War period[8] were clearly agitational, rather than propagandist but, as the twenties wore on and the Soviet cinema began to be organised on a more permanent basis, the distinction becomes more difficult to maintain. The elements of agitation and propaganda in a film such as Eisenstein's *Bronenosets Potëmkin* (Battleship Potemkin)[9] are inextricably intertwined. In a discussion of the Soviet cinema in the 1920s the distinction made between agitation and propaganda is not then on the whole a useful one. I am confirmed in this view by the manner in which Plekhanov attempted to define 'agitation' and 'propaganda' in terms of one another:

> In general it is not easy to draw the line between agitation and what is usually called propaganda. Agitation is also propaganda but propaganda taking place in particular circumstances, that is, in circumstances which compel even those people who would not normally have paid any attention to them to listen to the words of the propagandist. Propaganda is agitation conducted in the normal everyday course of the life of a particular country. Agitation is propaganda, occasioned by events which are not entirely ordinary and evoking a certain upsurge in the general mood. . .Propaganda, in the proper sense of the word, would lose all historical meaning if it were not accompanied by agitation.[10]

Save for the observation that there was a general tendency to move from agitation to propaganda as the cinema became more firmly established, I shall therefore use the English term 'propaganda' throughout this book to cover both Russian terms, 'agitation' and 'propaganda'.

The rôle of propaganda in the revolutionary struggle was also a commonplace of Russian socialist thought. The working class had had to be aroused to revolutionary consciousness: as the masthead of the Social Democratic newspaper *Iskra* (The Spark) had proclaimed, 'From this spark shall arise a flame.'[11] So too after the Revolution the masses would be aroused and actively involved in the struggle to create a new society. What *Iskra* had been to the underground Party, the cinema would be to the socialist society: a rallying-point, a unifying force.[12] This, at any rate, was the hope expressed by Lenin in the remark that I have quoted at the beginning of this chapter. But when Lenin said that, 'of all the arts for us the cinema is the most important', he was passing not an artistic, but rather a functional judgement. In an article written shortly before the outbreak of the First World War, Lenin had already noted the use of the cinema in capitalist society to improve productivity and therefore also profits in accordance with the so-called 'Taylor system' for the reduction of labour to its basic mechanical component movements:

> The cinema is systematically employed for studying the work of the best operatives and increasing its intensity, i.e., 'speeding up' the workers. . .A newly engaged worker is taken to the factory cinema where he is shown a 'model' performance of his job; the worker is made to 'catch up' with that performance. A week later he is taken to the cinema again and shown pictures of his own performance, which is then compared with the 'model'.
>
> All these vast improvements are introduced *to the detriment* of the workers, for they lead to their still greater oppression and exploitation.[13]

As Lenin had already observed in another article written slightly earlier: 'The capitalist cuts his expenditure by *half* or more; his profits grow. The bourgeoisie is delighted and cannot praise the Taylors enough!'[14] The cinema could thus have a practical economic function in that it could directly influence methods of work and lead to a more efficient use of resources. That Lenin felt that socialism could in this instance learn from capitalism is shown by his attitude towards the film *Gidrotorf*, an instructional film demonstrating a hydraulic method of lifting peat, which was made and shown to him in 1920.[15] The cinema was, quite clearly, the most appropriate medium for this type of propaganda, but why was it considered more generally to be 'of all the arts. . .the most important'?

To understand the importance of the cinema in its proper perspective we should first of all look at the other propaganda media that were available to the Bolsheviks at the time of the Revolution. Their pre-Revolutionary propaganda had been almost entirely confined to the spoken and the written word, the political meeting, the newspaper and the pamphlet. Written propaganda, especially in the form of a newspaper such as *Iskra* or, later, *Pravda*, had its place in preaching to the converted, who tended to be either members of the disaffected intelligentsia or literate members of the industrial proletariat. Spoken propaganda (or agitation, in Bolshevik terminology) was more appropriate to a specific situation, a case of alleged exploitation which could be developed into a strike or a demonstration of the kind that swept Russia in 1905. Although both these types of propaganda had their place after 1917, neither was entirely adequate for the task that confronted the new régime. The Bolsheviks had to find propaganda media that would appeal to the broad masses of the still largely illiterate population. This meant that written and printed propaganda had only limited value, at least in the early years, and their value was further limited by the confines of language in a multilingual country. Initially attempts were made to involve the population directly in the celebration of May Day and the anniversary of the Revolution.[16] But these attempts were limited in their scope and, therefore, also in their effect. The same could be said of attempts to utilise the theatre for revolutionary propaganda, but the theatre had its own limitations as well:

> The very nature of the theatre makes overnight changes impossible; a play cannot simply be mounted at a moment's notice. Even given the existence of a suitable play, there is bound to be a timelag for the rehearsals, training of actors, designing of sets.[17]

There was also the problem that the theatre was not entirely reliable; on the one hand a touring group might wander from the straight and narrow in the provinces, and the central authorities, even if they found out, would be powerless to act, while on the other hand the theatre was bound by conventions unfamiliar to the broad masses, conventions which might make the message of a play difficult to comprehend. Nevertheless efforts were made to break down these conventions and involve the masses in the actual performance. Events from revolutionary history such as the rebellion of Spartacus or the storming of the Bastille were re-enacted,[18] but perhaps the most extravagant gesture of this kind was the re-staging of the storming of the Winter Palace (*Vzyatie Zimnego dvortsa* – The Taking of the Winter Palace) *in situ* on 7 November 1920, with a cast including 2,500 performers, 500 musicians and some 35,000 spectators.[19] But the possibilities of such spectacles were clearly also limited, in both space and time, and such ephemera were scarcely worth the immense organisational effort involved.

The Bolsheviks needed a propaganda medium that was primarily and fundamentally visual in its appeal, one that would thus overcome differences of language and cultural development. In many ways the poster suited their purposes and they came to rely heavily upon it, both during the Civil War and afterwards.[20] The poster was, after all, visual, simple and universal in its appeal. It was used for educational[21] as well as agitational[22] purposes. The most important innovation in the poster field was the development of the ROSTA window, which provided a semi-satirical commentary on current events that could be displayed in the street or pasted on a factory wall.[23] There were some posters which became indelibly imprinted on the popular mind, such as Moor's *Ty zapisalsya dobrovol'tsem?* (Have you Volunteered?)[24] which owed more than a passing resemblance to the British 'Your Country Needs You',[25] and his appeal poster for the victims of the Volga famine *Pomogi!* (Help!),[26] but the poster was ultimately confined in its utility by its static imagery. The Revolution required a more dynamic, more modern medium of propaganda, and that medium was the cinema.

The cinema provided a medium that was not merely visual and dynamic but also mechanical. The cinema's essence, as the argument went, lay in movement: 'The soul of the cinema is in the movement of life.'[27] Its association with the machine underlined its novelty, especially in the outlying areas of the Soviet countryside, and its symbolic rôle as an agent of progress. The cinema was universal in its appeal: the 'great silent', as it was called,[28] could be viewed simultaneously in Petrograd and Vladivostok, in Murmansk and in Baku, and its message would be understood in all these places, unimpeded by language barriers.[29] This universality also meant that the cinema could be controlled more easily than, say, the theatre by the authorities at the centre. But to understand fully the attractions and limitations of the cinema as a propaganda medium we must examine the disputes that surrounded it throughout the period under discussion.

The disputes and polemics that took place in the 1920s between the various schools of film theoreticians, film makers and film critics must be seen against the background of a general preoccupation with three themes: the very legitimacy of the cinema as an art form, especially vis-à-vis the theatre; the rôle of the cinema as the art form of the machine age and therefore of the twentieth century; and, by extension, the rôle of the cinema as the art form of the Revolution itself.

The controversy that raged over the legitimacy of the cinema as an art form was very much a continuation of the debate that had been carried out in the period prior to the First World War.[30] Then theatrical interests had attacked the cinema largely because they were afraid that its rise would lead to the demise of the 'legitimate' theatre; but in the 1920s this possibility was acclaimed with glee. The essence of the argument lies in the words of the critic Pavel Poluyanov:

> The theatre's day is over and there is only one thing left for it to do – die... The theatre is for *a few epicures*, it is not for the people. The cinema belongs to everyone. The cinema does not talk, leaving us the chance to *complete* the spectacle, at the same time *training* our self-creativity. The theatre gives us long, boring, alien words which are 99 per cent banal and empty. Which of them do we need now? Of course there can be only one answer...The cinema and the theatre are enemies and every one of us knows where he stands; every one of us should say his yea or nay.[31]

In a pamphlet that he published himself in 1925 Poluyanov expanded his arguments. The title of the pamphlet was itself symptomatic of the style of the argument: *Gibel' teatra i torzhestvo kino* (The ruin of the theatre and the triumph of the cinema).[32] He thought that the demise of the theatre was inevitable because the cinema was better matched to the pace of contemporary change.[33] The amount of time spent theorising on the theatre and its rôle indicated its unhealthy state: 'The very fact of this controversy surrounding the theatre indicates that something is rotten in the state of Denmark.'[34] In addition Poluyanov quoted Eichenwald's argument that the theatre was not itself an art form but a combination of painting, architecture and literature; once a theatrical performance was completed, there was nothing left except the 'real arts' like the sets and the printed word.[35] The theatre was therefore dependent on 'real' art forms: 'If there were no literature, there would be no theatre, while, if there were no theatre, the play would nevertheless still exist.'[36]

Finally, he argued that it was the theatre, rather than the cinema, that was the vulgarising force: 'The theatre demeans man, making him into a mere...*actor*.'[37] The theatre had historically been in the hands of the ruling classes and had therefore always been a medium of entertainment rather than education.[38] The cinema, on the other hand, was a mass force:

> The curse of the theatre – *The Unrepeatability of the Spectacle* – does not frighten the cinema, which reproduces its spectacles for the whole world... Hence the colossal profitability of the cinema, which gives it the chance for the most powerful development and a tremendous advantage over the theatre – *Economy of Artistic Resources with an Infinite Auditorium.* In order to give millions of people the chance to enjoy a beautiful spectacle involving world artists the cinema has only to play once...And the great Asta Nielsen or Jackie Coogan excites and shakes simultaneously both Berlin and Singapore.[39]

The cinema could conquer time and space:

To tear dying life from the hands of all-destroying time and make it immortal, to preserve history for future generations – what a crushing victory over time and space![40]

This ability made the cinema a new teacher, particularly appropriate to the rush of modern life.

A similar point was made by the critic Voznesensky.[41] He recognised that the cinema had suffered from its origins in the market-place[42] and compared the attitude of many intellectuals towards the cinema with that of the Hottentots towards the first musical instrument.[43] Nevertheless he saw the cinema as a weapon for progress:

If the purpose of the world, of life, of every living thing, is to give birth to the new man, to ensure in such a way that tomorrow's man is today's with something else greater than today, then the art of the screen must be recognised as one of the most powerful methods on the road to this universal goal. . .Because in none of the old art forms is there that living flicker of the birth of new ideas, a new will, a new personality which those who know the screen sense to be amongst its future possibilities.[44]

Like Poluyanov, Voznesensky felt the cinema to be more 'real' than the theatre: the theatre for him was symbolised by the mask, whereas the cinema was concerned with the exposition of truth.[45] The cinema was also the 'art form of tomorrow' because of its connection with technology and the universality of time and space; here too Voznesensky was in accord with Poluyanov:

In truth all the rules of the past are broken here: Pickford or Chaplin act in America, but we see them in Nezhin or Mtsensk. The actor Polonsky or the actress Kholodnaya have died, but their living smiles, every wrinkle and every breath, can be seen with your own eyes and now the mystical secret of immortality has already become the concrete achievement of the screen.[46]

Other writers argued that the essence of the cinema's future lay in its connection with technology[47] but the majority emphasised the essentially visual nature of the film:

Literature seems to me to be the art which is most opposed to cinematograph art in as far as we bear in mind the very essence of these two arts. The means of expression of literature is the word. The cinema is the great silent. The word damages the cinema as such. . .The picture should speak for itself. . . And of course the ideal would be the picture that could be shown without subtitles.[48]

The absence of the word from the film meant that the audience was required to use its imagination and thus participate in the artistic process.[49] Literary adaptations were regarded as anathema: Eisenstein himself wrote:

On the question of what the cinema needs from literature, one thing can be said in every case with certainty:
Comrade littérateurs! Don't write screenplays!
Production organisations, make people buy your goods with novels.
Sell your rights to the novel.
And film directors must be made to find the *cinematographic* equivalent of these products.[50]

Osip Brik took a similar view: the screenplay should be written, not before, but after the film had been shot:

The screenplay should be written, not before shooting, but afterwards. The screenplay is not an order to shoot, but a method of organising what has already been shot. And we should therefore ask, not how a screenplay should be, but what should be photographed. The re-working of material in the screenplay is the last stage of the work.[51]

Unfortunately this extreme attitude contributed to the chronic shortage of screenplays that affected the Soviet cinema in the later twenties.

The cinema was also distinguished from the theatre by the scope of materials that it could encompass on the screen: 'the cinema is the organisation in time of the spatial elements of reality, taken on film...The theatre is the organisation of real people in the midst of reality.'[52] Or, as another critic put it, 'The theatre is a game. The cinema is life.'[53] Yet another argued that the only thing that the cinema and the theatre had in common was the auditorium.[54] For him the cinema's greatest advantage was the power of real movement.[55] He compared the film to a painting: 'The immobile chiaroscuro and line, as if frozen on to the painting, become mobile on the screen, as if alive. Their expressiveness is heightened.'[56] The painter could only produce 'the fiction of movement', but the film maker could produce real movement, using the painting as mere background.[57] The cinema's distinctive movement was produced by the manner in which the film was cut – by montage:

The film as a product of the art of the cinema originates from the time when words were replaced by images, when the unity of time and place was destroyed, when different concepts of the *combination of the order of separate scenes* appeared, when people began to introduce various plans for one and the same scene.[58]

In the theatre too the audience saw real people, whereas in the cinema it saw only illusions created by montage; the cinema, for this writer, was less realistic but more powerful.[59] He saw montage as having three purposes: it organised and directed the viewer's attention; it concentrated the imagination on essentials;

it retained the viewer's attention through the rhythm and dynamism of optical bombardment.[60] In all these, montage further distinguished the cinema from the theatre. This view was supported by Eichenbaum. For him the cinema deformed nature by giving the illusion of continuity: there was a contrast between the content of each individual frame and the impression left by a series of images – each frame attained its full significance only in the context of the surrounding frames.[61] Given the essentially visual nature of the cinema, fears were expressed that the introduction of sound would destroy the cinema; the director, Vsevolod Pudovkin, wrote in 1929:

At that time [i.e. the cinema's beginnings] people did not consider the cinema to be an art but a poor surrogate for the theatre – and they were right. Now the appearance of sound is once again driving us along the line of least resistance towards being a surrogate for the theatre.[62]

On the other hand, because of its dependence on visual imagery rather than words, the cinema was still attacked as illiterate:

Historically the cinema emerged as a substitute for the theatre. . .It's funny when people talk about 'the art of the screen'. . .Of course there is no 'art of the screen'. . .The cinema is untheatrical by its very nature. . .And it is not by chance that a fatal illiteracy weighs upon this dirty 'art'. Its terminology is not given to any language. . .Finally our Russian cinema. It beats the record for illiteracy.[63]

But, although this view had held sway before the First World War, it was now very much a minority opinion. The majority of critics agreed with Voznesensky:

The 'great silent' has literally become the hero of the day both abroad and here. In its triumphant progress it has left both the theatre and even literature some way behind it. It is increasingly gaining the audience of the broad masses, it is penetrating ever more deeply into such corners as would not in the near future be penetrated by other forms of art. It is therefore not surprising that the cinema, which even recently was slighted by every aesthete as a vulgar surrogate, has now become a subject for discussion amongst recognised art specialists.[64]

The cinema then, was a visual art form, the theatre a verbal one. In addition one of the cinema's principal distinctions from the theatre lay in its technological basis; in the Soviet Union in the 1920s technology was synonymous with progress, and hence the art form of the machine age would also be the art form of the Revolution.

As early as 1913 the cinema's connection with the pace of modern life had been noted by Shapotnikov: 'The tempo of dramatic action must correspond to the rapid tempo of contemporary life. The cinematographic pace of impressions.'[65] This central idea was taken up and developed in the 1920s, especially in the columns of the journal *Kino-Fot.* In the first issue of the journal, published in 1922, Lev Kuleshov proclaimed that any interest in the past was a sign of abnormality, that the cinema was *the* contemporary art form, and therefore the only one that was worthy of serious consideration.[66] Only the cinema could, through the techniques of montage, *organise* its material and its audience in such a way as to re-establish a connection whose loss had led contemporary art into what Kuleshov called 'a hopeless blind alley'.[67] In the very next article Ippolit Sokolov made even more extravagant claims for the cinema:

The cinema is the new philosophy.
The slow–analytical and rapid–synthetic language of the *cinema* is the new international visual Esperanto of the future.[68]

And further:

The style of our era is the style of straight lines and sharp corners.
Our contemporary psychology is constructed on sharp corners...
But the style of our contemporaneity is *the style of the cinema.*
Only the *cinema* is constructed exclusively on the straight line and the sharp corner...
The *cinema* is a universe constructed on straight lines and sharp corners.
The cinema is a new outlook on life.
The *cinema* is the triumph of the machine, electricity and industry.
The *cinema* alone can compel us to live with the wonders of technology at an ever more feverish pace. The latest cars, Canadian locomotives and ocean-going liners can rush furiously across the screen, and mills, machines, pistons and levers can work at a fantastic pace.
The Cinema is the Power of the Machine.[69]

Similar sentiments were expressed by Boltyansky in an article published in *Kino*, also in 1922, entitled 'The art of the future' ('Iskusstvo budushchego').[70] Boltyansky maintained that there had been a 'psychic revolution' in contemporary man induced by the introduction of the machine and the consequent broadening of human horizons; this had, of course, met with opposition from vested interests and, in the case of the cinema, those vested interests were to be found in the theatre:

But the young muse is armed, as a symbol of the New Man, with an adjunct in the shape of the machine, and it is already setting out on its independent path through the stormy waves of art.

But the sun cannot be stopped and the wheels of history cannot be turned back.

For every great historical epoch, regardless even of the parallel development of other forms of art, one art form has been the most characteristic, the most important and the most central. For the ancient Greek epoch it was sculpture, for the feudal period poetry and architecture; the bourgeois epoch also had its turn – painting, music and the theatre.

There can be no doubt that the cinema, this new art form, is the rightful heir for our time, for its melodiousness, its rhythm, refinement and its machine culture, and it therefore represents the central art form of the current epoch.

It is not yet the art of the present. The present is a transitional epoch in which the decrepit art of the theatre is writhing in terrible convulsions and fighting for its very existence, while the art of the cinema is growing triumphantly and becoming conscious of itself. The art of the cinema is all in the future.

All the more reason why we should approach it, recognise it and study it.[71]

Boltyansky's ideas were subsequently developed by Pavel Poluyanov in the two works already cited.[72] He expressed them most forcefully in his book:

The machine...That is the conqueror of our times! It drives its fellow machines and is controlled by more complex and surprising machines: in the air there is the sound of aeroplanes; with lightning speed radios bring the sound of world events from beyond the oceans. The machine...The tentacles of great cities compel us to transform the antiquated psychology of the feudal epoch into insolent, daring, tempestuous psychology of refutation, into the dynamic, into our *New Aesthetic of Struggle*, of heroic deed, of great adventure, of enterprise. We have been seized with a desire to tear ourselves away from our putrid way of life, always slow or static, into space, in pursuit of events, of the glittering happiness of a fundamentally new life.[73]

In Poluyanov's opinion, the only art form that was consonant with the machine age was the cinema: 'the real theatre of the people, the revolutionary, agitational, or simply *contemporary* theatre which really corresponds to the epoch and its tempo is the *cinema* alone'.[74] Boltyansky returned to this theme in a book published in 1927 and entitled *The culture of the cameraman* (*Kul'tura kino-operatora*).[75] The views expressed in this book by Boltyansky were very similar to those of the German school led by Walter Benjamin.[76] While emphasising the essentially visual nature of the cinema as an art form,[77] Boltyansky discerned a distinction between the cinema and other art forms that depended upon its capacity for mechanical reproduction:

The mechanical possibility of unending reproduction and distribution of the works of the cinema make it, as distinct from the other arts, the sole and exclusive *expression of the era of the new culture.*[78]

There were, of course, dissenting voices but they were few and far between. A typical counter-reaction to the enthusiasm expressed for the cinema appeared in the journal *Novyi zritel'* in August 1924:

> Life continues under the slogans of mechanisation and the automation of life. In art the actor is replaced by a biomechanical doll, the worker by a machine, the beast of burden by electricity or petrol traction. Many do not want a living theatre – but a mechanical apparatus.
>
> People have grown tired of words, speeches and books, their ears and their brains are sick, they are already bored with thinking and hearing, they want to look, and at the same time the 'great silent' comes to their rescue.[79]

But this particular author was merely expressing reservations, for he also referred to the cinema as 'the legitimate child of urban culture and of the twentieth century'.[80] Nonetheless he did point out what many saw to be the cinema's greatest weakness – its absence of words. What for some writers represented the very essence of the cinema, and of its strength, was for him its principal limitation: without words, he argued, the cinema could only be utilised to transmit extremely simple ideas.[81]

But, whatever the strengths of this view, it was atypical. The second issue of *Kino-Fot* carried an article by B. Arvatov which reiterated the mainstream view that the cinema was the appropriate art form for the machine age. The bourgeoisie, in his opinion, were obsessed with passive concepts of beauty; the proletariat, on the other hand, did not recognise the validity of the distinction between high and low art, but preferred to distinguish between progressive and reactionary art.[82] He held the American cinema up as an example whose techniques could well be copied: 'The American film is not merely constructive; it is, in addition, of maximum agitational value in its very forms.'[83] But Arvatov did not share the almost slavish worship of American films practised by some of his contemporaries:

> Agitation is not dreaming; agitation is practical action. And that is why the agitational cinema is the cinema not of adventures but of real people and objects.
>
> The realism of the material and the excitement of action are what we need.
>
> A fleeting train, a moving skyscraper, a strike on aeroplanes or an uprising of objects are fit themes not merely because of their entertainment value but also because of the possibilities that they present us with: *taking the very real and making of it what one will.*
>
> America has opted for pure entertainment.
>
> The R.S.F.S.R. must give entertainment its special, social purpose.[84]

But the attitude of Soviet film theorists and film-makers of the 1920s towards the American film is a matter to which we shall return later.[85]

There was thus a general feeling that the cinema was the most appropriate art form for the machine age. Further, since the machine had become the symbol of progress, the art form of the machine age was also deemed to be the art form of the Revolution. We can see here a direct parallel with the writings of Italian Futurism and, in particular, of Marinetti.[86] And in both countries it would be fair to say that the theory outstripped the practice.[87] The cinema's revolutionary rôle in Soviet Russia was primarily identified by complaints about its signal failure to fulfil expectations. In November 1923, in a review of the film *Krasnye d'yavolyata* (The Little Red Devils),[88] the journal *Kino-Gazeta* complained:

> For six years the Russian cinema has been in the hands of the workers' government.
> For six years we have waited for it to produce revolutionary films.
> And for all those six years instead of bread we have been given stones – German mysticism and, on rare occasions, a Soviet potboiler. . .
> And only now do we have the first, great and fine revolutionary film!
> A film of the Revolution![89]

In a poem published in *Kino-Fot* in October 1922 Mayakovsky expressed similar sentiments:

> For you a cinema spectacle.
> For me almost a *Weltanschauung*.
> The cinema – purveyor of movement.
> The cinema – renewer of literature.
> The cinema – destroyer of aesthetics.
> The cinema – fearlessness.
> The cinema – a sportsman.
> The cinema – a sower of ideas.
> But the cinema is sick. Capitalism has covered its eyes with gold. Deft entrepreneurs lead it through the street by the hand. They gather money by stirring the heart with whining little subjects.
> We must put an end to this.
> Communism must rescue the cinema from its speculating guides.
> Futurism must steam the dead water – slowness and morality.
> Without this we shall have either the imported tap-dance of
> America or the continuous 'tear-jerking' of the Mosjoukines.
> We are tired of the first.
> Even more tired of the second.[90]

In the same issue the Constructivist Alexei Gan stated more simply that, 'The cinema should depict our way of life!'[91] This was to become a common, and perhaps also a rather plaintive, cry.

These ideas were developed by Viktor Shklovsky in a book published in Berlin in the following year.[92] In it he argued that man was in danger of becoming insensitive to the world around him; he needed to renew his contact with it:

> Just as those who live by the sea do not hear the sound of the waves, so we do not even hear the words that we speak. We speak in the pitiful language of unspoken words. We look one another in the face but we do not see one another.[93]

This could be remedied by a periodic renewal of artistic consciousness through a concentration on new material, but, 'New material requires new forms.'[94] Shklovsky further observed that, 'Attempts to use literature for the cinema have come to nothing.'[95] Literature had been the art form of the bourgeois epoch, but it was no longer appropriate in the post-Revolutionary context:

> Art forms 'grow tired', burn themselves out, like flames. The change in forms is usually revolutionary.
>
> The cinema is the natural heir to the theatre and, possibly, literature. It may embrace the theatre, though probably not.[96]

For Shklovsky too, then, the cinema was the art form of the Revolution.

On 1 April 1924 the People's Commissar for Enlightenment, Lunacharsky, in an article in *Pravda*, lamented the cinema's failure to fulfil its function as the purveyor of the revolutionary message:

> The Soviet cinema cannot allow in its films either a political social–bourgeois tendency or the glorification of bourgeois virtues, nor elements of depravity or crime, presented in tempting form.[97]

In 1926 the journal *Kino-Front* printed an article by V. Kirshon which underlined the special responsibility of the Soviet Union for the production of revolutionary films:

> Is bourgeois ideology being propagated here in the cinema?
> Yes, it is.
> Every day in all our cinemas in the town and in the country, in the commercial cinema and in the club, bourgeois morality, bourgeois prejudices, the bourgeois gospel of faith in the 'Lord God' are presented from the screen with all possible Priscillas and Barbaras to the Soviet audience. . .The U.S.S.R. is the only country where revolutionary films can be made. . .The pursuit of philistine tastes, the preparation of films for the cinemas on the main streets, are *a crime which should be brought to trial.*[98]

Against this background there was some argument as to the exact revolutionary potential of fictional, as opposed to documentary, films; this is an argument to which I shall return in greater detail later,[99] but the origins of the dispute lay in this general discussion. Lunacharsky, in his *Pravda* article, had laid stress on the need for more *agitki*, or 'living posters' (*zhivye plakaty*) as he called them, because he felt that they were the most effective means of propagating Bolshevik ideology.[100] He was echoing Lenin's directive to Litkens of January 1922, which had also stressed the importance of documentary and newsreel films as a vehicle for propaganda.[101] By 1927 this had become the line that the Party had determined to push, for it emphasised the direct practical utility of the cinema; an editorial in *Sovetskoe kino* observed:

> We are not opposed to the fiction film, which should occupy a small place in the field of the cinema. *But we are opposed to the evaluation of the cinema in terms of art.*
>
> *The cinema is the condenser of human practice, of fact and insistence, not the literary teacher of life.*
>
> *The cinema is the ideological weapon of production of our time: its experience, its example, will forge new men, new achievements.*
>
> And we need not argue about the priority of the theatre or the cinema. To argue on such a level is like comparing the significance of electricity with . . .the Tretyakov Gallery.
>
> The fiction film is a good thing in a given period, necessary and profitable.
>
> *The constant broadening of the horizons and the experience of the human race – that is the task of the cinema.*
>
> *The way forward for the cinema is the cultural film.*[102]

There was then in certain quarters a strong feeling that it was not merely the cinema as such that was the appropriate art form of the Revolution, but more specifically the documentary cinema. But this is a debate that I shall return to later.[103]

Whatever individual attitudes might have been towards the specific qualities of the cinema, the attitude of the Party and government was made quite clear. At an early stage the significance of the cinema was underlined by the publication under official auspices of a collection of essays on the cinema and its social and political rôle.[104] In his introduction, Lunacharsky wrote: 'We must do what no-one else can do or wants to do. We must remember that the socialist state must imbue even cinema spectacles with a socialist spirit.'[105] But the exact nature of the task facing the cinema in a socialist society was spelled out in the contribution from V. Kerzhentsev entitled 'The social struggle and the screen':

> What then is the task of the state cinema in a socialist republic?
>
> To all appearances the answer is clear. The cinema must above all be utilised for the communist education of the broad masses. At the same time as cinema enterprises are nationalised and municipalised bit by bit and as they come under the general control and leadership of the People's Commissariat for Enlightenment and its local Departments, the transformation of

the cinema from a tool of amusement and entertainment into a means of education is achieved. But the task for our Commissariat for Enlightenment is not merely the communication to the population of a specific sphere of knowledge but the direction of education in a fully defined communist spirit.[106]

Kerzhentsev's remarks take us back to Lenin's statements on the eradication of illiteracy. The new government needed to educate the population, not merely in a general sense of cultural or intellectual enlightenment, but for the specific political purpose of winning their hearts and minds. Although military victory over the Whites was the first priority in the Civil War period, in the longer term the Soviet state could not survive without the support, however tacit and however passive, of the broad masses of the population. It was in this propaganda battle that it was envisaged that the cinema would play a major rôle.

3. REVOLUTION AND CIVIL WAR

Revolution releases all the forces that have hitherto been fettered and drives them up from the depths to the surface of life.

Lenin, 1920.[1]

The Bolsheviks needed to use propaganda and they chose the cinema as their principal weapon in the campaign to win the minds of the masses. But first they had to win control of the cinema, or what remained of it, in as far as that was possible. Just as the normal administrative structure of the Soviet state had been disrupted, so the production and distribution system of the existing cinema network in the R.S.F.S.R. had crumbled under the combined strain of political and economic pressures. It had thus become virtually impossible to realise the government's policy through conventional channels.

It was partly for this reason that the new government decided against the immediate and wholesale centralised nationalisation of the film industry, although in the chaotic conditions of the months following the October Revolution they had little power to do otherwise. Centralised organisations were established fairly rapidly but in the early stages their existence was largely confined to paper; Soviet power was not yet strong enough to realise its ambitions. For instance, on 9 November 1917 (Old Style), only two weeks after the Revolution, the Extra-Mural Section (Vneshkol'nyi otdel) of Narkompros (the acronym for Narodnyi komissariat po prosveshcheniyu or People's Commissariat for Enlightenment) was created.[2] It was eventually to play an important rôle in the development of the Soviet cinema but at the end of 1917 there seemed no way to give it power without frightening private enterprise into further spasms of flight and destruction. In December therefore the complete nationalisation of the cinema was considered and rejected, but even the mere consideration of the subject was enough to cause O.K.O. to declare war on what it described as the 'usurpers' (*zakhvatchiki*).[3] At the same time some of the Moscow entrepreneurs began to spread alarmist rumours about the impending confiscation of all cinema goods.[4]

As a tentative first step, however, a Cinema Subsection (Kinopodotdel) was established under the Extra-Mural Section of

Narkompros; this latter section was now headed by Krupskaya, Lenin's wife.[5] Instead of complete nationalisation, the Bolsheviks permitted, and at the local level encouraged, a somewhat random pattern of municipalisation by local soviets according to local circumstances. This issue was dealt with by a decree of the N.K.V.D. (Narodnyi Komissariat Vnutrennikh del – People's Commissariat for Internal Affairs) published on 18 January 1918:

1 Soviets of Workers' and Soldiers' Deputies are granted the right to requisition on behalf of the general public cinemas and their stock, together with the right of exhibition thereof.
2 In using requisitioned establishments compensation will be paid to the owners only in those cases where they have contributed with their own labour to the running of the business during the operation of the requisitioned establishment.[6]

But this measure provoked an immediate response from the journals *Kinonedelya* and *Mir ekrana*, which acted as the mouthpiece for what was now the opposition. *Mir ekrana* described the threat of nationalisation as the 'sword of Damocles' overshadowing the cinema;[7] on the other hand, the journal *Proektor* saw the problems facing the cinema industry as primarily economic, rather than political.[8] But in an ominous and prophetic article entitled 'An attempt to murder the cinema' ('Pokushenie na ubiistvo kinematografii'), published late in 1917, I. Ozerov wrote the following lines:

> The thought of a cinema monopoly has recently arisen here. Apparently the talk is of creating a monopoly of both film production and the theatres themselves.
>
> This is an extremely stupid idea.
>
> In fact a monopoly can be created only in those branches of production where production takes place in accordance with a definite and known pattern: thus railways are monopolised because the transport of freight and passengers keeps to a certain pattern; the production and sale of salt may be monopolised, for here again quality does not play a great rôle. But already with the monopoly of tobacco production, for example, doubts arise because there are many sorts of tobacco and a particular blend is required.
>
> What is more, the production of cinema films is an art, like painting, sculpture, music. Can a state monopoly be established in such a branch of production? Clearly this is madness...
>
> Cinema films cannot be produced according to a pattern. They must reflect the individuality of the artist, the director.[9]

These considerations raised by Ozerov are of course the exact inverse of those informing later Soviet film production, although there is no doubt that Lunacharsky, and probably Lenin as well, preferred a gradualist approach. However, as in the case of the decrees on land, peace and bread, the central authorities were not in complete control of events. In Moscow and Petrograd the local soviets had already established their own Cinema Commissions without reference to, or control by, Narkompros. On 4 March 1918 the Moscow City Soviet, in an attempt to control the remains of the industry and to prevent sabotage, issued the following decree, 'On the control of cinema enterprises' ('O kontrole v kinopredpriyatiyakh'):

1 In view of the false rumours that have been spread about the possible seizure of cinema enterprises, i.e. factories, offices, laboratories, theatres, warehouses, etc., in view of the attempts on the part of certain entrepreneurs to remove materials, equipment, film stock and means of production with a view to concealment, which could destroy the cinema industry at its roots and increase the number of unemployed, – the Presidium of the Soviet Workers', Soldiers' and Peasants' Deputies of the city of Moscow and its region declares publicly that no attempts whatsoever to seize cinema enterprises will be permitted, from whatever source they might come.
2 In order to preserve and regulate the cinema industry, workers' control over the industry is introduced.
3 Owners of all cinema enterprises are obliged to present to the Cinema Commission on 10 March details of their possessions and of the materials held in the said enterprise on 14 February this year.
4 All transfers to new ownership, curtailment or cessation of production, withdrawal from hire, and closure of offices, cinema theatres and laboratories without the permission of the Cinema Commission of the Artistic–Educational Section of the Soviet are forbidden.[10]

Whereas on 13 April 1918 Lunacharsky had announced that, at most, only one cinema in each town would be nationalised to secure an outlet for films produced by government organisations and to protect such films against abuse or sabotage,[11] only seventeen days later his own ministry established with the assistance of the Petrograd Soviet a 'Regional Cinema Committee for the Union of Northern Communes under the People's Commissariat for Enlightenment' (Oblastnoi kinematograficheskii komitet soyuza severnykh kommun pri Narkomprose). This Cinema Committee was empowered with the rights:

a to demand from establishments producing cinematograph films, apparatuses and their appurtenances, selling and hiring out the said objects, and also from cinema–theatre establishments, details of all, without exception, of the necessary information regarding the activity of the said institutions;
b to nationalise and requisition, and also to sequestrate, cinema establishments, either all together or each one separately, entrusting the direction of these establishments either to individual people or to boards appointed by the Cinema Committee;
c where necessary to remove from office members of the administration, directors and managers, and also owners of cinema establishments;

d to appoint government inspectors to observe the activity of cinema establishments.[12]

In May Narkompros assumed central control of the Film Section of the Moscow City Soviet, which had itself already absorbed the Skobelev Committee, and thus the control to be exercised by Krupskaya's Extra-Mural Section began to take shape. Government control was strengthened by a number of indirect measures, the most important of which was the Sovnarkom decree of 22 April 1918 which made foreign trade in all spheres a state monopoly. This particular measure provoked another strongly worded outburst from *Mir ekrana*:

> Our entire film industry, now standing so firmly on its feet, will inevitably collapse. . .as the new decree makes it quite impossible to import from abroad the materials needed for a film studio. . .The 'nationalisation' of foreign trade will lead to the paralysis of the film trade, turning Russia into an isolated state and the film industry into a corpse.[13]

It would be wrong to assume that the nationalisation of foreign trade was a purely political manoeuvre. Although ideological considerations and consequences were certainly not discounted, the primary motivation for such controls was economic necessity.[14] Russia's dependence on foreign products made her peculiarly vulnerable to disruptions in international trading patterns and some of the results of this dependence have been discussed in chapter 1.[15] There had been a severe shortage of film stock and other basic materials as early as 1916 when the effects of war and the action of various foreign governments in classifying film stock as a non-exportable strategic material drastically reduced the supply that could be imported into Russia.[16] The confusion that reigned in a period of Revolution and Civil War made the situation more critical; a number of entrepreneurs, optimistically regarding the Bolsheviks as merely a passing irritation, buried their supply of films to prevent them from falling into the hands of government sympathisers.[17] Others, who realised that the Bolsheviks had come to stay, fled to areas still controlled by the Whites, notably the Crimea, and from there they moved on to Paris, Berlin, or Hollywood.[18] In the White areas producers concentrated on the type of psychological drama that was later to be denounced by Soviet critics as either pre- or counter-revolutionary. In the Red areas private firms continued to exist, but they were largely engaged in fulfilling film contracts for state organisations.[19] In a sense this arrangement suited both sides: the government could be sure of a supply of films to order, without having to take the ultimate step of nationalisation, whilst the producers could be sure, or at least less unsure, of employment and materials.

Nevertheless the threat of complete nationalisation still hung over the industry and O.K.O. appealed both to its members and to the public at large to boycott cinemas that had been sequestrated by the government or its local organs.[20] Audiences were encouraged to prevent government films from being shown. In late January 1919 a Petrograd audience broke up a showing of the newsreel film of the Brest-Litovsk peace negotiations.[21] The attitude of the film world to the authorities had been soured by the constant and widespread power cuts which, it was felt, affected the cinema unfairly. The film press was full of complaints about these economy measures and there were periods when all the cinemas in Moscow were forced to close at the same time.[22] Matters came to a head in February when the electricity supply to cinemas in Moscow was cut off completely for a fortnight and only restored when Vserabis (Vserossiiskii soyuz rabotnikov iskusstv), the Union of Art Workers, pointed out that electricity consumption was in fact greater when people stayed at home.[23] The cinema, as well as filling people's minds, also warmed their bodies. In a period of chronic fuel shortages this function could not be ignored, particularly if it proved to be more economical than the alternative. A foreign writer has described a typical visit to a Moscow cinema at this time:

> I visited the 'Mirror' kino in Tverskoi, another of Moscow's fashionable thoroughfares. As the name implies, the 'Mirror' was once a hall of mirrors. When I saw it, it was the remains of mirrors, many of which got bent when the Reds and the antis were slaughtering each other. The decorated ceiling had been newly decorated by shot and shell, and had a special ventilating system introduced by the method of dropping eggs from aeroplanes. The windows were patched with odds and ends of timber, and the seats were in splints and looking unusually frowzy. Most of them were just plain wooden benches. Two dim lights made their appearance during the intervals which were pretty frequent. An ancient screen, suffering from jaundice, and a worn-out projector, buried in an emergency structure and half hidden by a dirty curtain as though ashamed of itself, completed the fitments.
>
> The film was a genuine antique of pre-war Russian manufacture. It was in rags, and the reel was so broken that the 'curtain fell' every few minutes.[24]

In these circumstances it is perhaps hardly surprising that the summer of 1918 saw a further wave of emigration by film-makers to the by now German-occupied southern Ukraine. Six months later Lunacharsky was to blame this movement for the 'catastrophic' state of the Soviet cinema.[25] The government felt itself forced to take more stringent measures to control this situation and it reacted by ordering the registration of all cinema equipment and forbidding its transfer without official permission.[26] The Moscow Cinema Committee was already one step ahead. Having introduced controls of this type in March, and tightened them early in June,[27] the local soviet now further strengthened its hold by a decree introducing film censorship on 17 June 1918[28] and another confirming registration on 17 July 1918.[29] But there was a constant danger that the more the Bolsheviks tightened their control over existing cinema institutions, the more their opponents would be inclined to flee, taking much-needed equipment and personnel with them.

However, the acquisition of the Skobelev Committee's film studios by the Moscow and Petrograd Cinema Committees had finally enabled the Soviet authorities to begin direct production of *agitki*, short agitational films which dealt with a particular topic in a strongly visual manner and with great simplicity. This type of film production was hampered only by a chronic shortage of film stock. In September 1918 Leshchenko, head of the Petrograd Cinema Committee, announced an agreement with the German Kodak firm for the immediate supply of film stock. This agreement would have alleviated the shortage but it was overruled by the government because it involved too many risks on the Soviet side.[30] Some film stock was however being imported through Latvia and sold illegally on the black market to private firms, but it was not enough to meet the demand. In November 1918 the Cinema Committee signed an agreement with N. A. Minervin for the re-emulsification of already exposed film stock.[31] This method involved the replacement of the exposed layer of emulsion on the film with a new layer so that the stock could be used more than once, thus obviating the need for further imports. But this agreement too had little practical effect because Minervin was only able to produce small quantities of re-emulsified stock that were of both poor quality and low sensitivity, but it is none the less an instructive example of the desperate measures that were being taken.

The first *agitki* were shown both by the agit-trains[32] and in the cities. Narkompros claimed that during this period its Cinema Subsection, despite the shortage of materials, produced six feature-length films, twenty-two *agitki* and forty-three newsreels, and that, 'All the most important moments in the life of our Republic have been immortalised on film, even if only on a small scale.'[33] It is hardly surprising to learn that these films were very popular with children. Between July and December 1918, 112,035 children attended special film shows in Moscow alone,[34] while reports from various agit-trains show a similar success in the villages. The *Lenin* train, for example, attracted an audience of 22,800 children in the period January to March 1919.[35]

In December 1918 the Narkompros board convened a conference with members of the Moscow and Petrograd Cinema Committees. Delegates included A. V. Lunacharsky, N. K. Krupskaya, D. I. Leshchenko, N. F. Preobrazhensky (head of the Moscow Committee), V. E. Meyerhold, D. P. Sternberg and V. E. Tatlin.[36] The conference recommended the establishment of a centralised organ under Narkompros which would control the local Cinema Committees, and suggested the opening of negotiations with Vesenkha (Vysshii sovet narodnogo khozyaistva or Supreme Council of the National Economy) for the transfer of all cinema affairs to Narkompros.[37] The resolution passed by this conference was considered by the Presidium of Vesenkha in January 1919. In March 1919 the 8th Party Congress adopted a resolution entitled 'On political propaganda and cultural–educational work in the countryside' (O politicheskoi propagande i kul'turno–prosvetitel'-noi rabote v derevne'), which stated that the cinema and other forms of communication 'must be used for communist propaganda'.[38]

By this time it had become apparent that the process of gradual nationalisation had reached its limits. Unless the government took a decisive step either there would be little left to nationalise or the central authorities would be presented with a *fait accompli* by the actions of the local soviets; either situation would be a recipe for chaos. To forestall further wastage of meagre resources Lenin signed the decree nationalising all cinema enterprises on 27 August 1919.[39] The All-Russian Cinema Committee was entrusted with overseeing the whole process of nationalisation.

Since the beginning of 1918, and particularly as the authority of the Bolshevik government had been extended beyond the confines of the large cities, the Moscow Cinema Committee, headed by Preobrazhensky, had tried to extend its influence too. Hence, by August 1919, the Committee's activities were no longer confined to Moscow and so it was re-named the All-Russian Cinema Committee. On 18 September a decree was published over the signature of Lunacharsky which transformed this Committee yet again into the All-Russian Photographic and Cinematographic

Section of Narkompros (Vserossiiskii fotokinematograficheskii otdel Narkomprosa, or V.F.K.O. for short).[40] V.F.K.O. was to be headed by D. I. Leshchenko, who also signed the document and had previously been chairman of the Petrograd Cinema Committee. Some sources maintain that the actual act of nationalisation was merely a recognition by the government of what had already been effected by the spontaneous activity of the masses.[41] However, Leshchenko was himself a proponent of the gradualist approach and the fact that as late as March 1920 Lenin had to send a telegram to local authorities which, among other things, asked for information about their progress in nationalising the cinema, would suggest that this is a misleading assertion.[42] Indeed it was only in November 1919 that the Moscow Cinema Committee was itself fully re-formed as an integral part of Narkompros, some of its lesser functions being assumed by the new Photographic and Cinematographic Section under the Moscow City Soviet (Fotokinosektsiya pri Mossovete).[43] This was the first of a network of such sections to be established by V.F.K.O.; the sections were subordinated to V.F.K.O. but also linked to the local soviet and they were intended to ensure that orders from the central authorities were being carried out. But even on paper the administrative centralisation of the cinema was not completed. On 29 January 1920 the V.F.K.O. board acted to nationalise the remaining rental offices in Moscow and on 5 November 1920 the process was concluded with a decision to pay cinema workers directly from state funds.[44] Even this was in any case only the beginning of a centralised film industry for there was little equipment left for production, the distribution network had broken down, the cinemas were in a bad state of repair and, even worse from the point of view of communications, the majority of cinemas had closed because of the shortage of films, fuel and electricity.

The shortage of film stock meant that virtually no new feature-length films were being produced. Film production in the years 1918–20 was concentrated almost entirely on the more urgently required documentary and newsreel films and the *agitki*.[45] The nationalisation decree had, it is true, uncovered a new supply of films that had been hoarded by entrepreneurs in the anticipation of a Bolshevik defeat in the Civil War and a subsequent return to full-scale private enterprise. However, the majority of these films were of pre-Revolutionary Russian origin, and the remainder had been imported: they consisted of so-called 'psychological' or 'salon' dramas of the type that Hollywood thrived, and the Bolsheviks frowned, on. Such films were considered ideologically unsuitable for a Soviet audience, but the shortage of new films was acute and the supply of acceptable old films worn and dwindling, so it was decided to show these films to the accompaniment of a lecture on their weaknesses by a party worker.[46] From the propaganda point of view this was a disaster, because the speaker was often ignored or shouted down. The practice was therefore soon discontinued.

The Soviet cinema, as a result of the emigration mentioned above, was also quite clearly going to suffer from a shortage of skilled and trained personnel in all spheres for some time to come. There were however plenty of unskilled volunteers, usually young and infused with revolutionary enthusiasm;[47] with the emigration of the entrepreneurs these new recruits could not be trained in the conventional manner through an apprenticeship in a well established studio. The only solution was to establish a film school to train these and other necessary technicians, actors, directors, etc. On the suggestion of the director Vladimir Gardin, a State Film School (Gosudarstvennaya kinoshkola) was established by V.F.K.O. in Moscow, with Gardin himself as its first director.[48] Lunacharsky remarked:

> We need cadres of workers who are free from the habits and strivings of the old bourgeois entrepreneurial hacks and are able to elevate the cinema to the heights of the artistic and socio-political tasks facing the proletariat, especially in the current period of intensified struggle.[49]

Initially the Film School produced two *agitki: V dni bor'by* (In the Days of Battle), using film from the Polish front, and *Serp i molot* (Hammer and Sickle), a meaningful tale of life in the countryside. Both were directed by Gardin, with Tisse as cameraman and Pudovkin playing the leading rôle.[50] Thus, like the agit-trains, the Film School in some ways represented the Soviet cinema in embryo. When the supply of film stock had been exhausted Lev Kuleshov and his Workshop of *naturshchiki* (actors with no conventional training) occupied themselves by trying out their theories of film and movement in miming so-called *fil'my bez plënki* (films without film).[51] In 1920 the Workshop produced its first *agitka* with the self-explanatory title *Na krasnom fronte* (At the Red Front). But the full effects of the Film School did not become apparent until the Civil War had been won and a more permanent organisational structure for the Soviet cinema established. Thus, accumulated difficulties had largely crippled the existing conventional network of cinema production and distribution so that the Bolsheviks had to create their own structures and methods of control and communication.

A vast country with a widely scattered population and a rapidly changing front required above all a mobile, flexible and reliable medium of communication between the centre and the regions, at least until the regions had become sufficiently stable to permit the establishment of more permanent and conventional organisations. The structure of the Soviet *agitprop* machine eventually developed to combine a network of stationary *agitpunkty* (from the Russian *agitatsionnyi punkt*, an agitational point or centre), placed at strategic points like railway junctions or large settlements, with an increasing number of travelling agitational trains (*agitpoezda*). The trains were to act as the standard-bearers of revolutionary agitation, moving wherever they were most urgently required, while the *agitpunkty* were to concentrate on propaganda saturation of the population in a given place. One hundred and forty *agitpunkty* were established in 1919 following a decree of 13 May[52] and a further two hundred and twenty were set up in 1920. The first *agitpunkty* were located in railway termini or junctions, but this arrangement severely disrupted the normal workings of the railway network and so a standard design for purpose-built *politdoma* (from *politicheskii dom*, literally 'political house'), stationary centres for in-depth propaganda saturation of the local population, was evolved. It is not known how many of these were eventually constructed but it is worth noting that the design included a library, schoolroom, canteen, cinema and stage, with, for larger centres of population, the addition of Komsomol and Party rooms, a chess room and a music room. In many ways the *politdom* resembled the concept of a modern community centre in its amenities, but its purpose in the context of the Civil War was, of course, essentially and overtly political.

The function of the mobile agitational centres, usually trains, was however altogether more dramatic and, in the short term, more important. The concept of the agit-train was a logical historical development, mixing the artistic tradition of the strolling player (*gastrolër*) and his later counterpart in the early history of the cinema[53] with some of the most modern technological capabilities. In the cinema the historical continuity of the concept was particularly noticeable, if only because the cinema had a more recent past. Before the construction of permanent cinema buildings, and the development of the regular distribution system associated with them, exhibitors had toured the country with a single projector and a selection of films, stopping in each town until their audience potential was exhausted, and then moving on.[54] The idea developed and there were several ambitious attempts to establish mobile cinemas on barges in the early 1900s,[55] but none was successful and with the construction of conventional permanent cinema buildings the practice died out. During the First World War mobile projection equipment was again used, this time for morale-boosting and propaganda purposes at the front. After the October Revolution the Bolsheviks set aside a compartment in their troop trains which was reserved for the propaganda section of the army. This section distributed leaflets, newspapers and posters. It was in the Military Department of the V.Ts.I.K. (Vserossiiskii Tsentral′nyi Ispolnitel′nyi Komitet – All-Russian Central Executive Committee) publishing house that the concept of the agit-train was born;[56] it represented both an amalgamation of previous techniques and a refinement of them.[57]

The first agit-train represented a direct experimental extension of the idea of the propaganda compartment to that of the full-length train. The *Voenno-podvizhnyi frontovyi poezd imeni V.I. Lenina* (V. I. Lenin Mobile Military Front Train) was hurriedly prepared and painted with pictorial slogans in the Kursk railway works, and it left Moscow for a trial run to Kazan on 13 August 1918. The train comprised between seven and nine coaches equipped with a bookshop, library, office and living quarters. The *Lenin* and its crew spent two weeks distributing pamphlets and newspapers to units of the Red Army stationed along the track, and returned to the capital in early September.[58] This experiment had been confined to agitational activity amongst the military; it was felt to have been so successful that Trotsky ordered five similar 'literary–instructional' trains from the Moscow regional railway, but production difficulties delayed the delivery of the last of these until 1920.[59]

On 31 January 1919 the Presidium of V.Ts.I.K. created a Special Commission to run its planned fleet of agit-trains and steamers and to study the problems of communication between the centre and the provinces that the project had exposed. The Commission officially had four members: Sosnovsky, Minin, Eremeev and Burov, but Burov later claimed that he and Eremeev had done all the work.[60] It is significant that the Commission was directly subordinated to V.Ts.I.K.; this was a further sign not only of the importance attached to the whole project but also an indication that the old machinery of government was being by-passed because of its inefficiency and unreliability. The Narkompros organisation, consisting of a thinly spread network of schools, 'people's houses' (*narodnye doma*), libraries and bookshops, was inert and unwieldy. Agit-trains, on the other hand, were a fast, flexible, more direct and dynamic method of communication with the masses. They had other advantages as well: a train carried with it a skilled team of *agitprop* officials, some of whom specialised in particular fields appropriate to the areas they were visiting. A Narkompros official was, as an individual in such circumstances had to be, very much a jack-of-all-trades, covering the whole range of subjects on which the central authorities might deem it fit to disseminate information. Similarly, his 'people's house' lacked the psychological advantages of a train, because it was always there, even when inactive. Trains, because they came and went and were based on Moscow, were regarded by the population at large as 'direct representatives of supreme power',[61] and became known as 'V.Ts.I.K. on rails'.[62] It was because of the status bestowed on them by their direct relationship with the centre that the agit-trains as a whole had to strike a balance between the twin tasks of agitation and in-depth propaganda; had their activities been too closely concentrated on the superficial, 'they would come, talk, and everything would remain unchanged'.[63]

As we shall see it was the cinema component that did much to make the visits of the train memorable, for most peasants had never before seen a moving film.[64] The Bolsheviks were able to take advantage of this in two ways; first, they associated themselves in the public mind with technology, modernisation and progress, and second, they could use the medium to bring pictures of the new leadership to the population at large. In these circumstances Lenin might appear as a god-like figure and indeed, following the attempt on his life in 1918, Lenin was shown in a widely distributed newsreel walking in the Kremlin with Bonch-Bruevich. This particular sequence was filmed and used quite specifically to scotch rumours that Lenin was dead.[65]

The second generation of agit-trains was more ambitious than the *Lenin*: these were composed of sixteen to eighteen coaches and each train had an internal telephone link and a radio transmitter-receiver for communication with their home base in Moscow. From fifteen to eighteen political workers were employed and in addition there were on average between eighty and eighty-five technical assistants. One of the contemporary criticisms levelled at the staffing policy was that agit-train journeys were seen as a kind of rest cure for ailing comrades, who then either refused to do their fair share of the work, or did it and destroyed their health completely.[66] The trains were distinctively and brightly decorated with paintings and slogans;[67] artists of the standing of Mayakovsky and El Lissitsky were involved, together with many others who, as a result of their Civil War experiences, later went into the cinema. Eisenstein and Kozintsev were amongst the latter. In the first burst of revolutionary artistic fervour the trains were covered with symbolic and futurist motifs representing the functions of the trains themselves,[68] but these were apparently either misunderstood by the peasantry or quite simply mystified them. More realistic imagery was subsequently adopted.[69] Inside, the trains were divided into different working compartments. The principal ones were the Political Department, which controlled instruction and agitational lectures, and the Information Department, which helped the Political Department to prepare the necessary propaganda material. There was also a Complaints Office which received petitions from the population and passed back information on the sources of political discontent both to its own Political Department and to the authorities in Moscow. Finally there was the ROSTA (Rossiiskoe telegrafnoe agentstvo – Russian Telegraph Agency) Department which was responsible for organising the publication of newspapers, leaflets, posters and appeals and for running the train's radio transmitter. In addition most trains had a film department, a book store, a shop and a space for exhibitions on various themes. The entire organisation of the train was supervised by a political commissar who was appointed directly by the V.Ts.I.K. Presidium.

While the supply of film stock permitted, the function of the film section was twofold: first, the demonstration in the provinces of agit-films produced at the centre (the Lenin newsreel sequence mentioned above would be included in this category), and, second, the supply of newsreel and documentary material from the provinces back to the centre where it was edited by Lev Kuleshov, Dziga Vertov, Esfir Shub and others who were to play a leading rôle in the later development of the Soviet cinema. Their experience at this time did much to shape the theories of the cinema that they developed separately later. Kuleshov used some of the footage he had shot himself in his film *Na krasnom fronte* (At the Red Front) in 1920, and much of the material brought back by the trains was incorporated into Dziga Vertov's series of newsreels, *Kinonedelya* (Cine-Week)[70] and later into his documentary feature films *Godovshchina revolyutsii* (The Anniversary of the Revolution) and *Istoriya Grazhdanskoi voiny* (The History of the Civil War).[71] Eduard Tisse, who later became the cameraman on some of Eisenstein's major films, was also involved in this work. The needs of the moment gave rise to two new genres of film: the agitational film-poster (*agitatsionnyi kinoplakat*) and the *agitka* proper. The former was quite simply what it claimed to be, a filmed version of a poster theme and in essence the cinema's equivalent of Mayakovsky's poster poems. The *agitka* proper was also short and explicit, conveying a simple message on a single subject with directness and economy. Of the ninety-two films produced by Soviet film organisations in the three years 1918–20 sixty-three were in this category and most of them were less than 600 metres in length, or less than thirty minutes when projected.[72] The *agitka* genre had a decisive influence on the stylistic development of the Soviet film: the essence of economy and dynamism in the visual presentation of material was developed in the principles of editing or, as Eisenstein was later to call it, 'dynamic montage'. The *agitka* had to convey its message entirely by simple, visual means. It had to attract and hold the attention of its audience and leave them with an impression of dynamism and strength. These principles were embodied in different ways in the theoretical teachings of Lev Kuleshov and his Workshop at the Film School, in the documentaries and manifestos of Dziga Vertov's Kinoglaz (Cine-Eye) group, in the films of Shub, Eisenstein, Pudovkin and others.

Sometimes the *agitka* was devoted to a topic of general interest, and sometimes to a more specialised problem. One of the most celebrated was *Gidrotorf* (Hydro-Peat), personally approved by Lenin, which explained the advantages of lifting peat by use of hydraulic power.[73] This film is typical of the later *agitka*. Made in 1920, *Gidrotorf* reflects a move away from the rather simplistic visual agitation of the first films towards an adaptation of the medium to encourage economic improvements. Of course this move also demonstrates the transformation of the Bolsheviks' position from that of a state of siege to the point where they could at last begin to concentrate on the details of government. But although the number of agitational and propaganda films that were intended to improve the efficiency of the Soviet economy was increasing, the majority of these films were still overtly political, depicting the trials of the Whites, the perils of counter-revolution, intervention and restoration, and the horrors inflicted on the toiling masses during the tsarist era. It was this latter type of film that was shown to the peasantry in large numbers. For propaganda purposes it was often sufficiently effective, for an audience that had never previously watched a film, to show a newsreel of the Bolshevik leaders, thus establishing a new kind of quasi-direct rapport between the rulers and the ruled. The trains themselves were also the subject of films. In 1919 the cameraman A. Lemberg made a film of the activities of the agit-steamer *Krasnaya zvezda* (Red Star) and in 1922 he followed this with a film entitled *Pervyi agropoezd imeni tovarishcha Lenina* (The First 'Comrade Lenin' Agro-Train).[74] Dziga Vertov wrote a script for a documentary film to be shot from the agit-train *Sovetskii Kavkaz* (Soviet Caucasus) but it was never made.[75] The shortage of materials and the resulting emphasis on newsreels and other films of more immediate political value meant that other, more ambitious plans had to be shelved as well, so that a series of films on the history of Russian and world culture, planned by a group which included Gorky, Blok, Bryusov, Alexei Tolstoy and A. Serafimovich was never started.[76]

The *agitki* were shown above all in areas where the need for active, and visual, *agitprop* work was perceived to be most urgent.[77] The *Lenin* train was sent through the parts of the North-Western province recently evacuated by the Germans on a six-week journey ending in mid March 1919. The train, headed by Sosnovsky, a member of the V.Ts.I.K. Commission established the previous January, visited Pskov, Riga, Vitebsk, Vilna, Minsk, Kharkov and Kursk, thus eventually covering the whole of the former front against the Germans, and entering what were still in some cases disputed territories. After a three-month wait in Moscow, which produced accusations of timewasting, the *Lenin* returned to the Ukrainian front where the Red Army was now fighting Denikin's troops. From October until the end of 1919 the train travelled through Siberia, visiting Samara, Omsk and Ekaterinburg. The aim was to improve the flow of grain to the cities and alleviate the worsening food situation there caused by Denikin's advance to Tula. In this respect agitation was intended to have an immediate and tangible result.

The *Krasnyi vostok* (Red East), equipped with a special section to deal with Moslem affairs, spent the first half of 1920 in Turkestan. The *Sovetskii Kavkaz* spent the three summer months in the malaria-infested regions of the Caucasus, while the *Krasnyi kazak* (Red Cossack) toured the Don area shortly after Denikin's defeat. However the two most important components of the operation were the train *Oktyabr'skaya revolyutsiya* (October Revolution) and the steamer *Krasnaya zvezda*, both of which were in differing ways atypical of the operation as a whole but illustrate the basic aim of taking a communications medium out into the field.

On 23 October 1919 Kalinin, who was acting as political commissar on the *Oktyabr'skaya revolyutsiya*, delivered a report on the train's activities to the Presidium of V.Ts.I.K. Its function was that of standard-bearer to the agit-train fleet, concentrating on political demonstration and only superficial instruction. Even more than the average agit-train it symbolised the presence of the central Bolshevik government in the remoter areas of the R.S.F.S.R. Between April 1919 and December 1920 the train made twelve forays into the countryside, all headed by Kalinin and each averaging three weeks in length, with a ten to twelve hour stop in each settlement. The other trains took up to three months for an average exercise and usually stopped for up to two days at a time. During its travels the *Oktyabr'skaya revolyutsiya* ranged as far as Minsk and Irkutsk, Petrograd and the Don Basin. In the course of 1919 the *Oktyabr'skaya revolyutsiya*, *Lenin*, and *Krasnaya zvezda* between them organised a total of 753 public meetings attended by 1,300,000 people.[78] By the end of 1920 the *Oktyabr'skaya revolyutsiya* alone had provided over 430 film shows which drew an audience in excess of 620,000 people.[79] Apart from the films mentioned above, the trains showed films specifically aimed at an audience of children in the daytime, such as *O rybake i rybke* (The Fisherman and the Little Fish), *Prazdnik kommunisticheskoi molodëzhi* (The Festival of Communist Youth), *Za krasnoe znamya* (For the Red Banner), and at an audience of adults in the evening, for example, *Spasiteli rodiny* (Saviours of the Homeland), *Za novyi mir* (For a New World), *Pobeda maya* (The Victory of May), *Glaza otkrylis'* (Eyes were Opened), and the anti-religious *Otkrytie moshchei Tikhona Zadonskogo* (The Exposure of the Relics of Tikhon of Zadonsk). These films were frequently accompanied by lectures from agitators, sent by the Party's Central Committee, or instructors sent by the various People's Commissariats.

The presence of cinema facilities on board fulfilled an additional function as a magnet; people who came initially and solely to watch films frequently became involved in other activities as well, ranging from purely political propaganda work to the campaigns for the eradication of illiteracy and for increased economic efficiency. There is however no evidence that at this stage film was used at anything more than a superficial level in the literacy campaigns; the cinema brought the message that illiteracy was undesirable but the medium itself was not employed as a teaching aid, probably because the shortage of appropriate facilities precluded the economies of scale that would have made the idea financially viable. In addition the agit-train workers were preoccupied with the more immediate problems facing the leadership: at one time, for example, the interval between film showings was used for appeals to the peasantry to send grain to the towns to alleviate the bread shortage there.[80]

The activities of the steamer *Krasnaya zvezda* are also well documented. On 31 May 1919 Molotov was appointed political commissar, and one month later Lenin gave him the following letter of introduction:

> The bearer of this, Comrade *Molotov,* is personally known to me as an old party worker and has been appointed plenipotentiary representative of V.Ts.I.K. on the literary–instructional steamer *Krasnaya zvezda.* I ask all authorities and organisations to afford him *every* assistance and, in order not to delay military information, to provide him with a direct [telephone] link.[81]

Nadezhda Krupskaya, Lenin's wife and head of the Extra-Mural Department of Narkompros, was appointed as Narkompros representative on the steamer and was therefore in charge of the film section.[82] The account that she wrote of her journey shortly afterwards[83] conveys a vivid impression of the way in which the fabric of a modern society, especially when it is not rooted in historical and national traditions, can easily be fragmented by the pressures of revolution and civil war. The reception that awaited the crew of the *Krasnaya zvezda* in Nizhny Novgorod, where it was to start its voyage down the Volga, was symptomatic of the generally chaotic conditions prevailing at the time and of the difficulties facing the government in its attempts to communicate with the provinces: 'The Red Army soldiers would not let us through even with passes from V.Ts.I.K.; they were not even aware of its existence.'[84] And this was eighteen months after the October Revolution! Local Party workers complained to the crew of 'apathy in the ranks of Party workers' and 'alienation from the masses'.[85] In Chistopol Krupskaya considered that the efforts of the Bolsheviks were being carefully undermined in the schools:

Scripture is not taught but the icons have been left in the schools so as 'not to perturb the population'; there is one teacher for extra-mural education and he considers that politics should not be mixed with cultural work. Nowhere have I seen such systematic sabotage of the measures of the Soviet authorities in the field of popular education.[86]

Shortly afterwards Krupskaya wrote to Z. P. Krzhizhanovskaya her deputy at *Narkompros*, asking for further supplies of 'wholesome' films, pamphlets of Lenin's speeches and writings and other similar forms of literature for distribution to the local population.[87] Both Krupskaya's letters of this period and the diary that she kept are valuable sources of information on the practical aspects of the steamer's journey and the problems encountered; they confirm too that Lenin himself was aware of the difficulties confronting Bolshevik propagandists in the field.

The *Krasnaya zvezda* itself was equipped with a printing press, bookshop and radio transmitter–receiver; this enabled the crew to maintain direct contact with Moscow, to produce a newspaper and to distribute it in towns and villages that had had no communication with the outside world for many months.[88] There was again a space for a travelling exhibition, the theme of which was changed according to the needs of the area visited: subjects ranged from the electrification of the countryside to advice for mothers on hygiene and the care of children. In addition the steamer towed a barge which served in effect as a floating cinema accommodating about a thousand people, and the presence of this was vital to the success of the whole enterprise. In sailing along the Volga and Kama rivers the crew were attempting to propagandise a population that was not only overwhelmingly illiterate but also multinational and, perhaps, more importantly, multilingual. The distribution of printed matter soon proved to be futile and, as the agit-workers sent from Moscow were Russian speaking, agitational speeches were also fraught with complications.[89] In these circumstances the cinema performed its unique function as a universal medium of communication: assuming that the film survived the process of projection, the same *agitka* could be shown to Chuvash, Bashkir, Tartar and other audiences, all of whom would stand an equal chance of grasping the point that was being made to them. At the time Nariman Narimanov, the Azerbaijani writer and a leading Party activist, remarked:

In the East, where people have grown accustomed to thinking primarily in images, the cinema is the sole possible means of propaganda because it does not require the preliminary, gradual preparation of the masses. The Eastern peasant accepts everything he sees on the screen as the most fundamental and genuine reality.[90]

In addition the cinema, being a totally new experience for the peasant, performed in itself a powerful propaganda function for the new régime. In the course of its three-month voyage the *Krasnaya zvezda* organised 196 film shows attended by a total of 225,000 people.[91] Like the agit-trains, the steamer played an essential rôle in establishing the film as an effective propaganda medium and in the longer term in spreading the cinema as a leading form of entertainment for the masses outside the cities, and the prominence of many of the people involved bore witness to the significance attached to the project by the central authorities.

Of course the whole scheme met with numerous difficulties. Lack of a coherent overall plan and a decision instead to respond pragmatically to immediate situations meant that the trains remained idle in Moscow when the need for their presence was considered less than urgent. This policy was dictated by circumstance; the number of reliable and effective agit-workers was limited in the initial stages before any training scheme had been started, equipment was in very short supply and communications were erratic. Hence the efforts of the V.Ts.I.K. Commission responsible had to be concentrated on areas where they would achieve maximum political impact, and these were primarily those regions that until recently had been occupied by the various counter-revolutionary forces and in which there lingered a residue of the anti-Bolshevik agitation and propaganda to which the population had been subjected. Despite their limitations, however, the agit-trains were deemed sufficiently successful to be continued on a larger scale and on a more permanent basis throughout the 1920s. Although there is evidence to suggest that they continued to be used into the 1930s (and that they are still used, albeit on a limited scale, in Siberia in the 1970s) the significance of their rôle has diminished as the network of conventional cinemas has spread to the remoter areas and as the film has yielded its position as the foremost medium of information and propaganda to the radio, which, despite its lack of any form of visual communications, and of the opportunity for mass experience, has the overwhelming advantages of immediacy and directness.

In 1920 the mechanisms of control over the trains were altered. In January Lenin issued a series of instructions designed to increase their effectiveness.[92] The existing V.Ts.I.K. Commission was demoted to a department which was concerned only with the more mundane administrative aspects of the project, while its overall policy functions were transferred to a special commission immediately under Sovnarkom (Sovet narodnykh komissarov – Council of People's Commissars) which was specifically given the right to refer to Lenin directly if the normal channels of communication through the governmental apparatus proved inadequate. Lenin also urged more detailed changes in the operation of the actual trains. He stressed the importance of increasing the supply of both literature and films on specific matters from anti-religious propaganda to methods of improving agricultural and industrial efficiency. Agit-workers were instructed to examine more scientifically the effectiveness of individual films and to report their findings back to V.F.K.O. so that a systematic programme of effective propaganda films could be produced. Litvinov was personally ordered to survey the foreign film scene with a view to the importation of suitable material. Finally, the range of the trains was to be made more flexible by providing them with fleets of bicycles, motorcycles and other locally available means of transport to improve the distribution of leaflets and other printed propaganda.

In March 1920 the Ninth Party Congress recommended that increased resources should be made available for propaganda work among the peasantry,[93] and in April the new department in charge of the agit-trains defined the areas within which the programme could most usefully be developed.[94] The aim was to increase and improve contact between the centre and the regions, thereby encouraging a more coherent and consistent implementation of policy overall; the principal methods of contact suggested were threefold:

1 The instruction and information of local organs of both party and state regarding the decisions taken at the centre.
2 Direct supervision of the conduct of local organs through the employment on a wider basis of specialists from Vesenkha, Glavkomtrud [Glavnyi komitet truda – Chief Labour Committee], Narkompros and other organisations.
3 The provision of an adequate supply of the literature issued at the centre.

Once an adequate degree of overall control had been established in this way and an effective governmental structure recreated, the task of everyday agitation and propaganda could safely be entrusted to the local representatives of Soviet power. This did not imply any relaxation of centralised control but was merely a reversion to the conventional hierarchical channels of the governmental process. Gradually the trains and their functions were replaced by an improved and vastly expanded network of *agitpunkty* and the type of workers' and peasants' clubs that survive to the present day. In this sense the agit-trains represented a spontaneous and temporary response to an emergency situation. Their rôle in assisting the Soviet state through the stormy years of its infancy was significant if not vital. Their greatest importance though lies in a longer term historical perspective: the agit-trains represented one of the earliest attempts at the creation and manipulation of a mass communications medium for political purposes and their requirements and techniques exerted a formative influence on the future development of the medium, the cinema, in both artistic and economic terms. Without the challenge of the Civil War it is unlikely that the Soviet cinema would have developed the forceful, distinctive and revolutionary visual style of the 1920s, and without that style the effectiveness of the cinema in transmitting the Bolshevik world-view both within and beyond the frontiers of the U.S.S.R. would have been severely restricted.

4. THE DISORGANISATION OF ORGANISATION: THE EARLY TWENTIES

Things are going badly in the cinema. The cinema is the greatest means of mass agitation. The task is to take it into our own hands.

Stalin, 1924.[1]

The conventional structures of the cinema industry in its three major aspects – production, distribution, and exhibition – had been shattered by the Civil War. The shortage of films and equipment meant that priority had to be given to the production of newsreels and *agitki* and the production of Soviet feature films was consequently neglected. As the existing supply of films was exhausted, as electricity supplies were interrupted, and as the economic crisis worsened, so the number of cinemas still in operation fell. This further reduced income which might have been used to stimulate production. The cinema was caught in a vicious circle. As late as 1923, the journal *Kino* observed:

We shall not deceive ourselves with faint hopes. The path of regeneration for a shattered industry is difficult. Not only are there no serious resources in the cinema, but the workers and producers are dispersed, disorganised and, to a significant extent, technically backward and unqualified.[2]

Two things above all else were needed for the regeneration of the cinema and for its use as an effective propaganda weapon: organisation and resources. The two principal Soviet film organisations to have survived the Civil War were V.F.K.O. in Moscow[3] and Sevzapkino (Severo–Zapadnoe oblastnoe upravlenie po delam fotografii i kinematografii – North Western Directorate for Photographic and Cinematographic Affairs), formerly P.O.F.K.O. (Petrogradskii oblastnoi fotokinokomitet or Petrograd Regional Photographic and Cinematographic Committee) in Petrograd. Both of these were basically regional organisations and neither was particularly powerful vis-à-vis the private sector that re-emerged, particularly in the fields of distribution and exhibition, under the New Economic Policy which had succeeded War Communism. The nationalisation decree of August 1919 had in effect transferred responsibility for distribution and exhibition not to any centralised organs of control but to the local representatives of Narkompros, subject only to somewhat vague and ineffective overall supervision from above. Such a state of affairs further weakened the nascent Soviet film industry, for it meant that the local cinemas had little incentive to perform their 'social duty' and very strong reasons for attempting to maintain their commercial viability. The continued existence of a tax on cinema seats, levied by the central government, made that commercial viability more difficult to attain but, at the same time, made the struggle to attain it all the more desperate. Hence, where possible, foreign 'hits' (*boeviki*) were shown.[4] In the early twenties these were almost entirely films that had been produced and imported before the Revolution,[5] but after 1924 the Soviet market came increasingly to be dominated by the Hollywood product. Mary Pickford,[6] Charlie Chaplin,[7] Buster Keaton, *inter alia*, were familiar figures in the pages of Soviet film journals. It was not until 1927 that box office receipts from Soviet films exceeded those from imported films,[8] and many of these Soviet films could hardly be classified as revolutionary in their ideological content.

The two problems of organisation and resources were closely related. It was no simple task to organise something that had only a shadowy existence. At the same time the situation could scarcely be improved without some form of direction and control. During the Civil War circumstances had imposed their own imperatives upon the cinema: the bulk of existing resources had been devoted to the specific and urgent tasks of the agit-trains. The resources not used for these tasks were also, on the whole, those that the Bolsheviks were unable to direct and control; private entrepreneurs from the pre-Revolutionary period were still active, especially in areas still held by the Whites.[9] This had left the conventional cinema network, and the studios that might have provided it with films, in a state of collapse. The normal structures of production, distribution and exhibition had broken down; the supply of basic equipment and film stock had been exhausted. Whereas during the Civil War there had been obvious short term priorities, now there were none. Only the longer term task of building up the Soviet film industry to serve the needs of the Revolution loomed on the horizon.

Lenin was not the only Bolshevik leader to extol the importance of the cinema;[10] in 1923 Trotsky suggested that, whereas in the feudal era the Church had been the opiate of the people, and in the capitalist period the tsarist government had created a state vodka monopoly to the same end, in a socialist society the cinema, instead of drugging the masses into submission, would emancipate them towards a new consciousness:

> In the daily life of capitalistic towns, the cinema has become just such an integral part of life as the bath, the beer-house, the Church and other indispensable institutions, commendable and otherwise. The passion for the cinema is rooted in the desire for distraction, the desire to see something new and improbable, to laugh and to cry, not at your own, but at other people's misfortunes. The cinema satisfies these demands in a very direct, visual, picturesque and vital way, requiring nothing from the audience; it does not even require them to be literate.[11]

Bemoaning the Bolsheviks' failure to take effective control of the cinema, Trotsky compared its potential effect with that of both the vodka monopoly and the Church:

> In attracting and amusing, the cinema already rivals the beer-shop and the public-house. . .it is manifest that, above everything, the cinema competes with the public-house in the matter of how the eight leisure hours are to be filled. Can we secure this incomparable weapon? Why not? The government of the Tsar, in a few years, established an intricate net of state public-houses. The business yielded a yearly revenue of almost a milliard gold roubles. Why should not the government of the workers establish a net of State cinemas? This apparatus of amusement could more and more be made to become an integral part of the national life, using it to combat alcoholism, it could, at the same time, be made into a revenue-yielding concern. . .
>
> The cinema competes not only with the public-house, but also with the Church. And this rivalry may become fatal for the Church if we make up for the separation of the Church from the socialist State by the fusion of the socialist State and the cinema.[12]

Trotsky lamented the Bolsheviks' failure to take advantage of the opportunities offered by the cinema, both as a propaganda weapon and, as Stalin was later to emphasise, as a source of government revenue:

> The fact that we have so far, i.e. in nearly six years, not taken possession of the cinema shows how slow and uneducated we are, not to say, frankly, stupid. This weapon which cries out to be used, is the best instrument for propaganda, technical, educational and industrial propaganda, propaganda against alcohol, propaganda for sanitation, political propaganda, any kind of propaganda you please, a propaganda which is accessible to everyone, which is attractive, cuts into the memory and may be made a possible source of revenue.[13]

Stalin paid lip-service to the rôle of the cinema, although at this stage he does not seem to have taken it as seriously as either Lenin or Trotsky did.[14] Indeed, one is tempted, from the evidence to hand, to the somewhat cynical view that it had perhaps become *de rigueur* for those in authority to make some pronouncement on the rôle of the film, while doing very little in effect to ensure that their pronouncements were realised. As a contemporary writer observed, 'Many people talk about the cinema, but few think about it.'[15]

The 7th Congress of the R.K.P.(b) (Rossiiskaya kommunisticheskaya partiya (bol'shevikov) – Russian Communist Party (Bolsheviks)), in March 1918 had made no mention at all of the cinema in any of its resolutions.[16] It may fairly be argued that the Congress had more urgent tasks in front of it. It had, after all, to deal with the Peace of Brest-Litovsk. The 8th Congress, meeting a year later in March 1919, passed a resolution 'On political propaganda and cultural–educational work in the countryside' ('O politicheskoi propagande i kul'turno–prosvetitel'noi rabote v derevne') which made only passing reference to the cinema as one of a list of possible weapons of propaganda and education.[17] The 9th Congress, in March and April 1920, acted in similar fashion but passed a general resolution recommending that increased resources should be devoted to propaganda work among the peasantry.[18] A year later, the 10th Congress heard a report from Preobrazhensky on the general problems facing the party in its agitation and propaganda work, given that it was starting from scratch and had available to it only embryonic organs like Glavpolitprosvet (Glavnyi politiko-prosvetitel'nyi komitet – Chief Committee for Political Education).[19] By the time of the 11th Congress in the spring of 1922 the Party could afford to devote more attention to the problems involved. At the tenth session Yakovlev read a report 'On the press and propaganda', ('O pechati i propagande') in which he made some general points about the fragmentation caused by the New Economic Policy and the hostility to the spread of education that apparently existed within certain sections of the Party:

> Then there's the point of view of the Yaroslavl *gubkom* [provincial committee]. In this Yaroslavl *gubkom*, so one of its leaders writes, they think that the more educated a peasant is, the more he'll think of his class interests as the interests of a smallholder, a petit bourgeois, and not the other way round. They say that the more educated a peasant is, the better he will understand his interests against us; hence the conclusion that we should not educate the peasant. All the more so, because the peasant wants to be both a hawk and a grass-snake. You choose – either a peasant or a communist.[20]

Clearly suspicions of the sort expressed in Yaroslavl did not make the Party's task any easier; nevertheless Yakovlev's point was not taken up by the other delegates in the ensuing discussion. Indeed the discussion concentrated almost entirely on the report read by Zinoviev, who had spoken before Yakovlev, entitled 'On the strengthening of the party' ('Ob ukreplenii partii').[21] Once more propaganda had been squeezed out by what were considered to be more urgent tasks.

The Party's apparent half-heartedness in practice about the cinema had obviously begun to irk those who were responsible for the cinema. Time and again, when the call had gone out, *Pravda* had devoted more column inches to the cinema, but it was only a short time before the Party organ lapsed into its usual state of apathy and reverted to theatre and concert reviews.[22]

In January 1922 Lenin, in a directive issued to E. A. Litkens, then Deputy People's Commissar for Enlightenment under Lunacharsky, indicated the path that Soviet film production should follow once it had got under way:

> Narkompros must organise the supervision of all institutions and systematise these matters. All films exhibited in the R.S.F.S.R. should be registered and catalogued by number in Narkompros. For every film programme a definite proportion should be determined:
> a entertainment films, especially for publicity purposes and their receipts (without, of course, any obscene or counter-revolutionary content), and
> b under the heading 'From the Life of the Peoples of the World', films of a particularly propagandist content, such as the colonial policy of the British in India, the work of the League of Nations, the starving in Berlin, etc., etc.[23]

More particularly, Lenin laid emphasis on the effectiveness of the cinema in relatively backward areas, saying. 'We should pay special attention to the organisation of cinemas in the countryside and in the East, where they are novelties and where, therefore, our propaganda will be particularly successful.'[24]

For the moment, however, these were to remain unrealised projects. While the cinema continued in a state of disarray there could scarcely be any alternative. On 24 December 1922 Lunacharsky, who, as People's Commissar for Enlightenment, had at least nominal charge of the cinema industry, reported to the 10th All-Russian Congress of Soviets in the following terms:

> In our resolution we have dealt with the cinema in earnest, and we ask you to show that the cinema is of gigantic importance and that we must not tolerate the confusion that exists at present. You will, of course, say that Narkompros is above all responsible for this confusion.[25]

While accepting, at least in part, Narkompros's responsibility, Lunacharsky went on to describe some of the difficulties that had arisen in the reorganisation and centralisation of the cinema. He frankly described the bureaucratic inertia of the Soviet administrative machine:

Even if we had paid more attention to this [the reorganisation], we should not have done anything, because even our decree has taken almost six months and only now have we received formal permission to start on the unification of the cinema; the decree on this only appeared in today's papers. But if you're going to blame anyone, don't blame us, but blame the fact that the cinema as an organ of political propaganda, of scientific propaganda, as a healthy entertainment, and even as a source of income, is a vast affair.[26]

Lunacharsky concluded with some observations on the rôle of foreign operators and an appeal to the Congress of Soviets to give a lead to the country in its proclamation of the cinema's importance:

Now German, Italian and American claws are stretching out towards us; they propose that we should give them rights over the cinema in Russia at a low price. Of course we can only attract them as shareholders under our leadership. In general, you know, comrades, that people now quite frequently watch showings of repulsive films, because there is no central censorship organisation, no administrative control over this matter; no attention is paid to it either in the provinces or in the centre. And now, when you here say that the cinema is a particularly important field of work, then we, both in the provinces and at the centre, shall start to take matters into our own hands, we shall begin to attract both private and foreign capital into mixed companies, leaving the commercial, technical, scientific and political leadership for ourselves.[27]

The resolution adopted by the Congress on 27 December is worth quoting in full because it is so typical of many others:

The Congress draws the most serious attention of all organs of Soviet power, and of the People's Commissariat for Enlightenment, to the tremendous agitational and educational significance which the cinema might and should have for the broad masses of the population. The Congress proposes to the People's Commissariat for Enlightenment that it should take immediate measures for the development of this matter in a spirit which corresponds to the interests of the cultural and political development of the workers and peasants.[28]

The subject was not discussed again.

In these circumstances the path towards the creation of a centralised cinema organisation was indeed a protracted one. V.F.K.O. was reorganised three times in the course of 1921 alone;[29] finally on 10 December 1921 both V.F.K.O. in Moscow and P.O.F.K.O. in Petrograd were transformed to the *khozraschët* system of accounting.[30] The effect of this was to transfer the cinema to the free play of market forces, so that it would cease to be a drain on state funds and should, at least in theory, become a profit-making industry and thus entirely self-sufficient. State funds could thus be devoted to more urgent and concrete tasks.[31] However, in the conditions prevailing, the cinema was to prove incapable of achieving self-sufficiency and became increasingly dependent on state funds.

The failure of the transfer to *khozraschët* to alleviate, let alone solve, the problems confronting the Soviet film industry, rapidly became apparent. Indeed there is some evidence to suggest that the transfer had only ever been regarded as a temporary measure. On 10 June 1921 and again on 21 June P. Voevodin, then head of V.F.K.O., had written to Lenin asking for state funds to be provided for the purchase of films and equipment abroad.[32] Voevodin suggested that the Soviet state might obtain as least part of the foreign currency needed (the equivalent of 15 million gold roubles in his estimate) by exporting some of the pre-Revolutionary films it had but felt it could not use for domestic consumption because of their 'bourgeois content'. Lenin passed the letters to N. Gorbunov, a member of Sovnarkom, with the telling comment, 'Deal with this. I haven't the time.'[33]

The leadership of V.F.K.O. was also pressing for a greater degree of centralisation to ensure overall rationalisation in a period of shortage. In September 1921 Sovnarkom considered a proposal that V.F.K.O. should exercise monopolistic control over cinema theatres and equipment with the right to lease them to other organisations.[34] This would have met the demands of V.F.K.O., while simultaneously passing the initiative to local groups in the hope that this might stimulate a greater income, which could then be ploughed back into production. This move would also have matched the transfer to *khozraschët*, but Sovnarkom rejected the proposal. On 1 December Voevodin suggested in another letter that, in accordance with the principles of *khozraschët*, V.F.K.O. should be transformed into a trust (*glavki*) with a capital of two thousand million gold roubles and an export fund.[35]

On 16 December 1921 Lenin suggested to Litkens that a commission be established to investigate complaints from Voevodin and consider the reorganisation of the cinema industry as a whole.[36] Lenin proposed that Litkens should chair the commission and that the other members should include Voevodin himself, P. A. Bogdanov (Chairman of Vesenkha) and A. M. Lezhava (Deputy Commissar at Narkomvneshtorg, Narodnyi komissariat vneshnei torgovli – People's Commissariat for Foreign Trade). In the event only Voevodin served on the commission, together with representatives from all the principal organisations concerned: Yu. Flakserman replaced Bogdanov as the Vesenkha representative and P. Gorodetsky replaced Litkens for Narkompros, while B. Kotsen represented the Central Committee of the Union of Workers in Culture and Education.[37] The Central Committee of the Party, Glavpolitprosvet, Rabkrin (Raboche-krest'yanskaya inspektsiya – Workers' and Peasants' Inspectorate), and Narkomvneshtorg were also represented.[38] The commission's report and recommendations were considered by the Presidium of Vesenkha in the spring of 1922 but no concrete measures were taken until the following December. It was this delay that Lunacharsky had complained of in his report to the 10th Congress of Soviets in the same month.[39]

The commission recommended the establishment of a central cinema organisation to control all forms of distribution throughout the R.S.F.S.R., while retaining the right to lease or rent equipment, studios, theatres etc. to other organisations, both state-owned and private, which could then continue with the production and exhibition of films.

On 19 December 1922 Sovnarkom finally adopted these proposals in its decree entitled 'On the Transformation of the Photographic and Cinematographic Section of the People's Commissariat for Enlightenment into the Central State Photographic and Cinematographic Enterprise (Goskino)' ('O preobrazovanii fotokinootdela Narodnogo Komissariata Prosveshcheniya v tsentral'noe gosudarstvennoe fotokinopredpriyatie (Goskino)').[40] It was assumed that the monopoly of distribution would give the new state organisation an adequate and steady source of funds which it could then plough back into the production of ideologically desirable feature films and perhaps also the acquisition of cinema theatres from private enterprise. In this way, the state sector of the Soviet cinema would gradually but inexorably overhaul the private sector. (Red Army cinemas and workers' clubs were to be excluded from the new arrangements as they were regarded as priority areas deserving of special attention.)

Goskino was based, as had been expected, on V.F.K.O. but, although this was the largest existing film organisation in the R.S.F.S.R., it still did not give Goskino sufficient capital resources to fulfil its tasks adequately. The new organisation had to compete with other, already established, cinema organisations which in different ways were stronger than Goskino. These included Sevzapkino and Kino-Sever, which both operated from Petrograd and covered the north-western and northern provinces respectively; Kino-Moskva, which had been started early in 1922 by the

Education Department of the Moscow City Soviet and had established its own distribution network;[41] Proletkino (Proletarskoe kino – Proletarian Cinema organisation), which served the workers' clubs, and Mezhrabpom-Rus, a mixed company with strong German connections.[42] Many of these organisations issued their own newsreels, some even produced their own feature films; they all arranged their own imports and local distribution networks. In this situation Goskino could not hope to accumulate the capital with which to pay for its own production and it therefore attempted to cover its own costs by profiting from these other organisations. Goskino surrendered its distribution monopoly to various local organisations, taking between 50 per cent and 70 per cent of their turnover in return. In this way it hoped to finance its own further development. But Goskino's fight for money led to higher seat prices and lower attendances, forcing local distribution organisations to expand outside their own areas.[43] Thus state organisation began to compete with state organisation; Goskino was unable even to supply films to its own theatres and an even stronger private sector emerged.

As Goskino had insufficient funds to embark upon large-scale production it was forced to import films from abroad, particularly from Hollywood and Neubabelsberg, the two greatest centres of capitalist film production. These films, not surprisingly, were considered to be ideologically harmful. In addition, as there was no planned system of importation and as neither Goskino nor its competitors had a monopoly over such imports, Soviet film organisations again found themselves competing with one another, forcing prices up and undermining their own financial position even further.[44]

The problem of imports had been a long-standing one for the Russian cinema: heavy dependence on imported raw and processed film and other materials and equipment had made Russia peculiarly vulnerable to fluctuations in the international trading position.[45] The First World War had also had a lasting effect. Because of the Allied embargo on trade during the Civil War period, it proved at first impossible to import any new film or equipment from abroad; Russia produced none of her own and thus depended almost entirely on what remained from before the Revolution. This of course could not continue indefinitely.

The first attempt to arrange an international deal came to grief when Jacques Cibrario absconded with Soviet government funds;[46] not surprisingly, this experience chastened the Soviet authorities and they were reluctant to authorise any further efforts of this kind. However, in August 1921 the International Workers' Aid movement was founded, with its headquarters in Berlin.[47] Its original aim was to provide international relief for the victims of the famine but, once that initial emergency had receded, the movement turned its attention to assisting the new Soviet state in every possible way. It issued an illustrated paper, *Sowjet-Russland in Bildern*, and established the Neue Deutsche Verlag to publish Soviet authors in translation. In the summer of 1922 it arranged an international loan through the specially established Aufbau organisation. It was Aufbau that also financed the bulk purchase of films, film stock and equipment in Germany on behalf of Soviet film organisations: it provided 80 per cent of these materials imported into the R.S.F.S.R. during 1922 and 1923 and supplied one million metres of negative and five million metres of positive film in this period.[48]

International Workers' Aid also set up Prometheus-Film A.G. to distribute and exhibit Soviet films within Germany (initially to attract funds for famine relief)[49] and later Weltfilm, which was to confine itself to the exhibition of Soviet films solely on the workers' club cinema circuit. Prometheus-Film provided an outlet for such films as *Bronenosets Potëmkin* (Battleship Potemkin) and *Oktyabr'* (October).[50]

Even this did not represent the full extent of Soviet–German collaboration in the field of the cinema. It was after all not unnatural that the two outcast nations of Europe should collaborate to their mutual advantage; the Treaty of Rapallo underlined that. As early as 1922 International Workers' Aid suggested a joint Soviet–German commission to censor and supervise the importation of films into the R.S.F.S.R., and later actively campaigned for the proposal that Goskino should have not merely a monopoly of distribution rights within the R.S.F.S.R., but also a monopoly right to importation. In this it did not succeed.

Despite this setback, and despite the difficulties caused by the effective devaluation of the rouble and the hyperinflation in Germany in 1923, cooperation continued to flourish. In March 1923 L. A. Liberman, Chairman of the Goskino directorate, returned from Berlin with agreements with V.U.F.K.U. and Goskinprom Gruzii (Vseukrainskoe fotokinoupravlenie and Gosudarstvennaya kinopromyshlennost' Gruzii, respectively the Ukrainian and Georgian equivalents of Goskino) on the joint purchase of film stock and films from Germany. Furthermore, he brought a proposal for the establishment of a joint Soviet–German film production company to be financed with German capital.[51] *Pravda* observed:

> Now the period of reorganisation is coming to an end and Goskino is entering a new phase of its activity. . .The prospects for further work are now becoming clearer. In the very near future Goskino is hoping to start a number of major productions, for which the screenplays are already completed.[52]

The plan for a joint company was approved by the authorities at Narkompros and on 1 August 1924 a joint production collective was established in Moscow employing capital provided by International Workers' Aid.[53] The collective was based on the Rus company, the largest surviving private firm, and was to be known as Mezhrabpom-Rus. (Mezhrabpom was the Russian acronym for Mezhdunarodnaya rabochaya pomoshch' or International Workers' Aid.) International Workers' Aid intended to take over the company gradually from the private interests that had previously controlled it, but was nevertheless attacked for allegedly selling out to *nepmen*.[54]

Mezhrabpom-Rus was responsible for the production of a number of important films which combined ideological rectitude with a strong streak of experimentation, for example: Yakov Protazanov's films, *Aelita* (1924),[55] *Sorok pervyi* (The Forty-First, 1926),[56] and the satirical comedy *Don Diego i Pelageya* (Don Diego and Pelagea, 1927),[57] Vsevolod Pudovkin's *Shakhmatnaya goryachka* (Chess Fever, 1925),[58] *Mat'* (Mother, 1926),[59] *Konets Sankt-Peterburga*[60] and *Potomok Chingis-khana*[61] and the satire in which Lunacharsky himself is reputed to have had a hand, Sergei Komarov's *Potselui, Meri Pikford* (The Kiss from Mary Pickford, 1927).[62] Mezhrabpom-Rus became the major exporter of Soviet films, partly because of its established German connections and partly because the type of film it produced had a wider appeal to foreign audiences.[63] Until 1927, however, the Soviet Union remained overwhelmingly a net importer of films.[64]

The continued importation of foreign films provided critics with a convenient weapon with which to attack the administration of the Soviet cinema industry for its repeated failure to produce suitable Soviet alternatives. It was primarily to establish a stronger basis for Soviet film production that Goskino had been established; and it was primarily to secure that basis that Goskino was eventually reorganised and finally replaced by Sovkino (Sovetskoe kino – Soviet Cinema enterprise).

In order to examine the record and to estimate the effectiveness of Goskino we must first look at exactly what it took over. Goskino's opponents consistently claimed that its directorate had squandered ample resources through corruption, inefficiency and sometimes even sheer stupidity. Goskino's advocates, on the other hand, argued that it had started with inadequate funds and had therefore been unable to cope with the situation that confronted it, especially as that situation was deteriorating all the time, while Goskino was simultaneously required to show a distinct improvement and expansion. As a *Pravda* correspondent observed in January 1923:

> As far as our own film production is concerned, it is on a level close to nothing. . .Unless the Party gives the cinema organisational forces in sufficient quantity and on the necessary scale, the prospects will remain as before, hazy and hopeless.[65]

But neither the Party nor the government gave Goskino the administrative and financial support that it needed to fulfil its tasks successfully. Anxious that the cinema should not become a drain on state funds, Sovnarkom permitted the establishment of limited companies to attract the investment of private capital, and forbade the closure or limitation of existing successful but rival state film organisations such as Sevzapkino.[66] Sevzapkino was, and remained, a more important distributor of films in both Moscow and Petrograd than Goskino and this strengthened its hand in negotiations with the new organisation. In these and similar negotiations Goskino, in exchange for waiving its distribution monopoly, aimed to acquire up to 50 per cent of the takings from films distributed by enterprises such as Sevzapkino or Kino-Moskva, in order to finance its own production. However, Goskino had, before it could embark upon such productions, to re-equip and modernise its studios, which had fallen into an advanced state of disrepair.

Thus in January 1923 Goskino applied to Sovnarkom for permission to establish a production company with a capital of 220,000 roubles; this plan was approved, with the suggestion that the new company should be a mixed enterprise. Goskino made unsuccessful attempts to attract capital from both Germany and America. It did however manage to come to an arrangement with a Russian entrepreneur, L. A. Azarkh, which was approved by Sovnarkom on 12 February 1923.[67] A new company, Russfilm, was to be established with a capital of 500,000 roubles, all provided by Azarkh. Goskino transferred its principal studio to him for twelve years; in return it was to receive 53 per cent of the shares and the government an annual income of 50,000 roubles. Azarkh undertook to provide Goskino with twenty films a year, each between 1,200 and 1,500 metres in length. For this he was to be guaranteed equal distribution rights throughout the Soviet Union. By this agreement Goskino, while hoping to ensure that film production was at least re-started, relinquished its position in three important areas: it gave away the material base for its own production, abandoned its distribution monopoly in exchange for the unrealisable asset of 53 per cent of the shares, and relinquished all control over the end product, the film. The Goskino directorate (and, by an implication that was not pursued, Sovnarkom, which had approved the agreement) was revealed as short-sighted and incompetent. Fortunately for Goskino, Azarkh soon failed to fulfil his part of the bargain and the agreement was promptly annulled.

In April 1923, E. S. Kadomtsev was appointed to replace Liberman as head of Goskino. But a change in personnel was not enough to rectify the basic structural faults of the organisation or the situation in which it found itself. Goskino's principal problem was lack of liquidity with which to repair its equipment, studios and cinemas and to finance the production of new films, the proceeds from which would have eased, if not solved, the problem. Hence the desperation with which Goskino dealt with Sevzapkino; hence also the abortive agreement with Azarkh. Goskino was also hampered by the high government tax on film equipment and on cinema tickets.[68] This led to higher seat prices, continued reliance on old films and, consequently, to lower attendances and to cinema closures. The old vicious circle continued; by 1924 in some areas of the Soviet Union only 20 per cent of the cinemas that had been in operation in 1917 were still functioning.[69] In Moscow in 1923 Goskino had only five cinemas; fifteen were run by other Soviet organisations, such as Sevzapkino, while the remainder, between fifty and sixty, were in private hands.[70] Lack of centralised control meant that private cinema owners vied with Goskino for the rights to foreign films,[71] thus increasing the pull away from the state sector and further diminishing state funds. Lack of control also meant that private entrepreneurs were able to smuggle equipment and banned films out of Moscow and Petrograd to the provinces, where they commanded exorbitant prices. This made effective censorship impossible.[72]

On 19 July 1923 *Pravda* reported a conference of Soviet film organisations and film workers ten days earlier which had failed to reach agreement on what the newspaper's correspondent regarded as the central problem – 'the creation of a central plan of production'.[73] *Pravda* pointed out:

> Although we are short of both means and personnel, we could nevertheless do many times more than we are doing at the moment if we were to work in an agreed and friendly manner, according to a single plan worked out to correspond exactly to the available resources of manpower and materials.[74]

In August 1923 Sovnarkom and the Central Committee of the Party ordered an investigation into the affairs of Goskino by the Central Control Commission and Rabkrin. Their report revealed that in its six months of existence Goskino had produced nothing apart from the occasional newsreel and that, while film distribution had produced an income of 76,834 roubles, and cinema operation 126,164 roubles, a total of only 23,172 roubles had been spent on this production. The report concluded: 'It follows that, even at the present time, Goskino is not a productive unit, but lives off its commercial operations, the income from which is barely sufficient to cover all its expenses.'[75]

On 4 September 1923 Sovnarkom discussed the state of the Soviet cinema, hearing reports from Lunacharsky and V. A. Avanesov, Deputy People's Commissar for Rabkrin, and decided that Goskino was not capable of fulfilling its responsibilities. A commission of inquiry was set up to find new and more appropriate forms of organisation for the Soviet film industry. The commission was chaired by V. N. Mantsev and amongst its members were included Lunacharsky, as representative of Narkompros, and Kadomtsev, for Goskino.[76]

The establishment of what came to be known as the Mantsev Commission unleashed a further flood of suggestions from the press. *Zhizn' iskusstva* echoed the common call for a centralised controlling organisation, which was, after all, what the already existing Goskino was supposed to be.[77] *Pravda* had suggested something similar in August,[78] but on 13 September V. Erofeev went further.[79] He rejected the existing system of centralised control of studios by Goskino as it had no funds to refurbish and reopen them, and he stressed that any plans for the unification of the industry must be agreed to by all the parties concerned. He proposed:

> We must:
> 1 Unite all the capital and material resources (factories, studios, labora-

tories etc.) of Soviet cinema undertakings into a single state cinema syndicate of the U.S.S.R.

2 Concentrate all production in three or four factories, equipping them with the last word in technology.

3 Grant autonomy to artistic collectives and production groups, regulating and directing their productive work.[80]

Erofeev followed this article with another on the state of Soviet newsreel films.[81] Here he urged that efforts should be centralised and rationalised and that, instead of the existing erratic competition, a single unified newsreel should appear on a weekly basis. The theme of all these articles was that effective use of resources could only be achieved through a centralised state-controlled organisation with the power of direction and rationalisation. Such an organisation also presupposed total abandonment of the commercial motive, and thus of *khozraschët*, and a return to admitted dependence on state funds; if the cinema was to attend to the social and political requirements of Party and state, then there could be no realistic alternative.

On 23 November 1923 the Mantsev Commission presented its report to A. D. Tsyurupa, the Deputy Chairman of Sovnarkom. It recommended the establishment of a limited company financed by a long-term loan of one million gold roubles. Following representations from Goskino and other organisations the Commission also recommended that film production should be exempted from normal taxation and that the tax levied on cinema seats should be reduced from 25 per cent of the purchase price to 10 per cent.[82]

Sovnarkom discussed the Mantsev Report on 27 November but referred it back to the Commission, asking it to look at the question of a state rental monopoly. At a meeting of the People's Commissars for Education of the individual union and autonomous republics, held in Moscow on 4 December, a resolution was adopted urging that each republican government should have a separate monopoly of film distribution. This would concentrate control in state hands at a manageable level and avoid both overcentralisation and bureaucratisation on the one hand, and unchecked competition from private enterprise on the other. This suggestion was adopted by the Mantsev Commission in its second report to Sovnarkom on 10 December 1923.[83] Its first report had recommended the establishment of a limited company to control the cinema throughout the U.S.S.R., but this proposal violated the existing constitutional provisions and the revised proposals confined the new company to the R.S.F.S.R., while suggesting some form of cinema syndicate for the union republics.[84]

The press still carried complaints about the existing state of affairs and suggested proposals for reorganisation. On 16 February 1924 N. Plastinin, director of Kino-Moskva, attacked Goskino in the columns of *Pravda* as 'the nationalised property of the cinematographic bourgeoisie'.[85] He blamed the state of the Soviet cinema on the stifling centralised control of Goskino and urged greater competition between the different Soviet film organisations throughout the U.S.S.R. His argument was backed up by another, anonymous article which appeared in the same issue. This asserted that, as far as production was concerned, 'Hitherto we have had no policy';[86] Soviet films were poor from both the ideological and the technical point of view and foreign films accounted for 99 per cent of total distribution. 'Distribution is in a state of complete anarchy',[87] the author asserted, and 'Cinemas, which had a major rôle in the fight against alcoholics, are dying out in this country.'[88]

In a rather more constructive article one month later Plastinin suggested certain definite measures to improve the situation:

1 The decree of December 1922 establishing Goskino should be repealed.
2 A new organisation with a distribution monopoly should be established as a safeguard against private capital. At the same time there should be competition between the different Soviet production companies on an all-union level. (This would safeguard the position of organisations like Kino-Moskva.)
3 All Soviet film organisations should be transformed into limited companies using both state and private capital.
4 All imports should be centrally controlled to avoid wasteful competitive bidding.
5 Every Soviet film organisation should have control over the exportation of its own productions.
6 Government taxation policy should be revised to discriminate in favour of cinemas as against shops and bars.[89]

To some extent Plastinin's proposals reflected his position as director of Kino-Moskva, but they did nevertheless represent a valid attempt at returning initiative to the production units while retaining overall state control.

Plastinin's articles brought a prompt reply from A. Goldobin, then a member of the Goskino directorate. Goldobin maintained that Goskino had already carried out most of Plastinin's suggestions and that the root cause of all the problems of the Soviet cinema lay with the failure of the People's Commissariat for Foreign Trade to consult Goskino on the funds necessary to finance an effective programme of imports of films and equipment. Goldobin also pointed out that Goskino had repeatedly asked the

Soviet government to lift the tax on cinema equipment and on tickets, that this suggestion had been supported by the Mantsev Commission in its report, but that Sovnarkom had still not discussed the matter. Finally he made it clear that there could be no solution to the problem of an effective state monopoly until the film famine had been overcome and private entrepreneurs put out of business.

At the end of March 1924 an All-Union Conference on Cinema Affairs (Vsesoyuznoe soveshchanie po kinodelu) was held in Moscow.[91] The conference heard two reports: the first, from Lunacharsky, was entitled 'On revolutionary ideology in the cinema' ('O revolyutsionnoi ideologii v kinodele'). He urged that the Soviet cinema should create its own genres of film to meet the urgent social and political tasks that faced it: 'The Soviet cinema cannot allow in its films either a political social–bourgeois tendency, or the glorification of bourgeois benefactors, or elements of treachery or crime presented in alluring form.'[92] These were the hallmarks of the Western import; the Soviet film industry, in Lunacharsky's view, should have been concentrating on the production of *agitki* or *zhivye plakaty* (living posters), as he called them.[93] These films should have a simple plot and a simple message, easily comprehensible to the broad masses of the population, and they should be augmented by a weekly newsreel. Thus Lunacharsky added his voice to those who proclaimed the overriding importance of the newsreel and the need to put newsreel production above all else on a firmer footing.

The second report, from Goldobin, was concerned with the economic position of the Soviet cinema and bore the title 'On the situation of the cinema' ('O polozhenii kinematografii'). As an indication of decline Goldobin pointed out that, whereas between 1915 and 1917 there had been about 2,000 cinemas within the present frontiers of the U.S.S.R., by January 1924 the number had still not recovered to more than 1,500.[94] While not disputing Lunacharsky's emphasis on the newsreel, Goldobin pointed out that in its current state the Soviet cinema had the resources to produce little else. A number of delegates echoed Goskino's complaints about the effects of heavy taxation. The example of the Crimea was quoted: in 1915–17 there had been thirty-five cinemas in that area; by January 1924 this number had fallen to twelve, and it declined further to six by March. The high cost of renting film was also blamed for the situation which resulted from the lack of an effective state monopoly of distribution.

The conference ended, ironically, by supporting all the major suggestions for reform that had been made by Goskino throughout the previous twelve months. It concluded, not surprisingly, that:

The cinema in the U.S.S.R. does not find itself in the position it deserves in view of its unique importance as the best and most powerful means of communist propaganda and agitation.[95]

It urged a reduction in taxation and rental charges, supported the right of monopoly of distribution for local film organisations and suggested that all Soviet film organisations should have the right to shoot film anywhere in the U.S.S.R. Finally, the conference passed a resolution:

The conference finds it advisable that all Soviet cinema organisations within the U.S.S.R. should be rapidly unified into a limited company. A necessary condition for such a unification is material support on the part of the state and the lowering of the taxes that are hampering the cinema industry.[96]

On 5 April 1924 the Mantsev Commission presented its final report to Sovnarkom and on 13 May Mantsev himself appeared before Sovnarkom with a full verbal account of the Commission's recommendations. These were approved by the meeting which entrusted Mantsev, L. B. Krasin and A. M. Lezhava with the task of reorganisation.[97]

Two weeks later, on 29 May, the tenth session of the 13th Party Congress finally gave the Party an opportunity to discuss the state of the cinema and its rôle as a weapon of agitation and propaganda. The organisational report of the Central Committee had been presented by Stalin on 24 May. He made reference to the sorry state of the Soviet cinema,[98] but discussion of the peculiar problems of the cinema was lost in a general discussion on questions of *agitprop* work amongst the peasants and the Red Army and the problem of the 'political literacy' (*politgramotnost'*) of Party members. A similar obfuscation occurred on 29 May. However the Congress did adopt a comprehensive resolution deploring the current state of the Soviet cinema and urging its reorganisation along more rational and effective lines.[99] Although the resolution remained generalised it did make a number of specific points, which supported the recommendations of the Mantsev Commission. The current position was blamed on a combination of shortage of working capital, lack of cooperation between rival Soviet film organisations, absence of ideological control and shortage of skilled personnel. The Congress resolved that existing organisations should be unified on the basis of the preservation of the state monopoly of distribution within each republic. It added that the new organisations should be strengthened by a reduction in taxation and an increase in ideologically trained personnel. In the four main republics, the Russian Federation, the Ukraine, Belorussia and the Transcaucasus, joint organs were to be established to control the content of films produced; at the same time cinema organisations were urged to redouble their efforts to provide workers' and Red Army clubs with a suitable diet of films. Once the Party Congress had broadly adopted the Mantsev Commission's recommendations there was little further delay in their implementation.

After another two weeks, on 13 June 1924, Sovnarkom considered the final version of the Mantsev Report and accepted its recommendations.[100] It was decided to form a limited company, rather than a syndicate, because this method was considered more likely to attract the necessary funds and create the necessary organisational unity.

The distribution monopoly was, in accordance with widespread suggestions, to be reserved for the individual republics. This was confirmed in a Sovnarkom decree of 17 July: 'The state monopoly of film rental shall belong to the Union Republics and be effected by each of them on their own territory.'[101] The assets of existing cinema organisations were to be exchanged for shares in the new company; an exception was made for both Proletkino and Mezhrabpom-Rus because of their special functions, and the new company was instructed to negotiate with these organisations to achieve a suitable *modus vivendi.* Sovnarkom decided to establish an organisational commission under the chairmanship of L. B. Krasin, with Lunacharsky, Mantsev and representatives of the Moscow and Leningrad Soviets and Goskino.[102]

On 12 December 1924 this organisational commission reported back to Sovnarkom, which decided to establish an all-union cinema company to be known as Sovkino.[103] The new company was to have a capital of one million roubles and only Soviet governmental organs were to be allowed to hold shares: 15 per cent were to be held by Vesenkha, and 55 per cent jointly by Narkompros and the Moscow and Leningrad provincial executive committees (*gubispolkomy*), while 30 per cent of the shares went to the People's Commissariat for Foreign Trade (Narkomvneshtorg). Krasin, who had chaired the organisational commission, was of course also People's Commissar for Foreign Trade, but it is probable that the Commissariat's financial interest in the Soviet cinema reflects the continued significance of imported foreign films rather than any improper activity on the part of its higher officials. Thus established, Sovkino was to begin work on 1 January 1925.

Although Goskino was now dead, it was far from buried, and the debate over its performance and the allocation of responsibility for its failures continued. In addition to the articles by Plastinin and Goldobin mentioned above, *Pravda* published a constant stream of criticism and counter-criticism by other authors. On 10 January 1924 A. Lvov complained of the rôle played by private entrepreneurs as middlemen in the film distribution process.[104] In March 1924 Lvov was commissioned by the South-Eastern Bureau of the Central Committee of the Party in Rostov-on-Don to examine the position of the cinema in that region of the Soviet Union, and his report was published.[105] He began by denying Goskino's assertions that the state of affairs had improved as a result of its efforts; placing words like 'work', 'production' and 'operations' in inverted commas, Lvov maintained that Goskino had on the contrary been criminally negligent and cited as a prime example the incompetence demonstrated during the filming of Lenin's funeral in January 1924.[106] He accused Goskino of placing sensationalism before political responsibility and observed, 'That same lack of talent and failure to understand matters, that absence of political and commercial sense that reigned two years ago still reign today.'[107] He further complained that Goskino's signal failure to produce any feature films meant that there was no regular system of film distribution for state-run cinemas; whereas the state cinemas in Rostov-on-Don required at least twenty programmes a month, they had in fact received only eight programmes in three months.[108] In this situation the door remained wide open for private profiteering: 'The theatres exist exclusively from the occasional picture which is supplied by private dealers.'[109]

In 1923, 62 per cent of the film rental in the South-East Region had gone to private individuals and Goskino's distribution monopoly had therefore become a farce: 'The monopoly of distribution means in fact that *private individuals have a monopoly of supply to the market* and pay Goskino for permission to show their pictures.'[110] As a result, of the 140 films available for distribution in the region, only four had any appreciable revolutionary content. Lvov was totally opposed to the use of private capital to finance the cinema, regarding it as an admission of failure.[111] He had earlier engaged in a polemic in the columns of *Pravda* with Lunacharsky on this subject.[112] He regarded the parlous state of the Soviet cinema as largely responsible for the delinquent element in society:

> The cinema has become a very important factor in the development of crime and the judicial organs are establishing a direct and indirect connection between one adolescent's crime or another and the picture he has seen at the cinema. The cinema, which in our hands can and must become a most powerful weapon for the spread of knowledge, education and propaganda, has been turned into a weapon for the corruption of adolescents.[113]

Lvov also dealt with the problem of taxation; whilst agreeing with Goskino's complaints and criticising Narkomfin (Narodnyi komissariat finansov – People's Commissariat for Finance) for its shortsightedness, he permitted himself this observation; 'In discussing this we must remember that the heaviest, most absurd and senseless tax on theatres is Goskino itself.'[114]

Attacks like this drew counter-attacks. In July Goldobin used the columns of *Zhizn' iskusstva* to complain about the campaign against Goskino.[115] He pointed out that the Mantsev Commission, Sovnarkom and the 13th Party Congress had all supported Goskino's complaints. He criticised the delay in implementing the changes recommended but blamed this on what he described as 'anti-state campaigns' by organisations such as Sevzapkino, Kino-Moskva and Proletkino. Goskino had, Goldobin maintained, fought single-handed against all odds to get its views accepted and had finally emerged triumphant. He concluded, with obvious satisfaction:

> People die as they have lived, according to the Russian proverb. The death of anti-state campaigns in the cinema will come with the compulsory unification of the Soviet cinema industry which is now being carried out.[116]

This was not, however, Goldobin's nor Goskino's, last word. Later in 1924 Gosizdat (Gosudarstvennoe izdatel'stvo), the State Publishing House published a study of the Soviet cinema compiled by Goldobin from material published in eighty-eight provincial newspapers between 13 June and 31 July 1924.[117] He took the opportunity to explain the financial reasons for Goskino's lack of production and the continued importation of unsuitable foreign films;[118] he also reiterated Goskino's call for the unification of all cinema organisations to ensure stricter control[119] and repeated his earlier claim that the delay in achieving this was the fault of rival Soviet film organisations like Kino-Moskva.[120]

The overall conclusions of the press were unsurprising. Provincial cinemas and newspapers constantly complained of erratic or inadequate distribution of films, and particularly of newsreels, which were supposed to constitute the vanguard of Bolshevik propaganda. In the period under examination only one issue of the Goskino newsreel, *Goskinokalendar'*, had reached the provinces, in an inadequate number of copies, and it was a newsreel that had been made the previous January.[121] In Ekaterinburg the press complained that the supply of films had broken down completely and that no attempt had been made to draw on stocks of suitable old films to fill the distribution gap in provincial cinemas.[122] The same newspaper complained that no Soviet films ever reached the provinces and the cinemas were forced to rely upon a diet of unsuitable melodramas: 'Despite the fact that Goskino has released many Soviet films, the cinemas in Ekaterinburg are showing old "love dramas" full of torment, tears and suffering.'[123] There had been a partially successful attempt to 'purge' the cinemas in Grozny[124] but on the whole the industry was caught in a vicious circle of cheap films leading to lower audiences and, in turn, to even cheaper films;[125] this was the same circle that had led to the establishment of Goskino. Now, two years later, it was leading to its replacement. In the face of all this evidence, and given his own personal views, Goldobin could not avoid the conclusion that 'as yet the cinema in this country is in no way playing its proper rôle'.[126]

However, Goldobin's initial defence of the Goskino position was strengthened by the publication in the spring of 1925 of Goskino's report for the period from October 1923 to October 1924.[127] This complained in detail about the government's refusal to reduce taxation and about Narkomfin's repeated attempts to reverse the Mantsev Commission's recommendations on this point, and noted that, as late as February 1925, the suggested reduction in taxation had still not been brought into effect.[128] Apart from this, Goskino had been obstructed by other governmental organisations. The initial allocation of funds for the importation of films and equipment had been reduced by Gosplan (Gosudarstvennyi plan S.S.S.R. – State Plan of the U.S.S.R.) from 250,000 to 100,000 roubles; after vigorous protests from Goskino the allocation had been significantly increased to 1,700,000 for film and 600,000 for equipment. However, political and economic events in Germany (the occupation of the Ruhr and the hyperinflation of 1923) had complicated the actual expenditure of these sums.[129] The report was concerned to defend Goskino against hostile allegations and to present the conclusions of the Mantsev Commission as a triumph for the arguments of Goskino against its rivals.

In both these tasks Goskino was largely justified. It had been given insufficient working capital with which to sort out the problems of production and distribution faced by the Soviet cinema in these years. It did not have sufficient funds to repair the damage to factory and plant resulting from years of disuse and neglect, let alone to compete effectively with a lively and profitable private sector. It did not receive much-needed government support in the field of taxation, nor was it backed by an effective centralised administration that could exert control throughout the country. Even at this period it is true to say that, in the cinema at least, the right hand of the Soviet administrative machine did not know what the left hand was doing.

In December 1922 Goskino had been established to put the Soviet cinema industry on a secure footing. It had failed. In December 1924 Sovkino was established to perform a fundamentally similar task.

5. THE ORGANISATION OF DISORGANISATION: THE LATER TWENTIES

The cinema is the only book that even the illiterate can read.

Soviet newspaper, 1924.[1]

Sovkino was faced with enormous tasks. At the centre it was required on the one hand to increase the quantity of Soviet film production so that the dependence on foreign imports could be first reduced and then eliminated; on the other hand Sovkino was expected to raise the quality of Soviet films which, in the circumstances, meant ensuring that the actual films produced were more closely tied to the ideological needs of the Party than had hitherto been the case. At the same time it was to concentrate on what were, for one reason or another, considered to be 'priority areas', the areas that had allegedly been neglected by Goskino and other Soviet film organisations. Sovkino was expected to provide cinema facilities and suitable films for the countryside, the network of workers' clubs, the armed forces and for the younger generation: in other words it was to ensure the allegiance of the pillars upon which the new state and society were supposed to rest. The problem was simply stated:

Here in Russia the cinemas are confined to the more or less large centres and aimed almost exclusively at the bourgeois classes. Even our urban workers are far from everywhere and always in a position to enjoy the benefits of the cinema, because the luxurious cinemas of the bourgeois type are inaccessible to them in terms of cost and uninteresting to them in terms of the content of the pictures, which here too are predominantly bourgeois.

The countryside however is completely unable to enjoy the benefits of the cinema.[2]

It was in the countryside therefore that Sovkino faced its most challenging task.

Sovkino's responsibility was to make the cinema accessible to the countryside and the countryside accessible to the cinema; although there was no precedent in practice for this, the new process had been anticipated before the Revolution and a new word invented. That new word was *kinofikatsiya* and we in turn must coin a new English word to translate it – 'cinefication'.[3] The cinefication of the countryside had for some time been regarded as an urgent priority; the agit-trains had been a temporary and partial response[4] and in his directive to Litkens of January 1922 Lenin had underlined the need for more permanent measures:

Special attention should be paid to the organisation of cinemas in the villages and in the East, where they are novelties and where our propaganda will therefore be particularly successful.[5]

The special effectiveness of the cinema in primitive and rural areas had been confirmed in Goldobin's study of 1924:

The cinema works directly on the imagination and the feelings of the spectator; that is why the silent film has a more powerful effect on the masses than the press and the spoken word. That is its strength and merit.

That is why the appearance of the cinema in the countryside must be welcomed as that of a great propagandist and agitator.[6]

That the rural areas of the Soviet Union were still both remote and primitive can hardly be doubted. The conditions described by Krupskaya in 1919[7] had shown little change. In some areas of Siberia, for instance, the peasants had no ready cash and paid for their admission in eggs and other produce, which were then sold to the village cooperative.[8] But, even more significantly, in the Volga region, which was traversed by Krupskaya, it is estimated that in the years 1921–2 over 80 per cent of the village youth had never seen a film.[9] The Bolsheviks hoped therefore that the spread of the cinema into such regions would, at least in the minds of the peasantry, equate Bolshevism with technology and modernisation.[10]

The formidable problems of equipment and resources had changed little since the October Revolution. Potential audiences were too widely scattered for the establishment of a network of permanent cinema theatres and yet Sovkino was charged with breaking down the barriers which divided the town from the country[11] and the cinema was to assist in unifying the whole of the Soviet Union into a coherent political entity.[12] Once again the revolutionaries turned to methods that had predated the Revolution. They returned to the mobile projector, which had served so well in the early years of the cinema, or at least to the idea of it.[13] Sovkino required supplies of mobile projectors on a scale that Soviet industry was not yet able to provide; it needed a projector that was simple to use, highly portable, and had its own generator, because only a projector of this type[14] could penetrate into what

Goldobin had called the 'areas of darkness and illiteracy'.[15] Foreign manufacturers were no longer gearing themselves to supply the backward Soviet market and were now concentrating their efforts on the richer pastures of mobile projectors that ran solely on mains electricity.[16] There were still some mobile projectors in private hands: these were either reconditioned pre-war KOK models[17] or some of a small number of petrol-driven machines that had been imported through Krupp in 1924.[18] Two handbooks for projectionists published at the time describe and illustrate only imported projection equipment with instructions in English or German;[19] these were the machines just mentioned. There was no Soviet mobile film projector in large-scale production to meet Sovkino's needs, although Soviet engineers had in fact designed a suitable machine. This was the GOZ, so called because it had been developed at the Gosudarstvennyi opticheskii zavod (State Optical Factory).[20] The GOZ was, by all accounts, far from ideal, but it was the best machine available if, as one contemporary noted, 'we exclude foreign apparatus, the ordering and purchasing of which would not be politically expedient'.[21]

The principal fault with the GOZ projector seems to have lain with its dynamo, which frequently broke down.[22] As it was the dynamo that distinguished the GOZ from other projectors, and made it particularly suitable for Soviet operating conditions, this was a very serious fault indeed. But it was not the only one: there was also a chronic lack of spare parts, particularly spare bulbs, of which none at all were provided at first.[23] One estimate suggested that by the autumn of 1925 there were about 1,500 projectors in the Soviet countryside,[24] but by the summer of 1926 over half were reported to be out of order and left idle.[25] Not all the blame for this sad state of affairs may, however, be laid with the projector. The organisation and administration of the cinefication programme through the local organs of Narkompros was largely responsible. There were very few trained personnel in the countryside and hence copies of the small number of films that did get through were often damaged beyond repair.[26] But sometimes their excesses were even more remarkable: 'Comrades of the Berezovka district. . .lubricated the projector with tar instead of oil and then complained that it was not fit for use.'[27] Faced with such appalling ignorance it was perhaps difficult to see what any organisation could do.

Sovkino was frequently blamed by contemporaries for its failure to produce films that were of specific value to rural audiences.[28]

One writer, realising the limitations of the peasantry, even went as far as suggesting that there should be two versions of Soviet films to cope with this problem:

The perception of montage raises a very serious question: the rural audience cannot grasp alternating parallel montage. Thus the movement is perceived but the essence of the action is lost; often rapid movement provokes laughter. Films for the countryside require re-editing and adaptation to the perception of the peasant.[29]

The accessibility or otherwise of Soviet films to the masses of the population in this sense was to become a major issue in some of the artistic controversies of the time.[30] But Sovkino was unable to provide the necessary films as much for reasons of finance as of organisational shortcomings. For this the Soviet government, and therefore ultimately the Party, could be held responsible.

The cinema's advocates at this period frequently complained about the high level of governmental taxation.[31] One writer went as far as to claim that the cinema was more highly taxed than any other Soviet industry.[32] Many others urged that more of the income from distribution and exhibition should be ploughed back into the areas where it was most urgently needed for the further development of the cinema.[33] In 1923 the Mantsev Commission had recognised the justice of earlier complaints about unfairly high levels of taxation and as a result Sovnarkom had reduced the tax levied on seat prices from 25 per cent to 10 per cent.[34] Part of the problem now lay in the large numbers of people, including children, veterans, soldiers, pensioners, and in the remoter areas, even women, who were exempted from paying any admission fees. One contemporary statistician put this figure as high as 42 per cent of cinema audiences.[35] But basically the government still wanted to use the cinema as a source of general tax income. Indeed one of the lesser known 'cultural' aspects of the First Five Year Plan was the proposal that tax income from the cinema should gradually phase out that from the consumption of vodka. Stalin said, 'I think that it might be possible to begin the gradual abolition of vodka by introducing instead of vodka such sources of revenue as the radio and the cinema.'[36] There was then a fundamental conflict of interest between the government's need for tax revenue from the cinema and the cinema's need to spend that same revenue on its own development.

Sovkino however cannot entirely escape responsibility for the situation. Admittedly it had inherited its problems and its difficulties but it had not lived up to its expectations in overcoming them. It is also true that it began life on 1 March 1925 purely as a distribution organisation for the films produced by others, and that it began its own film production only after its mergers with both Goskino and Sevzapino in 1926, when it acquired their studios.[37] Nevertheless Sovkino was responsible for the charges levied both on rural cinema installations and on workers' clubs for the hire of films; at first it did not give them preferential treatment and this in turn hampered their development.[38] Sovkino's principal fault was that, like its predecessor, it was developing into an unwieldy bureaucracy. Speaking on 15 October 1927 Mayakovsky criticised the growth of this phenomenon:

> Comrades, an administrative and financial apparatus sits on the whole cultural work of Sovkino. Unless we prepare qualified workers, a young cadre, unless we appreciate what cinema culture is, then we shall make no progress in the question of the cinema.[39]

But three points may be made in Sovkino's defence: first, the government was not willing to release the income from taxation on the cinema that would have enabled Sovkino to tackle some of its problems with greater energy and resources; second, without its own production facilities it could not itself produce the kind of films demanded by Party workers in the countryside, but had to rely on agreements with other organisations; third, when Sovkino took over the production studios of Goskino and Sevzapkino they were already committed to a programme of film production and it took some time for the new régime to have any practical effect.[40]

The problems that faced the cinefication programme in areas inhabited by the national minorities were even more acute than those that existed in the Soviet countryside generally. The linguistic diversity of the Soviet population was of course a lesser problem in the era of the silent film than it would have been only ten years later. Nevertheless the overwhelming majority of the film audience would have been illiterate, so that it would frequently have been essential for somebody to be present to read the titles out and, if necessary, translate them. On the other hand the cinema was still a technical marvel which inspired awe and admiration, and film plots were still relatively simple and could usually be followed without the assistance of the titles. The principal problem therefore concerned neither language nor literacy but quite simply the enormous cultural gulf between the cities where the films were produced and the settlements where they were to be shown. Russian, and even Ukrainian, production was aimed at a different and more sophisticated market, so that in Tashkent for instance the cinema had become an entertainment almost exclusively for the European sector of the population.[41] Films that were suitable for this European audience would not have been suitable for native audiences and *vice versa*. A contemporary study highlights the difference:

We recall a curious scene. In July 1923 we attended the opening of the Red Tea-House [*chaikhana*] in Tashkent, on the edge of the Old City. The highlight of the evening was a film show. The room, or rather the garden, because the show took place in the open air, was packed with Uzbeks and Kirghiz and resounded with cries of delight. It was strange, in a temperature of 50°C, to see on the screen the icy winter of northern Russia, its wooden houses etc...The socialist newsreels of Petrograd and Moscow, which we in the capital view with boredom, were watched with a lively interest in distant Tashkent.[42]

In an attempt to overcome these cultural differences, and where possible to turn them to advantage, separate studios were established in some of these areas. Film studios were first of all established in Armenia[43] and Georgia[44] but these produced very little. The Ukrainian film organisation, V.U.F.K.U. had produced a very small number of newsreels shot in Azerbaijan[45] and a local studio was started there in 1925; once more its production was minimal.[46] In the same year Uzbekistan had its first film studio in Tashkent.[47] But Sovkino's difficulties at the centre were echoed by similar difficulties at the periphery. It was estimated that, at a rate of one projector to every 10,000 of the population, it would need 11,000 projectors to cover the Soviet Union adequately.[48] This was clearly a target that it would take some years to accomplish.

The overwhelming majority of cinema installations in the Soviet Union in 1925, in fact around 75 per cent of them, were situated in workers' clubs.[49] There was actually a great deal of controversy within the organisation of workers' clubs as to whether film shows were beneficial, in that they attracted more people to use the clubs, or detrimental to the spirit of club meetings.[50] Film shows were however relatively easy to arrange, and they were profitable, and these seem to have been the conclusive arguments.[51] Sovkino, in response to complaints about the high cost of film rental, introduced a preferential tariff for mobile projectors (mostly installed in villages or workers' clubs) which reduced the average cost of renting a film from 10 roubles in 1925 to 5.83 roubles in 1928.[52] Sovkino also managed the ideologically desirable task of reducing the percentage of foreign films shown in the clubs from 79 per cent in the period March to October 1925, first to 65 per cent in the period October 1925 to October 1926 and then to 51 per cent in the year October 1926 to October 1927.[53] This was no mean feat. Although films were more popular than any of the clubs' other activities, and therefore acted as an attraction to other facilities, one obstacle to increased income lay in the large number of people (already mentioned) who did not have to pay to attend.[54] Another inhibiting factor was Sovkino's refusal to grant the clubs first-run rights to popular films.[55] From Sovkino's point of view this refusal is understandable, as it would have undermined that organisation's increasingly lucrative relationship with the commercial cinemas, particularly in the large cities where most of the workers' clubs were situated. But the clubs also suffered from a shortage of films on contemporary themes generally.[56]

In order to deal specifically with the problems posed by the workers' clubs, a special organisation, Proletkino, had been established in 1923.[57] The editorial of its journal, also called *Proletkino*, proclaimed the beliefs of the new organisation:

> Where capitalism is in power there can be no proletarian cinema.
>
> Only here in the R.S.F.S.R., where all the cultures of the past are being re-examined, where the culture of the future is being forged, can the dream of a proletarian cinema be realised...
>
> Our young Society must assist in this realisation.
>
> Leaning on the trades unions, supported by state organs, closely linked to the party, Proletkino goes cheerfully to work.
>
> The production of proletarian films is our first and basic slogan. This will be difficult in our situation. Colossal obstacles stand before us. We do not flatter ourselves and we shall not deceive others – there will be no sudden and glittering successes. The first steps of Proletkino will be slow and full of errors.
>
> But we believe in the achievement of success. Support for the Society must be strengthened and speeded up. And Proletkino will flourish.[58]

The editor's caution was justified; in the successor journal, *Proletarskoe kino*, two years later Bukharin lamented the lack of progress in developing a specifically proletarian cinema: 'Unfortunately however very little has been done so far in this field. More words than actions. More 'plans' and projects than living practice.'[59] One writer felt that the political functions of the cinema were quite specific: 'This mass does not expect entertainment in the cinema but the satisfactory resolution of those doubts which it would find difficult to resolve itself.'[60] The masses needed to be convinced by the cinema that 'we did not live, we do not and we shall not live in vain'.[61] But to instil revolutionary perseverance into the Soviet worker and peasant it was of course essential to produce the necessary films. As *Zhizn' iskusstva* observed:

> At the same time in our political and cultural conditions the cinema, like no other art, has colossal significance in the life of the toiling masses, and of course the first to suffer from the absence of the necessary Soviet films will be the cinema installations in workers' clubs and the network of mobile projectors in the countryside which has grown so much during the past year.[62]

One writer estimated that in the season 1926–7 the Soviet film industry would be able to produce only fifty feature films, whereas the distribution network now needed twenty-four such films *every month.*[63] Another, gloomier estimate assumed a total output of only twenty films.[64] But the industry was committed to a reduction in imports, which meant that cinemas had either to re-run old films or compile their programmes from short films and newsreels.[65]

The situation could have been partially alleviated had it not been for the 'mutual blockade' (*vzaimnaya blokada*) that had developed between Sovkino and its Ukrainian equivalent, V.U.F.K.U. The dispute had arisen over whether the two organisations should sell or hire their films to one another. V.U.F.K.U. wanted to sell its films at prices it fixed itself; Sovkino wanted a hiring arrangement, which would have left it with some control over the distribution of the film. The dispute came to a head over Eisenstein's film *Bronenosets Potëmkin*, which V.U.F.K.U. refused to hire even though Sovkino was prepared to guarantee its profits.[66] The 'mutual blockade' was brought to an end in the summer of 1927.[67] Although V.U.F.K.U. incurred much odium for its uncooperative attitude,[68] it had nonetheless managed to increase the proportion of Soviet films shown in the Ukraine to 40 per cent of the total, whereas Sovkino had managed a comparable figure of only 27 per cent.[69] But even 27 per cent was an improvement on the figures during Sovkino's first year of operation.[70]

It was also important to increase and improve the production of Soviet films for use as propaganda abroad. When in 1925 the film *Liki Krasnoi Rossii* (Images of Red Russia) was shown in Berlin, it was accepted as depicting the long awaited truth about Russia:

> On the first day that the film was shown, the theatre manager gave an introductory talk in which he observed, amongst other things, that 'We have heard many things about the U.S.S.R. which we were unable to confirm, but now the moving picture, *which cannot lie*, has the stage.'[71]

However, the great breakthrough for the Soviet cinema on world markets came of course with *Bronenosets Potëmkin* and the story of this film is a highly instructive one.

Potëmkin was billed as 'the pride of the Soviet cinema',[72] and was shown simultaneously at twelve Moscow cinemas.[73] The First Goskino cinema, where the première was held, was decorated so that it looked like a battleship, and the cinema staff were dressed as members of the crew.[74] Little effort was spared to popularise the film, but the authorities were obviously on the defensive; the journal *Kino-Gazeta* produced figures to show that in a twelve-day period 29,458 people had seen *Potëmkin*, while only 21,281 had seen the American hit *Robin Hood*, starring Douglas Fairbanks.[75] But these figures are open to question and were of course produced to prove a point, namely that Soviet cinema audiences wanted Soviet films. However, two weeks before the release of *Potëmkin*, *Robin Hood* was showing at eleven of the twelve first-run cinemas in the centre of Moscow[76] and the advertisements proclaimed 'All Moscow is watching *Robin Hood*.'[77] *Potëmkin* was released on 19 January 1926[78] but taken off on 16 February.[79] Meanwhile *Medvezh'ya svad'ba* (The Bear's Wedding), an adaptation by Lunacharsky of a short story by Prosper Mérimée, had been seen by 64,000 people[80] and was being hailed as 'the first hit of 1926'.[81] Clearly this was one Soviet film that Soviet audiences did want to see.

It was not until May that *Potëmkin* became a *cause célèbre* because of its phenomenal success in Berlin and the attempts by the German authorities to ban the film.[82] *Pravda* quoted German press reviews of the film under the title 'The Victory of the *Battleship*'.[83] On 2 June 1926 the film critic Khrisanf Khersonsky observed that it was easier to see *Potëmkin* in Germany than in the Soviet Union:

> *Battleship Potemkin* has also not been shown enough in the U.S.S.R. Until recently it had hardly been shown at all in the Ukraine,[84] while abroad in Berlin it is showing successfully at 150 cinemas.[85]

Following on the film's success in Germany it was re-released at the Second Goskino cinema on 15 June[86] but was replaced after a fortnight by Buster Keaton in *Our Hospitality*[87] and one week later, ironically enough, by yet another showing 'by public demand' of Douglas Fairbanks in *Robin Hood*.[88] Sovkino had to face the fact that, given a choice, Soviet audiences preferred foreign films and this was reflected by contemporary advertising in papers such as *Pravda*. Time and again a cinema would offer 'an American hit'[89] or 'foreign attractions'[90] and the foreignness was stressed rather than disguised.[91] Meanwhile, important Soviet films like Dziga Vertov's *Shagai, Sovet!* (Forward, Soviet!) were held back for months from release.[92]

The obvious conclusion for Sovkino to draw from the experience of *Potëmkin*, from its failure at the box-office despite all the publicity and backing that its release had received, was that Soviet audiences would continue to prefer imported films, or films of a similar, 'bourgeois' type, as long as the choice remained open to them. It came then to a question of removing that choice, but that meant increasing Soviet film production to replace the missing imports. Such an increase was hampered by the shortage of the necessary funds for the importation of raw film stock and equipment.[93] Nevertheless Sovkino managed to increase production from 77 feature films in the 1925–6 season to 122 in 1926–7.[94] These Soviet films were also obviously better attuned to the requirements of Soviet audiences: whereas in the 1926–7 season the income from the distribution of imported films exceeded that from Soviet films by 2,991,064 roubles, in the following season receipts from Soviet films exceeded those from foreign films by 627,829 roubles.[95] Thus for the first time in the history of the Russian cinema the native product had overhauled the import. It was of course quite another question to make these films ideologically acceptable to the Party.

Sovkino was constantly accused of commercialism[96] and even of a surrender to bourgeois ideology in order to increase the sales of Soviet films abroad.[97] As one critic observed, 'The Soviet cinema, like Soviet literature, is looking for its hero.'[98] Elsewhere he had written:

> In as far as the new way of life is still an abstract concept, we must show it in the process of creation. We must depict the sprouting shoots of the new way of life, the new relationships between people. We must romanticise the struggle between the birth of the new and the death of the old.[99]

And this was exactly what a whole string of Soviet films attempted to do from 1926 onwards. *Potëmkin* was by no means the first, though it may well have been the most famous, example.[100]

These films fell into four broad categories. In the vanguard came the films that romanticised the events of the October Revolution itself and those immediately associated with it: Eisenstein's *Oktyabr'* (1927)[101] is perhaps the most famous example, an account of the Revolution which is so vivid that it is taken by many to be a closely factual account, if not actually a documentary reconstruction. But other well-known films in this category include Pudovkin's *Konets Sankt-Peterburga* (1927);[102] Shub's compilation film, *Padenie dinastii Romanovykh* (The Fall of the Romanov Dynasty, 1927);[103] Dovzhenko's *Arsenal* (1929);[104] and Room's *Bukhta smerti* (Bay of Death, 1926).[105] The second wave of revolutionary films concerned themselves with the history of the revolutionary movement in Russia and with the revolutionary struggle in other countries. Foremost among this group were Pudovkin's two films, *Mat'* (Mother, 1926)[106] and *Potomok Chingis-khana.*[107] Kozintsev and Trauberg's *S.V.D.* (*Soyuz velikogo dela* or The Union for the Great Cause, 1927)[108] was based on the Decembrist Uprising of 1825, while their *Novyi Vavilon* (New Babylon, 1929)[109] dealt with the Paris Commune of 1871. Room's *Prividenie, kotoroe ne vozvrashchaetsya* (The Ghost that Never Returns, 1929)[110] depicted a revolutionary situation in a South American setting and Petrov's *Fritz Bauer* (1930)[111] was set in the Germany of 1923. Protazanov made *Belyi orël* (White Eagle, 1928)[112] around the events of 1905. All these films served to place the October Revolution in what was apparently a legitimate and coherent historical context.

The third category of films was concerned with contemporary problems and, in particular, with what Nedobrovo had described as 'the struggle between the birth of the new and the death of the old'. The two best known films in this group were concerned with the conflict between the old and the new in the countryside: Eisenstein's *Staroe i novoe* (The Old and the New, formerly *General'naya liniya* – The General Line, 1929)[113] and Dovzhenko's *Zemlya* (Earth, 1930).[114] Ermler's *Oblomok imperii* (Fragment of Empire, 1929)[115] dealt with the overall problem of change since the Revolution, but Room's *Tret'ya Meshchanskaya* (Third Meshchanskaya, also known as 'Bed and Sofa', 1927)[116] concentrated on conflict in the field of housing, and Yutkevich's *Kruzheva* (Lace, 1928)[117] on confrontation in a factory.

The fourth category of films comprised documentaries celebrating the new way of life in various ways. Vertov's *Shagai, Sovet!* (Forward, Soviet! 1926)[118] and *Shestaya chast' mira* (A Sixth Part of the World, 1926)[119] were paeans to the Soviet way of life. Shub's *Velikii put'* (The Great Way, 1927)[120] depicted the progress made since 1917, and Turin's *Turksib* (1929)[121] related the economic advantages that Soviet power had brought to Turkestan and Siberia by constructing a railway link between them.

In the latter half of the twenties then the Soviet film industry was beginning to produce the kind of films that the Party required. But there was still a long way to go; until deprived of the opportunity, Soviet audiences still preferred Chaplin, Keaton, Fairbanks and Pickford to tractors and the history of what was, after all, supposed to be their Revolution. In other words they preferred escapism to realism, however unreal that realism might in fact have been.

The problem was particularly serious in the field of the children's cinema. The potential of the cinema for educating and indoctrinating the younger generation, who were after all the generation upon whom the future of the country depended, was clear.[122] And yet once more it was alleged that the opportunity was being wasted. In as far as films aimed specifically at children were available, they consisted of endless fairy tales involving kings and queens.[123] The situation was described as 'worse than desperate'.[124] None the less children comprised a significant part of Soviet cinema audiences. A Kharkov survey revealed that the average child went to the cinema two or three times a week,[125] while in Leningrad children constituted 30 per cent of evening cinema audiences.[126] But the children's reasons were not particularly encouraging for the authorities: one child revealed that, 'I go to the cinema because I'm bored at home'.[127] Soviet writers were worried about the possible effects of sex and violence upon the young, as reflected in their allegedly unhealthy worship of film stars:

> The feeling of infatuation with film actors and actresses, which is so widespread amongst our youth, is related to the influence of the cinema on the sexual arousal of adolescents. We know, for example, of 10 to 15 visits to the same picture because of a feeling of sexual arousal stimulated by the appearance of the hero or heroine.[128]

Although in a period of transition the cinema might appear to encourage unhealthy aspects of children's behaviour, the same authors felt that the long-term outlook was brighter, and that the cinema could eventually be used to educate the younger generation:

> The cinema meets the everyday needs of children and adolescents; it satisfies their demand for romantic images, and the significance of the cinema is constantly growing.
>
> In the final analysis the cinema is becoming a necessity. It satisfies, it engulfs like drunkenness, and as a result we see innumerable thefts carried out by adolescents and juveniles to get the money for a cinema ticket.
>
> However, the cinemania of children and adolescents must not be wiped

out by severe laws but should be used as a magnet towards 'the most powerful medium of Communist education and agitation'.[129]

But, beyond criticising the existing situation, contemporary writers were unable to offer many positive suggestions for improvement. It was clear that the cinema was the most popular form of entertainment amongst the young[130] and that it could thus be used to entice children into participation in other activities approved by the Party.[131] But very few detailed suggestions were made as to the exact type of film that would appeal particularly to children, beyond observations of a very generalised nature, such as, 'No Marxist can fail to realise that new content demands new form',[132] and that this new form should be a synthesis of the feature and newsreel genres.[133] Synthesis was of course an acceptable concept, particularly as the schools of film-making were engaged in an unseemly battle for officially endowed legitimacy.[134] But at the Party Conference on the Cinema held in March 1928 complaints were still being made about the absence of suitable films. One speaker claimed:

In Irkutsk we have had cases of suicide under the influence of films. In a list drawn up by two Komsomol members they describe the ideal which they set themselves on the strength of viewing foreign films. They say that they would like to ride on horseback, fly in a plane, travel in a car, learn to fence, shoot, swim, dance the foxtrot, smoke, and own the clothes that they have seen in American films.[135]

Clearly the cinema had become isolated from the needs of the people, at least as far as those needs were perceived by the Party. Sovkino was, like Goskino before it, in danger of becoming a beached whale.

To bridge the gap between film producers, directors and audiences the N.K.V.D. established by a decree of 24 July 1925 the organisation known as O.D.S.K. (Obshchestvo druzei sovetskogo kino – Society of Friends of the Soviet Cinema).[136] O.D.S.K. was to have the widest possible membership and its foundation was welcomed by representatives of Sovkino:

We cannot have a situation in which the cinema organisation merely shows the film and the audience, our Soviet audience, merely watches. Intimate contact with the mass audience is necessary; they will help us to a successful fulfilment of the task we are trying to achieve, i.e. the construction of the Soviet cinema.[137]

On 12 November 1925 Felix Dzerzhinsky, then President of Vesenkha, was appointed head of O.D.S.K.[138] In his speech of acceptance he outlined the task that lay before the Society:

The cinema can and must become a powerful tool for the cultural elevation of our workers' and peasants' country. We are tired, uncultured, illiterate, but we have given ourselves the very difficult task of becoming in a short time the most progressive, the most cultured, the most literate country. The first successes in the development of our economy and the prospect of a further rapid growth in our industry and our economy furnish a strong base for the cultural development of the masses of workers and peasants. In this cause the cinema must play an important rôle.[139]

O.D.S.K. was supposed to reform the cinema through mass involvement[140] but it faced difficulties in recruiting its membership because there was by this time a surfeit of voluntary organisations in the Soviet Union.[141]

O.D.S.K. was to be organised on a 'non-bureaucratic' basis, that is membership cells were to be allowed to grow up in places like factories and offices, rather than being established by government or Party fiat.[142] The cinema, it was felt, could not perform its proper educational function without the active support of the masses:

The cinema, more than any other field of our work, needs public support. The cinema is not merely a medium of agitation and propaganda, but is a powerful and a key factor with the aid of which we shall raise the masses to a higher cultural level. The tasks which face the cinema in this respect are so great and so complex that without public assistance they would not be possible. O.D.S.K. is the only organisation which has formed around the cinema that can help it to pave the way and that in addition should do much to transform the cinema into a real weapon for the cultural influencing of the masses.[143]

O.D.S.K. was to be composed of strong local organisations with only a guiding and coordinating central organisation; this would prevent the growth of bureaucratism and the consequent stifling of initiative.[144] But at the same time it was expected to undertake the task of furnishing the countryside with projection equipment and films and to provide courses in equipment repair and related matters.[145] It was required to maintain close links with the local branches of the Party; at the same time it needed funds greater than those accruing from membership funds and it was expected to supplement its income by producing local newsreels for commercial ends.[146] Finally it was suggested that O.D.S.K. should operate in workers' clubs and that it should in fact take over the management of the film sections of the network of workers' clubs.[147] And all this without falling into the trap of bureaucratism that had hitherto ensnared every Soviet film organisation.

It is not possible to measure with any accuracy the degree of success that can be attributed to O.D.S.K. rather than to any of the other Soviet film organisations in the process of cinefication of the countryside. Nevertheless, in as far as O.D.S.K. comprised the leading cadres of film workers in these areas, those with the greatest commitment and enthusiasm, it acted as a vanguard and a focal point for the subsequent ideological indoctrination of the population, especially in the rural areas:

> The local cells of O.D.S.K. constitute a rural pressure-group (Komsomoltsy,[148] progressive peasants, the doctor, the teacher, the agricultural expert, the village librarian, etc.); they find the means and explain the rôle of the cinema in the economic and cultural life of the countryside.[149]

Members of O.D.S.K., being an educated or trained elite, were also to introduce films, explain the titles and lead any ensuing discussion, much as the workers on the agit-trains had done during the Civil War period.[150] The rôle played by O.D.S.K., both at the very basic level and as a link between the central organisation and the masses was thus potentially a very important one, but in practice the Society hardly lived up to the promises made on its behalf in 1925:

> The establishment of O.D.S.K. should correspond to the final completion of the construction of the Soviet cinema as a weapon of class enlightenment for the proletariat.[151]

This task was left to the Party Conference on the Cinema, held eventually in March 1928.

6. THE PARTY TAKES CONTROL

Although we all share Lenin's view that the cinema is the most important agitational and propaganda weapon for influencing the masses, we have nonetheless hitherto allowed this art form to drift on the Soviet sea 'rudderless and without sails'. . .The forthcoming conference will work out a 'single' platform for the 'unification of the socialist state with the cinema on proletarian foundations'.

Soviet cultural journal, 1927.[1]

Sovkino had not had to wait long before it, like Goskino before it, became the butt for general criticisms of the weaknesses in the organisation of the Soviet cinema. But to a considerable extent Sovkino became a scapegoat because official cultural policy was changing. The end of the New Economic Policy, and the period of reconstruction associated with it, meant, as far as the Party was concerned, that the material base for the transition to socialism had now been achieved and that attention could therefore be concentrated on ideological matters and in particular on an emphasis on the leading rôle of the working class in cultural affairs. This change in attitude was signalled by the resolution adopted by the Central Committee on 18 June 1925 concerning Soviet literature: 'Leadership in the field of literature belongs to the working class . . .There is not yet a hegemony of proletarian writers.'[2] The exact nature of the 'proletarian cultural revolution'[3] that was to accompany the economic revolution of the Five Year Plan was to be decided in a series of Party conferences on the arts.[4] The last of these conferences was that on the cinema, held in Moscow after some delay[5] from 15 to 21 March 1928.[6]

The conference came at the end of a prolonged press campaign against Sovkino and its policies and clearly marked a watershed in the development of the Soviet cinema. One has only to turn the pages of the Soviet film press for the latter half of the 1920s to notice an enormous change in atmosphere in 1927–8; this change was given more concrete form by the Party conference on the cinema.

The press campaign against Sovkino's policies began in earnest in the middle of 1926 with the publication in *Sovetskii ekran* of a rather vicious poem satirising the reaction of the stereotyped

'Nepman' to *Potëmkin* following its enormous success abroad.[7] According to the poem the general public at first received the film with indifference, boredom, even distaste:

> Who praises it? The film writer,
> And the Party member praise it –
> But the Soviet man in the street[8]
> Is dissatisfied and scandalised:

The film is then shown abroad, where it is a tremendous commercial success. Fresh from its foreign success, *Potëmkin* returns to a more enthusiastic Soviet reception:

> The soul of the audience is a mystery.[9]
> Weep, Shklovsky; cry, Brik,
> *Potëmkin* comes to the U.S.S.R.
> As a *foreign* hit.

It was of course still foreign hits that Soviet audiences wanted to see.[10]

In the first weeks of 1927 the attack on Sovkino and its alleged obsession with box-office success at the expense of ideological content was renewed. Sovkino was accused of 'philistinism'[11] and dire consequences were predicted if no effective action were taken to control the origin and content of the films shown on Soviet screens:

> Enough has been written about the ideological worth of foreign films, and the best that can be said for the best of them is that they are harmless. . .In my opinion *decisive* measures must be taken in this matter. If not, the cinema, as the most popular art among the broad masses of the population of the U.S.S.R., will be compromised for a long time. This would be a severe blow to our cinema industry, which is still not strong enough, and it would be cruelly reflected in our cinema network.[12]

A third writer, criticising existing Soviet film production, suggested that the authorities should ensure that 'a place of honour is given to short political–educational and cultural films'.[13] These could be shown with a feature film and presumably mitigate its harmful effects. But these criticisms and suggestions were only the beginning. The press campaign was intensified with the issue of *Novyi zritel'* dated 13 September 1927, which merely informed its readers that a Party conference on the cinema 'will be called in January'[14] and gave the bare details.

This issue of the journal signalled the opening of a debate on all aspects of cinema policy in the Soviet Union. That the debate was not entirely orchestrated by the Party is demonstrated by the first trumpet blast in the campaign from *Zhizn' iskusstva* quoted at the head of this chapter. However it is scarcely surprising that it was Sovkino rather than the Party which came in for the greatest volume and strength of criticism: the aforementioned article went on to criticise Sovkino for its obsession with commercial considerations.[15] In a later issue one critic reiterated the by now familiar points about the lack of trained cadres of film workers, the shortage of film and equipment and the absence of a solid financial basis for the further development of the Soviet cinema.[16] He expected the forthcoming conference to be a 'turning point'.[17] But perhaps the most forthright and blistering attack came in the next issue from Adrian Piotrovsky, a leading film critic.[18] He started from the premise that the cinema, unlike the theatre and literature, had no classical tradition: the existing, or 'bourgeois' cinema was the product of the 'militant bourgeoisie'. For this reason Soviet film-makers should brook no compromise but should instead reject the past completely:

> The cinema was born among the bourgeoisie as the last of its arts and the first art of socialism. . .[The conference] should take a categorical stand *for* the specifically Soviet and socialist tendencies and directions in our cinema and *against* half-heartedness, *against* the 'academicism' of the past, *against* attempts to turn the Soviet cinema into an ideological colony of bourgeois cinematography, which is socially harmful and formally reactionary. . .So let us be clear: there is no place in our cinema for halfheartedness, for complicated tacking manoeuvres. Here we can and must be maximalists. Here we can and must stake everything on the socialist art of the cinema and, perhaps, on the socialist industry of the cinema. Here we must speak with one voice, with the voice of the Five Year Plan, a voice which speaks of industrialisation and the electrification of our country.[19]

These themes were echoed in an article published almost simultaneously in *Novyi zritel'*. Having attacked the alleged preoccupation of the Soviet cinema with '90 per cent commerce – 10 per cent ideology' the writer reiterated the need to carry through a cultural revolution in the cinema:

> The Soviet cinema must look for commercial success in new Soviet themes, in ideology. It must help the Party and Soviet power to carry out the cultural revolution, the transformation of our way of life, and socialist construction.[20]

He then went on to suggest that scriptwriting should be reorganised on collective lines to reflect the new collective way of life. In the next issue of *Zhizn' iskusstva* there were further complaints that the interests of the workers' clubs were being ignored, that they were being treated as 'poor relatives' and even that they were being sent copies of films 'that are in such a state that it is impossible to tell which is the beginning and which is the end'.[21] In other words commercial interests were once more being given precedence over ideological ones.

Piotrovsky returned to the attack in the following issue of *Zhizn' iskusstva* with the assertion that the division between commerce and ideology was in itself a misleading one. He claimed that such a division reflected a lack of faith in the ability of Soviet films to attract audiences; this lack of confidence could go a long way to explaining the apparent failure of Soviet films in competition with imported ones.[22] But in his next article Piotrovsky took up and developed the point made by Blyakhin about the need to reorganise scriptwriting procedures. He claimed that the basic problem in 1927–8 was that which had dogged the Russian cinema ever since 1912–13, a shortage of suitable screenplays. His remedy was simple, if not simplistic:

> This collaboration of literature should be on a mass scale. Life should gush out into the cinema along the canals of literature, refreshing, renewing, enriching the formal fabric of our cinema. Mass literary conferences under the slogan 'To the aid of the cinema', prolonged campaigns should bring about the mass involvement of writers in the work of the cinema.[23]

The 15th Party Congress in December 1927 passed the usual resolution about strengthening Party control over Soviet cultural life, although the general circumstances gave the resolution greater significance on this occasion.[24] At this Congress Stalin first made his remark about using the cinema to combat alcoholism,[25] although on closer examination it would seem that his words have been misinterpreted.[26] It is clear from the official stenographic report of the Congress that Stalin was concerned not so much with the direct use of the cinema in a propaganda campaign against the consumption of alcohol as with its usefulness as an alternative source of tax revenue to vodka:

> I think that it might be possible to begin the gradual abolition of vodka by introducing instead of vodka such sources of revenue as the radio and the cinema. In fact, why don't we take these very important media into our own hands and people them with shock workers from among the real Bolsheviks, who could blow the whole thing up successfully and give us the chance to do away with the whole vodka business at last.[27]

Clearly the effects of this policy on alcoholism were considered very much as a side issue.

In January 1928 Lunacharsky, then still People's Commissar for Enlightenment, made a courageous speech to the All-Union Conference of Cinematographic and Photographic Workers.[28] He attacked conspiracy theories and the selection of scapegoats and rejected calls for purges in the personnel of cinema organisations. He took up Stalin's remarks to the Party Congress but compared the cinema to a healthy infant that needed to be nurtured with care and consideration. Lunacharsky was acutely aware of the danger of an adverse public reaction that would render Party-directed propaganda counter-productive:

> Many of us do not appreciate that our cinema must stimulate the public appetite, that, if there is no public interest, then the films that we show become boring agitation and we are transformed into boring agitators. But it is well known that boring agitation is counter-agitation. We must search out and find a line *in accordance with which the film is both ideologically sound and artistic, in which there is both romantic experience and experience of an intimate and psychological character.*[29]

As the author of a number of 'romantic' screenplays, Lunacharsky was in an unusually strong position to put forward the view that romance and ideology could be satisfactorily combined, although his interest and experience may well have counted against him in the longer term.[30]

The last articles to appear before the conference finally began merely reiterated points that had already been made. One writer claimed quite sensibly that Soviet cinema organisations could reduce their costs by cooperating with one another rather than competing as they had done hitherto.[31] Another urged a greater effort to export Soviet films to spread the Bolshevik message abroad. But his opening remark may serve to underline the stark fact behind the whole debate: 'The 15th Party Congress linked questions of cultural revolution closely with the fundamental problems of socialist construction.'[32] In other words the Party had finally decided to realise the proposal made by Stalin at the 13th Party Congress in May 1924: 'The cinema is the greatest means of mass agitation. The task is to take it into our own hands.'[33] The realisation of this proposal, the extension of the cultural revolution to the Soviet cinema, was the task set by the Party for the conference in March 1928.

Everything was done to encourage the view that the First All-Union Party Conference on the Cinema was to mark a turning point in the development of the Soviet cinema. This attitude was underlined in the introduction to the official stenographic report of the conference proceedings:

> The All-Union Party Conference marks the completion and underlines the results of that wide-ranging discussion of the questions of Soviet cinematography which has lasted for almost half a year. The materials and reso-

lutions of the conference represent, for the Party, Komsomol [Vsesoyuznyi leninskii kommunisticheskii soyuz molodëzhi – All-Union Leninist Communist League of Youth] and trades union organisations, as for the film organisations and for practical workers in the field of the cinema, a most valuable guide in the resolution of the colossal significance of the task of cinefication of the U.S.S.R., of the transformation of the cinema in practice into a weapon of communist education and agitation, of the realisation of the slogan: 'the cinema instead of vodka'.[34]

At the opening session S. V. Kosior, who made the introductory speech, claimed that the conference was a focus of mass interest for two reasons: first, because the cinema was so important and, second, because the Soviet cinema had reached this turning point.[35] He stated quite clearly where he thought the blame for past failures lay:

We feel that we have now come to such a point that all these questions must be put and discussed at a fundamental level...The Party paid improbably little attention to this, if not no attention at all. (Voices: That's right.) And, comrades, I think we can say this without being at all embarrassed. We all, and the Communist especially, understand that this is the principal cause of all the misfortunes and inadequacies of our cinema. If our Party and the Party organisations had given immediate, direct and close guidance in this matter there is no doubt that we should have had much greater successes.[36]

But Kosior seemed as unclear as others had been previously as to the exact rôle of ideology in the development of the cinema. On the one hand he argued that commercial considerations were legitimate: 'The cinema is a cultural–commercial undertaking and should develop as such.'[37] On the other hand he quite clearly regarded the cinema as perhaps the Party's most important weapon of class warfare:

In our Soviet Union we cannot for one minute turn away from regarding not just the cinema but every other art as a weapon for the influence of the proletariat on the non-proletarian part of the population.[38]

The first report to be read to the conference, by A. I. Krinitsky, head of the Agitprop Department of the Central Committee, on 'The results of the construction of the cinema in the U.S.S.R. and the tasks of Soviet cinematography', echoed this last point of view by citing Bukharin:

As Comrade Bukharin has said, 'We are emerging from the cells of "chamber" culture on to the city streets and squares and we are sending the heralds of culture into the villages and the countryside'; we are creating a 'great mass cultural movement', we are 'calling into life the vast, broad and profound flow of mass cultural construction'.[39]

In this process of transformation the cinema's rôle was clear:

The mass aspect of all forms of art, and especially of the cinema, the force of example and great conviction, the capacity for influencing profoundly the most outmoded strata of society – all this transforms art into one of the most powerful instruments of the struggle for cultural improvement, an enormous factor in the cultural revolution and the socialist transformation of the country.[40]

The cinema was to lead the way in providing the 'high cultural level' that Krinitsky believed to be a necessary corollary to the economic transformations envisaged in the Five Year Plan.[41] Using the old Plekhanovite distinction between agitation and propaganda, Krinitsky saw the tasks of the cinema in its new situation as twofold:

The cinema must be a weapon for the *organisation of the masses* around the task of the revolutionary struggle of the proletariat and socialist construction, and a means of *agitation* for the current slogans of the Party.[42]

He commented on the success and the high standard of films depicting the history of the Revolution and the Revolutionary movement; this kind of film, in his eyes, 'gives a class assessment of historical events'.[43] But the Soviet cinema had signally failed to produce worthwhile films on contemporary Soviet life and its problems:[44] in Sovkino's production plan for 1927–8 there were, for instance, no films on 'the union [*smychka*] of the workers and peasants, the fight for collective forms of agriculture, our nationalities policy, the work of the trades unions as schools of communism, the significance of cooperation in the cause of socialist construction, questions of rationalisation, of the old and the new school, *et al.*'.[45] There was a particular need for agitational shorts on themes such as bread production and elections to the soviets,[46] while the newsreel should be employed as a means for the transmission of 'graphic *political information*'.[47]

Krinitsky criticised the crude distinction that had been made by others between commerce and ideology, claiming that, if the cinema were to 'serve widely the demands of the worker and the peasant',[48] then it could 'stand firmly on the feet of a healthy economic and organisational policy'.[49] The key to success lay in producing films that were 'comprehensible to the millions' (*ponyatna millionam*),[50] an expression that was to become something of a catch-phrase.[51] Krinitsky maintained that a healthy economic basis for the Soviet cinema depended also on an expansion of the cinema network, on which matter he described himself as a 'maximalist',[52] and on an increase in the number of copies made of each Soviet film; at present the average Soviet film was produced in only forty-two copies but it was technically feasible to raise this to between 150 and 300 copies with the resulting advantages of economies of scale.[53] He reiterated Stalin's remarks to the 15th Party Congress,[54] underlining them by pointing out that the tax revenue obtained by the Soviet state from vodka sales during the tax year 1927–8 had been 644,000,000 roubles, compared with a mere 20,000,000 roubles from the cinema in the same period.[55] This statistic was not only a measure of the task ahead if the cinema was indeed to replace vodka as a source of tax revenue; it was also intended as an answer to those who complained that the Soviet cinema was overtaxed.

Despite his comments on the compatibility of commercial and ideological aims, Krinitsky did criticise what many regarded as the somewhat vulgar and sensual Western influence on Soviet film posters.[56] This kind of thing only pandered to the lowest common denominator and encouraged people to see Soviet films for the wrong reasons. Krinitsky, like Kosior in his introductory speech, laid the blame for this state of affairs at the feet of the Party itself:

> At the Party conference we must pose in all seriousness the question of the causes of those great inadequacies and distortions of the Party line from which our cinema is suffering.
>
> One of the most important causes – we must confess this without reservation – is the hitherto inadequate attention paid to the problems of the cinema by the Party and the broad Soviet public.[57]

But, unlike Kosior, Krinitsky was unequivocal in his estimation of the task to which the Soviet cinema should apply itself:

> In all its cultural work under the leadership of the proletariat there stands before Soviet art – in this case before the cinema – the enormous task of the transformation of the masses. The Soviet cinema must not follow in the wake of the audience, but must move ahead of it; it must lead the audience, support the beginnings in it of the new man, instil into it new views, tastes, habits, which correspond to the task of the socialist reconstruction of the whole of society. In this we can see the striking difference between the Soviet cinema and the bourgeois cinema which, in its relationship to its audience, indulges and supports in its views, tastes and attitudes which are reactionary, anti-revolutionary, directed against the interests of the workers, and are cultivated by capitalism in its own interests.[58]

The debate which followed Krinitsky's report did little to illuminate the problems of the Soviet cinema, although much to confirm one delegate's view that the Soviet cinema was in a 'state of civil war'.[59] Kostrov, the delegate from *Komsomol'skaya pravda* echoed Krinitsky's complaints about the direction and standards of Soviet film advertisements[60] and other speakers reiterated many of the points that he had made in his report, or in the earlier press campaign: the shortage of Soviet films overall, the shortage in particular of films on contemporary themes or on themes of special relevance to children or to rural audiences. The delegate from the North Caucasus, Tsekher, pointed out that the distribution of poor copies of poor films could well be counterproductive: 'Because of these worn films the countryside is turning not merely against Sovkino but also against Soviet power.'[61] Ananev, a delegate from Siberia, demanded more immediate measures: in Irkutsk, he claimed, 60 per cent of the films shown were still of foreign origin and there was a clear case for a complete ban on such films in certain areas, particularly where the cinema was still regarded as a technical marvel. He complained about the depiction of the peasantry in Soviet films: *Lyubov' vtroem* (Three-Way Love)[62] had depicted peasant women as spitting: 'That is how Sovkino promotes the *smychka* between the town and the countryside.'[63]

On the whole the debate degenerated into a confrontation between those, like Ananev, who were critical of Sovkino, and those, like Kosior and Ivanov (a Leningrad delegate), who felt that Sovkino was being used as a scapegoat. Rafes, Trainin and Shvedchikov, the three Sovkino delegates, not surprisingly defended their organisation, Rafes claiming that the pressure for ideologically weak films came from the audiences themselves:

> There is a tradition in the cinema, although it is young. It is the tradition of obscenity, emptiness, vulgarity. These traditions surround the Soviet cinema and act on it from below upwards.[64]

He attacked the 'cinema opposition' for its rashness and compared the so-called 'maximalists' with the initial advocates of industrialisation;[65] this was either a very brave or a very foolish thing for a man in his position to say, but at the time all it produced was laughter and a voice shouting, 'Pie in the sky!'[66] However Rafes was attacked by another delegate, S. N. Krylov, for his complacency,[67] and Krylov alleged that the existing leadership of the Soviet cinema had led it 'into a petit bourgeois commercial cul-de-sac'.[68] His remarks were immediately refuted by Ivanov who felt that the fault lay higher up in the Soviet political hierarchy: he attacked Lunacharsky himself for 'ideologically disarming the proletarian public' and argued that the task ahead was too great for Sovkino alone.[69] This was not the first attack on the People's Commissar for Enlightenment: he had previously been criticised by Meshcheryakov, the Glavpolitprosvet delegate, for being two-faced.[70] The Sovkino representatives defended themselves by pointing out the tremendous technical and financial difficulties that the Soviet cinema had faced, and was still facing.[71] Their attitude was vigorously attacked by two of the representatives of the Agitprop Department of the Central Committee, Olkhovy and Kerzhentsev. Olkhovy described Sovkino's policies as a 'rotten compromise' (*gniloi kompromiss*);[72] the problem, in his view, was not shortages of technical and financial resources but an absence of ideological leadership.[73] Kerzhentsev went further and argued that Sovkino should not need the Communist Party to tell it that *Potëmkin* was a good revolutionary film.[74] He claimed of Sovkino that, 'It has conducted no agitation, produced no agitational films.'[75] The debate continued with a repetition, from N. I. Smirnov, of the claim that the current problems of the Soviet cinema stemmed from its past neglect by the Party.[76] Following this, Krinitsky was faced with the unenviable task of summing up the discussions.

In his closing speech to this session of the conference Krinitsky argued that the Party must move from abstractions to concrete acts: 'It is time to translate the cultural revolution from the skies of general judgements to the soil of systematic practical work.'[77] He went on to argue that there was insufficient propaganda content in Soviet films and that commercial considerations must yield to ideological ones.[78] He divided existing films into three categories: those which were ideologically satisfactory; those which were ideologically unsatisfactory but not harmful; and those which were both ideologically unsatisfactory and harmful.[79] He cited in particular Eisenstein's *Oktyabr'* as an example of a film that, while it was ideologically satisfactory in terms of content, was too difficult, because of its advanced experimental technique, to be properly appreciated by Soviet audiences without a certain amount of prior explanatory work.[80] Krinitsky attacked many of the criticisms that had been made during the debate for being too negative, although he did admit:

> It seems to me that one of the most important conclusions that we must draw from all our conversations at the conference and from the discussions beforehand is to answer truthfully the question of who is responsible for the situation in the cinema.[81]

He avoided giving his own answer and did not repeat the answer that he had suggested in his original report;[82] perhaps he had sensed the way the Soviet wind was blowing.

Krinitsky concluded his speech, and thus the session, by outlining what he saw as the principal tasks facing the Soviet cinema industry in the future. These were: to make the cinema into a weapon of communist agitation and propaganda; to attract greater talent; to instil greater comprehension among the film-going public; to organise the worker audience; and finally to arrange for closer Party supervision not merely of Sovkino but also of the various national film studios.[83] He did not mention the problem of the cinema's relationship with the countryside, not because it was not important, but because it was to be the subject of one of the reports to be given to the following session.

The second session of the conference opened with a report from Shvedchikov on 'Organisational and economic questions of Soviet cinematography'. He complained about the heavy burden of taxation that, in his view, the Soviet cinema had to bear: most industries in the U.S.S.R. paid between 3 and 5 per cent of their turnover in taxation, but the twenty million roubles previously cited for the cinema[84] represented 27 per cent of its turnover for that year.[85] The larger cinema network required an increase in the number of films produced and in the number of copies made of each film. But Sovkino had been unable to attract the capital from outside sources that was needed to do this.[86] Sovkino therefore needed either loans from Gosbank (Gosudarstvennyi bank S.S.S.R. – State Bank of the U.S.S.R.)[87] or, preferably, a reduction in taxation so that the money previously raised in tax revenue should be ploughed back into investment in the cinema.[88] Shvedchikov also argued that the situation had been made worse by recent decisions of Glavrepertkom (Glavnyi repertuarnyi komitet), the organ responsible for censorship, which had virtually excluded all foreign films and thus created an even larger gap for Sovkino to fill; this it was unable to do, quite simply because the Soviet film industry was not producing enough films.[89] He felt that the situation could be resolved by the centralisation of production, distribution and exhibition throughout the Soviet Union into a single organisation (i.e. Sovkino)[90] and the simultaneous establishment of a close link between Sovkino and Vesenkha, so that the economic needs of the cinema were no longer ignored.[91]

Before Shvedchikov's report was throw open to debate, the conference heard another report, from Meshcheryakov, on 'The cinema in the countryside'.[92] He said nothing that had not been said many times before in the Soviet film press during the latter half of the 1920s. He began by criticising what he regarded as the prejudiced view that the countryside was only interested in films about the countryside, although he did admit that urban life was often misunderstood in country areas and that counter-revolutionary sympathies could thus be unintentionally encouraged:

> In the countryside many films are not understood. . .And it must be said that the more widely the Soviet cinema develops, the greater will be the percentage of films that are completely incomprehensible to the peasantry. I am talking about a film like *October*'. There's nothing to be said for *Zvenigora,* which we all had the misfortune to see.[93]

Meshcheryakov argued that there were two ways in which the Soviet cinema network could develop: either a commercial network could be established to accumulate capital rapidly, or a broader network could be set up, especially in rural and working class areas.[94] The latter course would reduce costs through economies of scale, rather than leading to an accumulation of capital. Sovkino, in his view, was arguing for the first course; in its demand that the cinema network should be handed over to it, it was assuming that Narkompros, which at present exerted ultimate control over the cinema network, was concerned with education, while Sovkino itself was concerned purely with trade.[95] But this course of action would make the Soviet cinema once more heavily dependent on imports.[96] Meshcheryakov believed that the second course was preferable: it would enable Sovkino to extend the showing of old films to places where they had never been shown before and the money thus saved could be used to pay for imported film stock with which to expand current production.[97]

Following Meshcheryakov's report the session was opened to general debate. The first speaker was Arustanov, the delegate of Goskinprom Gruzii, which was the Georgian equivalent of Sovkino; he underlined Meshcheryakov's point about the possibility of using old films in remote areas by revealing just how inefficient the Soviet film distribution network still was, at least at the edges:

> In distribution things are extremely bad. Perhaps in Moscow this isn't felt so strongly. The conference won't believe this, but for example, a film like *The Fall of the Romanov Dynasty* hasn't got to the Transcaucasus yet. The pity is not just that in the lower levels of the distribution organisations we don't have our workers but more than 90 per cent of the immediate purveyors of the pictures – cinema managers – are either the former owners or uncultured workers. And these are the people who are supposed to show our *October* to the Soviet audience.[98]

Arustanov argued that this vacuum must be filled from above by qualified cultural workers,[99] but the next speaker, Maltsev, the delegate from O.D.S.K.,[100] not unnaturally disagreed and expressed the view that Sovkino was already stifling local initiative.[101] But he was to have his full say in the following session of the conference.[102] The rest of the debate consisted of the various delegates putting forward the views and interests of the organisations that they represented: for example, Kameneva, the delegate from V.O.K.S. (Vsesoyuznoe obshchestvo kul'turnykh svyazei s zarubezhnymi stranami or All-Union Society for Cultural Relations with Foreign Countries) argued that there was a need for films demonstrating the success of the Revolution for distribution amongst Western intellectuals[103] and that friendship societies abroad could be used to stimulate the market for Soviet films and thus reduce the need for expensive advertising.[104] Apart from these rather narrow views only two points of general significance emerged: that the cinema was a very powerful weapon, and that it was being abused. The first point was made graphically by Kolesnikova, a delegate from Yaroslavl:

A few words to show how important the cinema is in the countryside. In one of our villages, at just the time the vespers were supposed to start, we began a film show and the priest had to postpone the vespers because the church remained empty.[105]

On the other hand, Annenkova, the delegate of *Pionerskaya pravda*, alleged that, in the cities at least, the cinema was attracting quite the wrong kind of audience:

Or take Belgoskino's cinema, the Ars on the Arbat. This cinema, starting with the advertisements and finishing with the foyer, is a qualifying school for hooligans. The manager of the Belgiya himself proudly declares, 'Hooligans come here from all over Moscow.'[106]

If one can draw any conclusions from this session of the conference, they must be those that can be drawn from the first session: the Soviet cinema was potentially an extremely powerful propaganda weapon, but its potential was as yet nowhere near being realised.

The third session of the conference also heard two reports: one from K. A. Maltsev on 'The public and the cinema', and one from N. I. Smirnov on 'The press and the cinema'. Maltsev began by attacking the view that there was an autonomous entity that could be described as the 'cinema public':

We use the term 'cinema public'. I think that this term is misleading. It defines that public on which the Soviet cinema is supposed to depend. It seems to me that the entire Soviet public should, in one way or another, help the Soviet cinema, for the cinema is such an important and powerful means of cultural influence upon the masses that the matter of the cinema's development should be the concern of the entire Soviet public.[107]

There were, in his opinion, five ways in which the interest of the public at large could be stimulated: first, through the trades union movement and the workers' clubs and cultural work amongst the proletariat; second, through his own organisation, O.D.S.K.; third, through the specialist associations of cinema workers; fourth, through the Party, Komsomol and other cells that existed within the cinema organisations; and last and least, through the institutions of scientific research into the cinema.[108] He cited several examples of Sovkino's lack of cooperation with organisations such as O.D.S.K.,[109] blaming it in a large part for the failure hitherto to involve the Soviet public with the cinema to any significant organisational extent. He also complained about the lack of ideological control in the film studios.[110] In Maltsev's opinion, the solution to all these problems lay in the further expansion of O.D.S.K., which already had 400 cells, 35,000 members (of whom 35 per cent were classified as working-class), and a network of mobile projectors 'which operate in all corners of the U.S.S.R.'.[111] He also made reference to A.R.K. (Assotsiyatsiya revolyutsionnoi kinematografii – Association of Revolutionary Cinematography)[112] which, he urged against some interruption from the floor, should become the cinema's equivalent of V.A.P.P. (Vsesoyuznaya assotsiyatsiya proletarskikh pisatelei – All-Union Association of Proletarian Writers), whose ideological position it had already adopted.[113] That position was the one that, in the 1930s, was to subjugate all the arts in the Soviet Union to the dead hand of 'socialist realism'; this degree of control and direction is already indicated in Maltsev's closing remarks:

If we wish to have a healthy cinema that will serve the workers and peasants, then we must surround it above all with a healthy public. We must place this public under the leadership of the proletariat, under the leadership of Party organisations, because only in this way can we be sure that all our decisions passed at this conference will be realised, and that the Soviet cinema will stand on wider, solid and public foundations.[114]

The final report to the conference was that by Smirnov on the press and the cinema.[115] He launched a strong attack on the quality and content of the books and leaflets published by Tea-Kino-Pechat, the relevant state publishing house, citing as a typical example the pamphlet on Douglas Fairbanks and Mary

Pickford entitled *They are here* (*Oni u nas*), which was printed in an edition of 45,000 copies and which Smirnov described as 'a masterpiece of banality'.[116] He also criticised the quality and purpose of film reviews.[117] The film press reflected too closely the ideological weaknesses of the Soviet cinema, whereas it should have been criticising them: 'In the cinema press there is no ideological unity. It is divorced from the Soviet public and is at times dependent on the film production organisations.'[118] Smirnov reserved particular words of criticism for two of the leading film journals, *Sovetskii ekran*, and *Kino*, which had become the official mouthpiece for O.D.S.K. He maintained that an examination of the contents of *Sovetskii ekran* for the year 1927 revealed that 54 per cent of the material could be classified as 'entertainment';[119] the ideological weaknesses of the journal were further underlined by the hostile review that it had given to *Potëmkin* in contrast to other films.[120] *Sovetskii ekran* was far too dependent on the film production organisations and, like them, it ignored both the countryside and the workers' clubs.[121] *Kino*, as the organ of O.D.S.K., had a particular rôle to play in the education of the proletarian cinema audience, but it was taking far too passive a view of this rôle.[122] It too had failed to mention the specific interests of the rural audience[123] and was failing to reflect what Smirnov regarded as the proper functions of O.D.S.K.[124]

The final debate on the reports by Maltsev and Smirnov again produced little that was new. The delegate representing the Ukrainian O.D.S.K., Govtvan, supported Maltsev's assertion that Soviet film organisations were unwilling to cooperate with O.D.S.K., which was therefore fighting an uphill struggle in its attempts to prepare villages for the cinema.[125] However, the most significant contribution to the debate came from Obnorsky, the delegate of the Leningrad committee of the Party. He stated in effect that the Party itself must take control of the cinema, and thus brought the proceedings of the conference full circle:

> In the first place we must turn our attention to the mass organisations, to the proletarian organisations of the Soviet public so that, by bringing them closer to the cinema, by linking them closely with the cinema, we shall realise through the cinema the task of exerting the influence of the working class on the non-proletarian strata of the population. From this point of view we must first of all speak of strengthening the link between the film organisations, the Party and the trade unions.[126]

All that was now left was for the conference to pass its resolutions. One resolution was passed to deal with the issues raised in each report that had been presented. In one sense the resolutions walked a tightrope between the different views that had been expressed during the debates, for example on the question of whether the cinema was an art form, an industry or some other form of commercial enterprise,[127] but in another sense the message of the conference to the cinema was quite clear and was best expressed in the first resolution, which was a response to Krinitsky's report:

> The cinema, 'the most important of all the arts', can and must play a large rôle in the cultural revolution as a medium for broad educational work and communist propaganda, for the organisation and education of the masses around the slogans and tasks of the Party, their artistic education, and their wholesome relaxation and entertainment.
>
> The cinema, like every art, cannot be apolitical. The cinema must be a weapon of the proletariat in its struggle for hegemony, leadership and influence in relation to the other classes, it 'should be, in the hands of the Party, the most powerful medium of communist enlightenment and agitation' (in the resolution of the 13th Congress of the V.K.P.(b). [Vsesoyuznaya kommunisticheskaya partiya (bol'shevikov) – All-Union Communist Party (Bolsheviks)]).[128]

The cinema's rôle was particularly vital at a period of transition when, in the eyes of the Party, reactionary elements in society were making what amounted to a last-ditch stand.[129] The Party and the Soviet public were advised to concentrate on the ideological control of the cinema, on its economic organisation, and on strengthening the cadres of trained film workers.[130] The resolutions on the role of the cinema in the countryside (in response to Meshcheryakov's report)[131] and on the relationships between the Soviet public, the press and the cinema (in response to the reports from Maltsev and Smirnov)[132] were both uncontroversial and were passed unanimously.[133] However the resolution on the organisational and economic aspects of the cinema (in response to the report from Shvedchikov)[134] was passed against the thirteen votes of the Ukrainian delegation,[135] who objected to the fourteenth paragraph, which made allowances for one Soviet film organisation (e.g. Sovkino) to rent its films to another (e.g. V.U.F.K.U.), rather than selling them outright.[136] This issue had been the one that had led to the 'mutual blockade' of films between the Ukraine and the R.S.F.S.R. earlier in the decade.[137] Apart from this paragraph this resolution too was uncontroversial, but the general message of the conference was unambiguous: the Party and the Soviet public must take the Soviet cinema in hand. The cinema must be made into a weapon of the internal class struggle being waged during the cultural revolution of the First Five Year Plan. The cinema network must be extended,[138] the films produced improved,[139] and at the same time the Soviet Union must be made independent of imported films and raw materials.[140] In short:

> The cinema exerts a very strong influence on the viewer. The cinema is the most portable art; it is cheap and unusually visual. The cinema has a more numerous audience, the cinema is by nature the most democratic and mass art. The cinema, by its example, is capable of attracting and influencing the consciousness of the viewer who is culturally most backward. In the variety and richness of its formal and technical resources, the cinema has no rivals.[141]

The problem then was to harness the cinema at last to the purposes of the Party.

What then were the consequences of the First Party Conference on the Cinema and how far did it represent the 'turning point' that had been predicted? There is no doubt that the conference presaged a change in atmosphere and in attitudes as well, a change summed up in the title of an article by R. Pikel on the conference that appeared shortly afterwards in *Zhizn' iskusstva*: 'From following in the tail of events to a clear class line'.[142] Pikel reflected the general press reaction to the conference, although in view of Smirnov's report the degree of spontaneity in that response was probably very small indeed:

> The philistine [*meshchanin*] in the Soviet cinema has not infrequently felt himself to be master of the situation. The conference sharply underlined the inadmissibility in future of a similar slide into the philistine quagmire and gave clear directives to cinema organisations on the strengthening of the political and ideological heights. The cinema should become a powerful weapon of political education and organisation of the broad millions of the masses. The cinema should be one of the most serious proletarian forward posts in the front line of the cultural revolution. The cinema must have its own clear class line and must march in step with the political and cultural rise of the country. That is the fundamental political task that the conference has placed before our cinema and concretely detailed in a series of resolutions taken by the conference.[143]

Pikel rejected the view that the cinema was in a state of crisis and that there was a chronic shortage of screenplays; the difficulties arose from the uncooperative attitude of certain sectors:

> The vain attempts of several film ideologists to isolate literature from the cinema, to demonstrate the impossibility of using it in the forms and laws peculiar to the cinema, met from the side of the conference the most decisive condemnations. They themselves appear to be the best illustration of the fact that the 'screenplay crisis' exists not 'in nature' but in the minds of idle pseudo-theoreticians.[144]

He also supported the conference's view that, for the time being at least, the Soviet cinema would have to depend upon a mixture of old-established talent and young blood; this situation would create fewer ideological difficulties in the cinema than in other forms of artistic activity:

> The cinema, as the youngest art form, does not have those long-standing traditions, those conservative statutes, which could slow down its progressive forward movement. In this respect the use of the best cadre of old workers and the education of the new appears as the most beneficial and productive, unlike in the other branches of the arts.[145]

The conference, he argued, had given its support to a variety of artistic approaches to the cinema and to the encouragement of healthy competition between them, subject only to the caveat that the competing groups should always 'produce a film which was accessible and comprehensible to the millions in the form of its conception'.[146] Pikel concluded by attempting to dispel the impression that the Party conference had been yet another talking-shop which would have no practical effects. He cited Krinitsky's closing remarks, although in fact his citation was a paraphrase:

> The cinema already stands under the gaze of the Party and the Soviet public. And if some cinema workers suppose that our resolution will turn out to be a worthless scrap of paper, then they are cruelly mistaken. We shall ensure that in fact the resolutions of our conference and the directives of the Party are fulfilled.[147]

In Pikel's view then the conference was to mark a turning point in the development of the Soviet cinema.

The journal *Kommunisticheskaya revolyutsiya*, in its comments on the conference, not surprisingly laid stress upon the ideological implications of its resolutions. The conference had brought the attention of the Party and the public to the importance of the cinema as an ideological weapon, and the past faults of the Soviet cinema resulted from ideological misguidance from the top and an obsession with commercial interests.[148] The period of reconstruction was now over and there was a definite need for a decisive step forward; the cinema could replace vodka as a source of tax revenue, but only gradually and over an extended period of time during which the cinema would reorientate itself towards the interests of the worker and peasant and a broad network of cinemas would be established;[149] this was the course of action that had been favoured by Meshcheryakov.[150] This wider network of 'proletarian' cinemas would give rise to a greater demand for proletarian films, and this in turn would necessitate the training of new cadres of film workers; the first, and most fundamental step therefore was to institute such training.[151]

Sovetskii ekran, taking Smirnov's comments[152] to heart, called enthusiastically for the centralisation of the cinema under a single organisation,[153] and published a violent denunciation of the kind of imported films to which it had previously been giving relatively favourable reviews:

> We can and must fight this cine-rubbish. Parallel with the strengthening of our own production, we must curtail decisively the importation of the foreign product, if we cannot dispense with it altogether.
>
> We must intensify our struggle against foreign trash, which has always been harmful and poisonous to us.
>
> We must declare an unconditional boycott of foreign production. Here there should be no agreements but merciless warfare!
>
> Down with foreign rubbish![154]

If the Soviet cinema as a whole had not yet been brought under strict ideological control, at least *Sovetskii ekran* obviously had.

The response of *Zhizn' iskusstva* to the conference was as usual more constructive and responsible. It called for the realisation of the conference resolution on cinefication, especially of the countryside,[155] for the increased production of Soviet film equipment[156] and of films suitable for audiences of children.[157] The latter plea was made by Piotrovsky, who once more played a prominent part in the discussions on the current state of the cinema. A later issue of *Zhizn' iskusstva* carried a review by him of the year 1928 in the Soviet cinema:

> Now we are witnessing an organic transformation of our cinema, which is entering, one might say, the period of its reconstruction. . .Our cinema is still being constructed as a socialist art.[158]

Piotrovsky returned to his theme three weeks later in the columns of the same journal. He argued that, contrary to some allegations, there was in fact no real crisis in the Soviet cinema, only the normal growing pains.[159] The plans for the development of the cinema demanded an increase in the number of films on contemporary themes, but these plans had met with little response:

> Pudovkin has made an exotic Mongolian picture,[160] Kozintsev and Trauberg are making a Parisian film,[161] Kuleshov is making *The Happy Little Canary* in Odessa,[162] Room a Mexican picture;[163] all this should be regarded as a mistake. This obsession with the exotic is nothing other than a refusal of our central masters to resolve the most difficult tasks. These tasks have fallen upon the less experienced, but clearly more courageous, shoulders of the young directors.[164]

Piotrovsky's article represented yet another plea for facilities to train this younger generation of film makers and to give them both better opportunities and more experience.

On 11 January 1929 the Central Committee of the Party took the first practical step towards the realisation of the conference resolutions: it issued a decree entitled 'On the strengthening of the cadres of the cinema'.[165] Its aim was to strengthen not so much the cadres themselves as the Party's ideological control over them:

> The heightening of the class struggle on the ideological front cannot fail to evoke from petit bourgeois groups the desire to influence the most important lever for the cultural improvement and education of the masses. The task of the Party is to use all measures to strengthen its leadership of the work of the cinema organisations and, by preserving the ideological consistency of the films produced, to combat decisively the attempts to bring the Soviet cinema nearer to the ideology of the non-proletarian strata. . .Party, professional, Komsomol, social and scientific organisations should play a more active part in the work of the cinema.[166]

The decree was also partly intended to attract new writers to the cinema,[167] but this aim was to some extent frustrated by the iron grip that V.A.P.P. was soon to exert on cinema workers through its connection with A.R.K.[168]

The new decree was welcomed by the film press, and the first journal to declare its approval was *Sovetskii ekran.* It reprinted the resolution passed by a closed conference of Sovkino in December 1928 under the heading 'Sovkino's New Course' and emphasised that the quality of films produced could only be improved if there were much tighter control over all stages of film production,[169] and if there were much closer links between the people who made the films and the people who watched them:

> We must link the cadres of artistic workers with the proletarian public, with powerful economic and cultural construction, in order to destroy the isolationism of the basic mass of artistic workers which exists at the present time and in which such decadent views can take root.[170]

Although *Kino i kul'tura* produced figures to show that in the season 1927–8 58.5 per cent of all Soviet films, and 80 per cent of Sovkino films (the discrepancy being accounted for by V.U.F.K.U., Mezhrabpom and Goskinprom Gruzii amongst others) dealt with contemporary themes,[171] *Zhizn' iskusstva* still felt that there was room for improvement. In an editorial entitled 'For a Soviet Screenplay' the journal urged film writers to overcome the ideological weaknesses of their work by collective group efforts:[172] this was to become a popular cry in Soviet literature during the period of the First Five Year Plan.[173] One month later *Zhizn' iskusstva* published a blistering attack by Petrov-Bytov on some of the best known Soviet films:

When we talk of the Soviet cinema we wave a banner on which is written: *Strike,*[174] *Battleship Potemkin,*[175] *October,*[176] *Mother,*[177] *The End of St Petersburg,*[178] and we have recently added *New Babylon,*[179] *Zvenigora,*[180] *Arsenal.*[181] *Do 120 million workers and peasants march beneath this banner? I know very well that they don't.*[182]

He attacked the arrogance of those who maintained that, although the Soviet cinema audience might not understand Soviet films at the current time, they would understand them after five or ten years:

This is an elitist point of view. Who is supposed to carry out the donkey work of raising the masses to an understanding of these films? *The principal task of the Soviet cinema is to raise the cultural level of the masses now, urgently, immediately.* We must think of the future, but for 90 per cent of the time we must think of the present.[183]

Petrov-Bytov then repeated the plea implicit in the Central Committee's decree that film makers who were 'inexperienced in life'[184] would have to get to know their audiences better:

The people who make the Soviet cinema are 95 per cent alien, aesthetes or unprincipled. . .*You will not lead with 'Octobers' and 'New Babylons', simply because people do not want to watch these pictures. Before you lead the masses behind you, you must either be of the masses yourself, or have studied them thoroughly, and not just studied, but also experienced what the masses experience*. . .I repeat, we must speak in their own comprehensible, native language. Our heart and mind must be in it. We must not look down on the masses from above, but the artist himself must think and feel fundamentally and positively at one with the masses and be in the vanguard. . . *Every picture must be useful, comprehensible and familiar to the masses, otherwise neither it nor the artist who made it are worth twopence*. . .With the help of art that is not separated from the masses we shall fight all the base aspects of life, so that not only art but life itself shall become beautiful.[185]

Zhizn' iskusstva soon published a reply from Piotrovsky, who argued that Petrov-Bytov's views were both factually erroneous and politically harmful.[186] In effect he was saying that the Soviet cinema had to make do with the talent that it had, and in a subsequent article he went further and argued that, although the Soviet cinema had now turned away from Western imports, it still had some lessons to learn from them.[187] Piotrovsky was supported in his more moderate views by another contributor to *Zhizn' iskusstva*, Podolsky, who, while criticising liberal interpretations of the resolutions of the Party conference, attacked Petrov-Bytov for his extremism:

Such an attitude towards the best pictures of our cinema characterises the ultra-left views of Petrov-Bytov, which are in reality no less dangerous than the reactionary views of the rightists.[188]

With this article in May 1929 the vocabulary of Soviet political rhetoric had finally and irrevocably entered the arena of the cinema. As one writer put it:

And so from this point of view 1929 appears to us as the initial period of an organic transformation of the methods of artistic influence of the Soviet cinema, of a transformation resting on the basis of socialist reconstruction.[189]

In his speech to the 14th Congress of Soviets on 15 May 1929 Lunacharsky observed that, although the cinema was a powerful propaganda weapon, the pace of its development as such in the U.S.S.R. had been too slow; but now, 'At last, great steps have been taken in the development of the cinema.'[190] The Party conference had been held and the decree on film workers had been issued; all that now remained was for Sovkino, which had been subjected to so much criticism, to be reorganised, and that was done in 1930.[191]

7. THEORY AND FILM

The cinema's misfortune is that there are very few literate people in it.
Soviet film journal, 1922.[1]

By the end of the 1920s discussions within the Soviet cinema were being conducted primarily, if not yet exclusively, in Party terminology. This was a new phenomenon. Although the arguments about the cinema's rôle in relation to the theatre and about its function as the art form of the machine age had been put in political terms, against the background of a belief in the cinema as the art form of the Revolution itself, these terms had not previously been imposed on the cinema world from outside. The views expressed in these polemics reflected a genuine and spontaneous desire to assist the revolutionary cause and the construction of the new society.

Lenin had laid great stress on the particular importance of the newsreel and documentary film for Bolshevik propaganda.[2] In November 1920 he suggested that Soviet newsreels should concentrate on three themes: the welfare of mothers and children, the Wrangel front and 'palaces transformed into children's homes'.[3] By selecting and emphasising these issues Bolshevik propaganda would make the maximum impact on its audience and the meagre resources available would thus be used to optimum effect.[4]

Documentary film makers were of course to seize on the encouragement that Lenin had given them to claim for themselves the legitimacy thus bestowed upon the art form of the Revolution. The leading exponents of the documentary school of film-making were Dziga Vertov and his Kinoglaz or Cine-Eye movement. The essence of their stated philosophy was contained in two documents: *My. Variant manifesta* (We. Variant of a Manifesto), published in 1922,[5] and *Kinoki. Perevorot* (The Cine-Eyes. A Revolution), published in 1923.[6]

The first manifesto began with a total rejection of the past and present of the cinema:

WE consider the old films, the romantic, theatricalised etc., to be leprous.
— Don't come near!

— Don't look!
— Dangerous to life!
— Infectious.

WE assert that the future of cinema art lies in a rejection of its present.
The death of 'cinematography' is necessary for the life of the cinema art. WE *call for the acceleration of its death.*
WE protest against the *mixing* of the arts that many call synthesis. The mixing of bad colours, even those ideally matched to the colours of the spectrum, gives not white, but dirt.[7]

The Cine-Eye group saw the cinema as a 'pure' art form in its own right, which should not be polluted by the theatre, literature or other art forms:

WE cleanse the cine-eye from its hangers-on, from music, literature and the theatre, we look for its own, never stolen rhythm, and find it in the movement of objects.
WE declare:
— *away* –
from the sweet embraces of romance,
from the poisons of the psychological novel,
from the clutches of the theatre lover,
with our backsides to music,
— away –
into the open country, into space with four dimensions (3 + time), in search of our own material, metre and rhythm.[8]

But the really revolutionary aspect of the Cine-Eye approach came in its rejection of the conventional method of depicting man on the screen: Vertov stated that, 'The "psychological" prevents man from being as exact as a stop-watch and hinders his striving to approach the machine.'[9] Man was not considered perfect or regular enough to be the subject of films; he fell far short of the standards of the machine:

WE *exclude for the time being man as an object of filming because of his inability to conduct his own movements.*
Our path – from a dawdling citizen through the poetry of the machine to the perfect electric man.
Revealing the souls of machines, enthusing the worker with the lathe, the peasant with the tractor, the driver with his engine, –
we bring creative joy to every mechanical labour,
we join men with machines,
we educate the new men.
The new man, liberated from heaviness and awkwardness, with the exact and light movements of the machine, will be the grateful object of the cine-camera.
WE openly recognise the rhythm of the machine, the pleasure of mechanical labour, the perception of the beauty of chemical processes, we hymn earthquakes, compose cine-poems to the flame and to power-stations, revel in the movements of the comets and meteors and the star-blinding gestures of the projectors.[10]

The essence of the cinema, for the Cine-Eye group, lay in *movement* and, more particularly, in the way in which that movement was arranged on film through editing or *montage*:

The cine-eye is the art of organising the necessary movements of objects in space and time into a rhythmic artistic whole, according to the characteristics of the whole and the internal rhythm of each object.

The material – the elements of the art of movement – is comprised of the *intervals* (the transitions from one movement to another), and by no means of the movements themselves. They (the intervals) attract action to kinetic resolution.[11]

Because of montage the cinema could also go beyond reality and create, in a sense, a *new reality*:

The cinema is also *the art of invention of the movement* of objects in space in accordance with the demands of science; it is the incarnation of the dream of the inventor, whether he be a scientist, an artist, an engineer or a carpenter, the realisation by the cine-eye of the unrealisable in life.[12]

This first manifesto ended with a paean to the machine, underlining once more that the Cine-Eyes regarded the cinema as the art form of the machine age:

Long live *dynamic geometry*, the runs of points, lines, surfaces, volumes, long live the poetry of the moving and the moved machine, the poetry of levers, wheels and steel wings, the iron cry of movements, the blinding grimaces of red-hot jets.[13]

Vertov had distinguished between cinematography (the existing state of affairs) and the cinema (what the Cine-Eyes stood for). In the same issue of *Kino-Fot* the Constructivist Alexei Gan echoed this distinction. In his view the machine (cinematograph) had not yet produced the art form (cinematography):

The cinematograph, as living photography and as the technical apparatus of mass production of the theatrical art, is the old cinematograph, the cinematograph of the capitalist system of exploitation, the cinematograph of the private owner.

Cinematography, as the materially labouring apparatus of social technology, as the extended 'organs' of society, is a matter for the proletarian state.

Those are the two paths which are being followed on the other side of the screen.

The cinematograph or cinematography?
Yesterday the cinematograph.
Tomorrow cinematography!
Today we are clearing the path for tomorrow.[14]

The second manifesto of the Cine-Eye group reiterated many of the points made in the first. It contained the same rejection of the existing type of film:

Looking at the pictures that come to us from the West and from America, considering the evidence that we have on work and plans both abroad and here, I have come to the conclusion that:
the death sentence pronounced by the Cine-Eyes in 1919 on all films without exception is still valid today.[15]

It also repeated the claim that the new cinema could create a new reality:

I am the Cine-Eye, I create a man more perfect than Adam was created, I create thousands of different men according to different preliminary drafts and schemes.
I am the Cine-Eye.
I take the strongest and most agile hands from one man, the fastest and best proportioned legs from another, the most handsome and expressive head from a third and through montage I create a new, perfect man. . .
I am the Cine-Eye. I am the mechanical eye.
I, the machine, show you the world as only I can see it.[16]

The cinema was also distinguished by its associations with the machine and with movement:

From today I liberate myself from human immobility forever. *I am in constant movement,* I approach objects and move away from them, I creep up to them, I clamber over them, I move alongside the muzzle of a running horse, I cut at full speed into the crowd, I flee before fleeing soldiers, I turn over on my back, I rise up with aeroplanes, I fall and rise with falling and rising bodies.[17]

The idea that the cinema was a synthesis of other art forms was again rejected:

We, the Cine-Eyes, determined opponents of the current synthesis ('towards synthesis as the zenith of achievement!') realise that it is futile to mix the fragments of achievement: the little pieces will perish straight away in the crush and the confusion.[18]

Documentary material organised through montage was to be the essence of the new cinema:

Not a Pathé or Gaumont newsreel (a newsreel of record), nor even a *Kino-Pravda* (a political newsreel), but a real Cine-Eye newsreel – *a rapid survey of* VISUAL *events interpreted by the film-camera, pieces of* REAL *energy* (as distinct from theatrical), *brought by intervals to an accumulated whole by the great skill of montage.*

Such a cinematic structure permits one to develop any theme, whether comic, tragic, trick or otherwise.

The whole secret lies in one or another correlation of the visual moments, in the intervals.

The unusual flexibility of montage construction permits the introduction into the film-study of any political, economic or other motif. And so

FROM TODAY *neither psychological nor detective dramas are needed in the cinema,*
FROM TODAY *filmed theatrical productions are unnecessary,*
FROM TODAY *neither Dostoevsky nor Nat Pinkerton will be filmed.*
Everything will be included in the new definition of film newsreel.
Into the confusion of life enter with determination;

1 the *Cine-Eye*, calling into question the human eye's conception of the world and presenting its own 'I see!' and
2 the *Cine-Eye editor*, who first arranged the moments of life seen in this way.[19]

Again the cinema was to create, or at least organise, a new reality.

Although these two manifestoes were the principal statements of the Cine-Eye group, their ideas were developed in articles elsewhere. One of the most important of these was the concept of *zhizn' vrasplokh* (literally 'life caught unawares' and the equivalent of what we might now call 'candid camera'): 'We shoot only facts and bring them through the screen to the consciousness of the workers. We consider that to explain the world as it is is our principal task.'[20] This concept was in direct contradiction to the idea expressed in both manifestoes that the cinema's function was the organisation of raw material through montage. Nevertheless Vertov repeated it unambiguously: 'Of course we should prefer a dry newsreel to the interference of the scenario in life and the work of people living on our planet.'[21] Vertov regarded the film *Kino-Glaz*,[22] made in 1924, as the realisation of the principles of *zhizn' vrasplokh*, but others regarded the film as disorganised and incomprehensible.[23] The use of associative montage and trick photography in *Shestaya chast' mira* (A Sixth Part of the World)[24] represented a departure from absolute principles. Vertov saw the use of titles as a means towards the active involvement of the masses: the titles were the skeleton of the film, the images were the flesh. But the contradiction between the use of montage and the concept of *zhizn' vrasplokh* was underlined by the critic Ippolit Sokolov: 'Montage deforms facts. The rearrangement of pieces changes their sense.'[25] This contradiction was never overcome. As a recent historian of Soviet film theory in the 1920s has observed:

The self-styled Columbus of the 1920s, Dziga Vertov set off in search of the concrete India of the 'pure fact' and found the America of cine-journalism. Repeating the discovery, he repeated the mistake of the original discoverer. He called a newsreel that which was not a newsreel, but something new and different, which he himself did not understand and whose significance was defined decades later.[26]

Although Vertov and the Cine-Eye group became involved with

other documentary film-makers in polemical arguments the main force of their attack was directed against the fictional film-makers and the concept of art, which the group regarded as a relic of the bourgeois era. As there was no classical tradition in the cinema, it was that much easier to effect a revolution, and the revolution would be that much more complete. Art, in the bourgeois sense, had led to the unconsciousness of the masses; hence emotion and art must be eliminated:

> We must once and for all eradicate from the picture all its Romanticism, all its psychological emotionalism. We must state quite openly that in the film we do not intend to arouse either joy or sadness, that we want to show the necessary facts and events.[27]

Vertov himself had gone further and proclaimed that 'the very term "art" is essentially counter-revolutionary'.[28] He regarded the fiction film too as dangerous and counter-revolutionary:

> The film drama is the opium of the people. The film drama and religion are a fatal weapon in the hands of the capitalists. The screenplay is a fairy-tale thought out by literature for us...Down with bourgeois screenplay fairy-tales! Long live life as it is![29]

Vertov predicted that the days of the art film were numbered:

> The world conflagration of 'art' is at hand. With a premonition of disaster theatre workers, artists, littérateurs, ballet-masters and other canaries are fleeing in panic. In search of a refuge they run to the cinema. The cinema studio is the last bulwark of art. Sooner or later long-haired quacks of all sorts will gather them in. The art film will receive colossal reinforcements, but it will not be saved, but will perish together with all the array of people saving their souls.
>
> The Tower of Babel that is art will be torn down.[30]

For him the task of the Soviet cinema was quite clear:

> Only in the U.S.S.R., where the cinema is a tool in the hands of the state can and should the battle against the blinding of the popular masses begin, the battle for sight...
>
> *To see and show the world in the name of the world proletarian revolution – that is the simple formula of the Cine-Eye.*[31]

This was not strictly speaking the formula of 'life as it is' but that of 'life as it ought to be', the formula that subsequently developed into socialist realism. As the journal *Novyi zritel'* observed, the film *Chelovek s kinoapparatom* (The Man with the Movie Camera)[32] 'contrasts sharply "life as it is" from the viewpoint of the eye armed with the camera (*the Cine-Eye*) with "life as it is" from the viewpoint of the imperfect *human eye*'.[33] In other words, the Cine-Eyes aimed to improve upon reality. Vertov clearly felt that the Soviet authorities should give greater support to their efforts. In 1922 he complained of lack of equipment, money and facilities,[34] and in the following year pointed out the immense propaganda potential of the Cine-Eye methods:

Kino-Pravda only exists, but it must *live.*
The government and Comintern have not yet realised that, by giving serious support to *Kino-Pravda* they could find a new mouthpiece, a visual radio to the world.[35]

Not surprisingly, there were those who supported the Cine-Eyes. Alexander Fevralsky, writing in *Molodaya gvardiya* in 1925, stated:

Radio-cinema should come to the aid of the printed word and sometimes even replace the book or newspaper. At the present time it is impossible to appreciate fully the enormous significance which the radio-cinema might have as a tool *for education and propaganda.* Imagine a newspaper in which events are not read but seen and heard, a newspaper which at the moment of its publication serves people in the most widely separated places. With what giant strides will cultural work in the U.S.S.R. advance, and what a powerful medium for the strengthening of its international unity the proletariat will receive. What will be the significance of even one correct visual source of information on the U.S.S.R. for the workers and peasants of the West and East. Apart from this the radio-cinema can play a large role in the *direction of the economy, in bringing together different people* etc. etc. The prospects are unlimited.[36]

Others wrote in even more eulogistic terminology, from the poem published in *Kino-Fot* in 1922:

Welcome to you.
You are the leaders of the cinema of tomorrow!
I call upon all revolutionaries in the art of the cinema to respond to the start made by the Cine-Eyes.[37]

And in 1929 *Sovetskii ekran* published the following somewhat exaggerated claims:

The machine, like a work of art, is higher and more important than the master who has made it. Man is only an engineer, a pilot directing it. . .The whole world was shaken when cultural monuments were destroyed during the war. But it is true that, while the cathedral at Rheims could be replaced by other Gothic monuments, nothing can replace a destroyed copy of the *Lenin Kino-Pravda,* for the photographic newsreel of our days is a document of first-rate importance, through which future generations will be able to study the living history of our days.[38]

But in the longer term the Cine-Eyes proved to have been too experimental for their own time and too rigid in their theorising for practical effect.

Boltyansky, in his book on newsreel photography published in

1926, cites Lenin's remark to Lunacharsky: 'We must begin the production of new films which are imbued with Communist ideas and reflect Soviet reality with newsreels.'[39] Here again we find the basic dichotomy in the Cine-Eye approach: on the one hand the film is to 'reflect reality' but on the other it is to be 'imbued with Communist ideas'. Belenson attacked the Cine-Eyes for their belief that the cinema could be reduced to a series of laws:

> The cinema has no laws; the best proof of this is that in our language only one brochure in all has been written on the 'laws of the cinema' (by V. Shklovsky), while one could as a joke write a whole encyclopaedia on the lawlessness of the cinema. Ask the filmgoer – he is at the heart of these questions.[40]

But, ironically enough, it was Shklovsky who launched the main attack on the Cine-Eyes. In 1925 he argued that, 'The Cine-Eye and the cine-eyes do not want to understand the basic essence of cinematography';[41] the cinema was like a sentence whose direction was, at least to some extent, imposed by the words of which it was composed:

> Their eyes are situated at an unnatural distance from their brains. They do not appreciate that the cinema is the most abstract of the arts, close in its fundamentals to some aspects of mathematics. The cinema lacks actions, a sense of direction, in the sense that literature is lacking in words. Cinematography is lacking in subject just as a picture is lacking in a sense of direction. Without this it would be difficult to orientate the viewer, to give a single direction to his view. . .The fundamental material of cinematography is not the photographed object, but the particular method by which it is photographed. Only a certain approach by the cameraman will give the image desired.[42]

Shklovsky attacked the very idea of *zhizn' vrasplokh* and stressed that the essence of the cinema lay in movement and, in particular in movement organised through montage:

> The Cine-Eyes reject the actor and think that by this action they are separating themselves from art, but the actual selection of moments of photography is already an act of will power. The juxtaposition of one moment with another, montage, is already work done in accordance with artistic, only unified principles. . .In the work of the Cine-Eyes cinema art is not entering a new field, but merely narrowing its old field. . .In their images objects are impoverished because there is no bias, in the artistic sense of the word, in the *relationship to objects*.
>
> Cinematography is the art of meaningful movement. The basic material of cinematography is its graphic cine-word, the fragment of photographic material which has a certain significance. For this reason cinematographic material in its very essence gravitates towards the subject as a means of organising the cine-word, the cine-phrase.[43]

In other words, the structure of a series of images is dictated neither purely by the subject-matter (*zhizn' vrasplokh*) nor by the editor (montage). Shklovsky also pointed out the importance not only of the way in which a sequence of frames was ordered, but also of the content of each particular frame:

Places within the cine-frame do not have equal weight. A separate alteration in sense, changing one two-hundredths of the height of the frame, can radically alter its whole meaning, all the more radically because all around it nothing has altered.[44]

In a later article Shklovsky reiterated the importance both of context and content:

Montage of life? Life caught unawares. Not material of world importance. But I think that newsreel material in Vertov's treatment is devoid of its soul – documentary quality.

A newsreel needs titles and dates.

There is a difference between an idle factory and the Tryokhgorny workshops idle on 5 August 1919.

Mussolini talking interests me. But a straightforward plump and bald-headed man who talks can go and talk behind the screen. The whole sense of a newsreel is in the date, time and place. A newsreel without this is like a card catalogue in the gutter.[45]

Shklovsky did concede that in actual fact Vertov did not apply his theoretical principle of *zhizn' vrasplokh* in practice:

He takes newsreel as material. But we must admit that the very frames of Vertov are more interesting than what he has found in the newsreel. There is a director there. There is aesthetic consideration and invention.[46]

Nevertheless Shklovsky continued to attack the concept of *zhizn' vrasplokh*. In an article written in the following year he claimed that the concept was unrealisable, and in practice even fraudulent.[47] He underlined the practical difficulties: 'To teach someone to walk in front of the camera as if he hadn't noticed it is very difficult.'[48] There were, Shklovsky felt, two possible solutions to the problem of this artificial realism: either everyone should be taught to act on film, which was clearly impracticable, or a process of selecting the most suitable people should be employed. This latter course clearly implied the use of actors: actors represented, and were trained to represent convincingly, an ideal which the audience could follow, and it was therefore perfectly legitimate for the revolutionary Soviet cinema to employ them: 'The film actor now is usually biologically and socially the ideal of his audience, and to replace the actor by a passer-by would be to turn back from industrialisation.'[49] Shklovsky was not however the only person to attack the Cine-Eyes, although his attack was the most sustained and coherently argued.

The Cine-Eyes had been subjected to attack from the very beginning. Probably the most abusively hostile remarks were contained in an article published in *Kinonedelya* in 1924 and written by A. Anoshchenko:

> The Cine-Eyes [*kinoki*] or Cinecocci [*kinokoki*] are the contemporary variety of the bacteria of Futurism, weakened by its degeneration in the Revolution, but finding a disturbed source of nourishment in the new-born cinema and starting to multiply in its still weak organism. The Cinecocci bacteria, despite their terrible appearance, are harmless to life, but nonetheless their actions cause harm and sometimes give an original pathological result.[50]

Boltyansky also attacked the Cine-Eyes for their assumption that they alone had the answer to the problems of the cinema; although he himself was closely concerned with the production of newsreels and documentaries, he criticised the Cine-Eyes in particular for their view that the fiction film was inherently valueless:

> Communist policy in art cannot be ruled by a preference for one form rather than another. For us, all forms are good which fulfil their aim. Of course it is true that realism and conviction are among the most important conditions for a work of art. This applies to newsreels but it can also apply to fiction films.[51]

Although the Cine-Eyes played a prominent and important rôle in the development of the Soviet documentary cinema, they were, despite their own claims, not the only Soviet documentary filmmakers.

The films of Esfir Shub and her associates were less experimental than those of the Cine-Eyes but far more typical of the Soviet documentary film. Esfir Shub has herself admitted her debt to Dziga Vertov:

> The path of my generation, coming to work in the cinema, was not linked to a higher cinematographic education. There was nowhere in fact where you could get it.
>
> My universities were different ones: the cutting table, cameramen, the directors of fictional feature films – and *Dziga Vertov*.[52]

But Shub was practical where Vertov was theoretical: the task that she set herself was the compilation of newsreel footage.[53] Shub's initial experience on the re-editing of foreign films[54] gave her an understanding of the techniques of Western film-making and made her appreciate the need to keep a filmed record of early Soviet life.[55] Although Shub was not averse to making a point by contrasting one frame with another, she renounced Vertov's method of rhythmic montage, believing in the superior needs of the truth.[56] She considered that montage not only united the parts and unfolded a flow of events, but also revealed the contradictions inherent in the parts and in life itself.[57] Shub's practical problem was that of how 'to achieve the emotionalisation of the arousal of people with the material of actual reality'.[58] Here again Shub was confronted with a potential conflict between the interests of film-making and those of truth.[59] She could not always authenticate a particular frame, or place it in its proper context. As a contemporary critic commented: 'The objective–authentic meaning of a frame may not correspond to that particular concrete authenticity in the conditions in which it was filmed.'[60]

Shub's technique has since come to be known as that of the 'compilation film'; she compiled films from footage taken by other people, whereas Vertov established a direct link between cameraman and director.[61] The three films that Shub made in the 1920s were all 'compilation films' of this genre: *Padenie dinastii Romanovykh* (The Fall of the Romanov Dynasty), made in 1927, *Velikii put'* (The Great Way), also made in 1927 to celebrate the tenth anniversary of the October Revolution, and *Rossiya Nikolaya II i Lev Tolstoi* (Lev Tolstoy and the Russia of Nicholas II), made in 1928.[62] Whilst Shub's contribution to the theory of documentary film-making was minimal, her practical activities did much to preserve valuable film footage of the Soviet Union during the 1920s, and her films themselves stand as a useful record for the historian of that epoch. The films were useful to the Soviet authorities as well for, unlike those of the Cine-Eyes, there was no doubt whatsoever that the productions of Esfir Shub were 'comprehensible to the millions'.

In spite of the emphasis placed by Lenin,[63] amongst others, on the importance of documentary and newsreel films, by far the largest number of films produced in the Soviet Union during the 1920s fell into the fictional category. But whereas Vertov and the Cine-Eyes dominated, or at least set the pace for, the documentary film-makers, fictional film-making was by no means the preserve of any single group. There were various schools, often overlapping, of fictional film-makers and they revolved around Lev Kuleshov, Sergei Eisenstein, Vsevolod Pudovkin, and the group of young men known as FEKS, the acronym for Fabrika ekstsentricheskogo aktëra, the Factory of the Eccentric Actor. One of the least well known, but also the most influential, of these schools was the Workshop of Lev Kuleshov.

A contemporary critic, writing of Kuleshov, said that he 'gave birth to Eisenstein and Pudovkin'.[64] Pudovkin himself went even further:

We had no cinematography – now we have. The establishment of cinematography stems from Kuleshov.

The formal problems were unavoidable and Kuleshov took it upon himself to resolve them...

Kuleshov was the first cinematographer to begin to talk of an alphabet, organising inarticulate material, and he busied himself with syllables, not words...

We make pictures – Kuleshov made cinematography.[65]

This view was shared by another critic reviewing Kuleshov's film *Po zakonu* (By the Law, also known as Dura Lex):[66]

For Soviet artists of the screen Kuleshov is a trampoline without which they could not make a jump, but from which they have to take off because, if they did not take off, there would be no jump.[67]

Kuleshov's distinction lay in the fact that he was the first to unravel the importance to the cinema of montage, and he did this as early as 1918:

By reason of its artistic structure the cinema as an independent art form can have nothing in common with the dramatic stage. A plus in the cinema is a minus in the theatre, and *vice versa*. For this reason there should not be a single director, designer or anyone acquainted with the footlights in the cinema...

Actors, directors, designers, write on your banners in clear letters the most important commandment of the cinema: the inspiration of the cinema should be cinematographic inspiration...In the cinema such a means of expression of artistic thought is the rhythmic alternation between separate immobile frames or short sequences with an expression of movement, i.e. what is technically known as montage. Montage in the cinema is the same as the composition of the colours in painting or a harmonic sequence of notes in music.[68]

During the Civil War period, when the shortage of film stock made the production of full-length films excessively difficult, if not impossible, Kuleshov set about establishing his Workshop and experimenting with various techniques. As he himself later observed, 'An experiment for the true cinematographer is more important than bread.'[69] These experiments were known collectively as *fil'my bez plënki* (films without film)[70] and gave rise to the discovery of what has become known as the 'Kuleshov effect'.[71] Through the acting out of various scenes Kuleshov and his Workshop came to the view that the content of each individual frame should be kept as simple and direct as possible and that, through montage, both the context and the meaning of the frame could be altered: 'The content of the frames themselves is not as important as the joining of two frames of differing content and the manner of their joining and interchange.'[72] Instead of rejecting the existing cinema, Kuleshov studied and learned from it: 'We had to find the very means of cinematographic impressiveness and we knew that, if we found this means, then we should be able to direct it wherever necessary.'[73]

The Soviet Union needed a cinema that was 'simple, comprehensible, heroic',[74] one that would 'save the audience's energy'.[75] The Soviet cinema would, in Kuleshov's view, be rejuvenated through learning lessons from the American film.[76] 'Americanism' was to become the rallying cry of the Kuleshov Workshop.

Montage was the key to Kuleshov's 'Americanism':

The essence of the cinema lies in composition, the alternation of sequences which have been shot. For the organisation of the impression the main thing on the whole is not what has been shot in a particular sequence, but the way in which one piece of film is juxtaposed with another, how they are constructed. *The organisational foundation of the cinema must be sought, not within the limits of the filmed frame but in the alternation of these frames.*[77]

But the individual frame must be in itself straightforward in order not to confuse the viewer:

The frame should act as a sign, as a letter, so that it can be read immediately and so that the viewer should be clear immediately and comprehensively about what is being said in the given frame.[78]

Man was to be given equal treatment to objects in Kuleshov's cinema.[79] But Kuleshov did not believe in using conventional actors. Instead he developed the concept of the *naturshchik*, who was defined as 'a real person, real life, in whatever fantastic forms, but unfailingly real'.[80] Kuleshov felt that the hero of a film was very important, that he should be 'brave, quick and strong',[81] as in an American Western, and that the film should have a happy ending (or, in Russian, *kheppi end!*) so that the audience's sympathy for the hero was adequately rewarded. The Soviet cinema, he wrote, needed, 'adventure films set in the U.S.S.R. in which the strong people overcome all obstacles and enemies'.[82] The paradigm of this type of film was *Neobychainye priklyucheniya Mistera Vesta v strane Bol'shevikov* (The Unusual Adventures of Mr West in the Land of the Bolsheviks).[83] A contemporary critic wrote:

In his conception of 'film material' Kuleshov included human material – the actors of his collective. And he strove so that his actors – above all Khokhlova – showed what the human body is from the point of view of the camera lens.[84]

The *naturshchik* acted through gestures and had to know the significance of his own movements in their particular context.[85] Kuleshov rejected theatricality in all its forms: 'To imagine, to pretend, to act – is useless, because it turns out very badly on the screen.'[86] The term *naturshchik* was applied to 'people who in themselves. . .present some interest for cinema treatment'.[87] It was, as Shklovsky observed, 'a question of the molecule of cinematography, the molecule of its artistic tangibility, of the bricks of cinematographic feeling'.[88] But the *naturshchik* was to be at least as thoroughly trained as the conventional cinema actor:

In training the *kino-naturshchik* the teacher turns his whole attention to external criticism, to the expressiveness of the body, to its litheness, flexibility and rhythmic quality. He needs 'man' in the frame as object, construction, nature – a piece equal to the other pieces. In this case all attempts at emotional education are expunged.[89]

But the actor would be trained to fill 'the *centre* of the frame, its most important part'.[90] The actor's rôle was not reduced by montage in the same way as that of the *naturshchik* was:

Not 'him' amongst the objects, machines, constructions, cars and trains, but the objects, machines, constructions, cars, trains *for him*; these things are a secondary background, against which he should be as important as against a background of black velvet.[91]

Therefore the training of the actor and the flexibility of his rôle differed from that of the *naturshchik*:

The actor is at the same time both master and material. His body, thoughts, emotions, desires, these are his material. With this material he speaks from the screen to the masses, transmits scientific, artistic, ideological, social and historical truths; he arouses, he inspires, he agitates. To be fit for such work he must start off by working for a long time, not on excerpts, rôles and images, *but on himself*. . .The actor can serve directors of all tendencies; the *kino-naturshchik* only the director who has taught him and a small circle of like-minded people.[92]

It was the character and individuality of the *naturshchik* that gave him his distinctive identity. Kuleshov himself wrote: 'A man with a characteristic appearance, with a definite sharply defined character is a cinematographic *naturshchik*. . .Individuality is exceptionally important in a *naturshchik*.'[93] Such characters are to be seen in all the films made by the Kuleshov Workshop during this period, from the character of Mr West in *Neobychainye priklyucheniya Mistera Vesta v strane Bol'shevikov* to the rôle played by Kuleshov's wife Alexandra Khokhlova, in *Po zakonu*. In an abject article published in 1930 Kuleshov described *Po zakonu* as 'the swansong of our collective'.[94] The whole article could well be described as an *apologia pro vita sua*; the fact that it was deemed necessary for the leading experimenter of the Soviet cinema of the 1920s to pen such sentences in 1930 is a sad comment on the effects of increased Party control: 'We must create a new proletarian cinema. A cinema which will help the masses in the construction of our socialist future.'[95] Kuleshov's contribution to the theory and practice of the Soviet cinema was undoubtedly of great significance: above all he was responsible for establishing the distinctive identity of the cinema, in contrast to the theatre in particular, through an emphasis on dynamic movement and montage.

Kuleshov's most influential follower in the development of the theory of montage was probably Sergei Eisenstein, whose name, more than that of any other film-maker, is popularly associated with the revolutionary cinema of Soviet Russia. Eisenstein was closely connected with the group that published the collection of essays entitled *Poetika kino* (The poetics of the cinema) in 1927.[96] He developed the theory of cinematographic conflict based on montage: 'The essence of the cinema must be found, not in the frames but in the interrelationship between the frames.'[97] Eisenstein's montage, in contrast to Kuleshov's, was to be the so-called 'montage of attractions' (*montazh attraktsionov*). Eisenstein used the word 'attraction' in the sense of a fairground attraction, something that caught the attention and conveyed a point succinctly. Montage that was purely academic, or failed to move the audience, was useless: 'It is more important to catch mass moods and infect the viewing masses with them.'[98] Elsewhere he further defined an 'attraction' as a 'striking moment' (*udarnyi moment*).[99] Examples of such striking moments may be cited from two of Eisenstein's films of the 1920s. First, from *Bronenosets Potëmkin*,[100] where both the famous Odessa Steps sequence and the red flag on the battleship in the last sequence (which was hand-tinted in red in the original version) are evidence of the techniques that he was developing. Secondly, the mating sequence and 'marriage ceremony' in *Staroe i novoe* (The Old and the New)[101] provide more clear evidence of Eisenstein's intentions. Yuri Tynyanov shared Eisenstein's enthusiasm for cinematographic conflict. He wrote 'The cinema jumps from frame to frame as a poem jumps from line to line.'[102] Eisenstein preferred a mechanical simile: 'The phalanx of montage piece-'frames' should be compared to the series of explosions of the internal combustion engine which are multiplied into the dynamic of montage by the jolts of the speeding car or tractor.'[103]

The concept of the 'attraction' was further clarified by the critic Alexander Belenson:

An attraction in this sense is every demonstrable fact (action, subject, phenomenon, conscious combination etc.), known and tried as the pressure of a certain effect on the attention and the emotion of the viewer, in combination with other things possessed of the characteristic of exaggerating this emotion in one direction or another, dictated by the aim of what is being shown.[104]

In Belenson's view it was the overall pattern of a sequence that determined the choice of individual frames and 'attractions', but Eisenstein argued the reverse: 'Movement within the frame impels the montage of movement from frame to frame.'[105] But there was no disagreement between them on the position of the cinema in relationship to the theatre. Eisenstein, perhaps projecting the pattern of his own career on to a general historical process, saw four stages in the collapse of the theatre into the cinema: 'In other words the cinema is the contemporary stage of the theatre. The next consecutive phase.'[106] But the theatre was not completely dead, only reduced in stature: 'And the theatre will go back to its good old position. It will once more become a church, a school, a library. As you please. But no longer the apparatus of independent aggressive possibilities.'[107] The cinema was clearly distinguished from the theatre, for one critic, not only by the possibilities of montage, but also by the rôle of the masses:

In *Potemkin* there is no hero–individualist as in the old theatre. The mass is active. The battleship with its sailors and the town with its population predisposed towards revolution. The one and the other are constructed with the greatest mastery and brought into a complex construction. . .the victory of *Potemkin* is a victory for the revolutionary leftist art of Soviet Russia.[108]

The same critic praised the film for the absence of the 'normal' cinematographic conventions:

Potemkin is a phenomenon of immense social significance, for here form and content have merged into a strong whole and a film which is revolutionary in subject has found its revolutionary artistic formulation. . .It has been said of *Potemkin* that here there is a direct rejection of the concepts of the theatre and an affirmation of the specific concepts of the cinema. Yes, really there is no actor in the usual sense of the word. There is no theatrical 'hero' with his experiences of a 'salon' nature, no love melodrama, sentimentalism or even psychologism, with which the theatre is satiated, as is the cinema of the usual formulation which is dependent upon it. At the beginning of the film stands the 'beat of the waves' and the rhythm of the sea waves is then developed in the ensuing frames, revealing with ever-increasing strength the energy which is involved in the beat and movement of the waves. In the theatre this is impossible...With Eisenstein it is objects that act and not actor 'heroes'. The battleship with its machines, its steps, the muzzles of its guns – or the town with its pier, its bridges, streets and terraces. And this would be impossible in the theatre...In an Eisenstein film objects, not actors, act.[109]

Eisenstein believed in what he called the 'intellectual cinema', which had considerable affinities with Piscator's 'epic theatre' and Brecht's *Verfremdungseffekt*; this 'intellectual cinema' was connected with the absence of emotionalism and individuality, both of which were regarded as bourgeois: 'At the basis of the film lies the incarnate idea. It develops in its contradictions, in its contrasts.'[110] But Eisenstein went further and saw his 'intellectual cinema' as a means of breaking down the conventionally accepted barriers between reason and emotion:

The new art should place a limit on the dualism of the spheres 'emotion' and 'reason'.

Return to science its sensitivity.

To the intellectual process its ardour and passion.

Plunge the abstract process of thought into the cauldron of practical reality.

Restore to the emasculated speculative *formula* all the splendour and wealth of gut-felt *form*.[111]

Eisenstein further declared war on the individual or 'living man' (*zhivoi chelovek*):

Someone is standing on the path to the intellectual cinema.

Across the path.

Who is he? He is 'living man'.

He requests entry into literature. He is already half-way into the theatre at the entrance to M.Kh.A.T.[112]

He is knocking on the door of the cinema.

Comrade 'living man'! I cannot speak for literature. Nor for the theatre. But you have no place in the cinema. To the cinema you are a 'rightist deviation'.[113]

Eisenstein became embroiled in a polemical argument with the Hungarian-born critic Béla Balázs, whose book *Der sichtbare Mensch* (Visible Man) depicted the actor as the object of the cinema.[114] In a 1926 article entitled 'Béla Forgets the Scissors' ('Bela zabyvaet nozhnitsu')[115] Eisenstein reiterated his view that montage was the key to cinematography. Indeed, on this occasion he went further and expounded the argument that montage led to synthesis; for this reason, he was later able to claim that the cinema of montage was, because of its dialectical nature, the only truly Marxist art form: 'Any two frames juxtaposed inevitably combine into a new concept, arising from this juxtaposition like a new characteristic.'[116]

But Eisenstein's 'intellectual cinema' was not short of critics. His fellow director, Abram Room, accused him of making films that suffered from an 'absence of people'.[117] Other critics were quick to note the absence of an individual hero and the problems that this caused for audience identification.[118] Mayakovsky expressed his distaste for the portrayal of Lenin in *Oktyabr'*[119] because he regarded it as cold and uninspiring.[120] Curiously enough the film brought to another critic's mind Lenin's remark about Mayakovsky's verse: 'I've tried to read Mayakovsky several times but I've never managed more than three lines. I always fall asleep.'[121] Perhaps Khersonsky's comment on *Potëmkin* summed up the critical reaction to Eisenstein's films: '*Potëmkin* is made by a fine brain but inside it is cold somewhere.'[122]

Eisenstein's contribution to the theoretical debate on the technical side of fiction film-making was enormous. There is however a certain irony in the fact that he became so closely identified with the concept of Party art, when one considers what was to happen to him in the 1930s and 1940s. *Kinozhurnal A.R.K.* defended *Stachka* (Strike)[123] in an editorial entitled 'A Warning' ('Preduprezhdenie'):

> In our young cinema there are clear signs of impending reaction. . .The one-sided discussion 'with or without a hero' had the character of a masked persecution of the best revolutionary film *Strike*. . .Our *films should in any case be at least as agitational as bourgeois films*. There was and is no non-Party art.[124]

Lenin's widow, Krupskaya, closely identified *Oktyabr'* with the art that the Party should encourage:

> Now an art is emerging that is near to the masses, that depicts the fundamental experiences of the masses. This art has a colossal future. The film *October* is a fragment of this art of the future. There is much that is fine in it.[125]

Eisenstein, despite his clearly acknowledged faults, was then considered to be the leading director of fiction films, although the basis of his theoretical writings can be traced back to Kuleshov.

Eisenstein's greatest rival, both in theory and in practice, was Vsevolod Pudovkin. Whereas Eisenstein had entered the cinema through the world of the theatre and set decoration, Pudovkin had started as an engineer. The French historian of the Soviet cinema, Léon Moussinac, feels that this difference is reflected in their respective films: 'An Eisenstein film resembles a shout, a

Pudovkin film evokes a song. . .Pudovkin incorporates in his films more study, more science, more intellectual effort than Eisenstein. He relies on method rather than inspiration.'[126] Like Eisenstein, Pudovkin felt liberated by his work in the cinema: 'In the exact sciences. . .I always feel myself to be a slave. The cinema allows me to create!'[127] But, unlike Eisenstein, Pudovkin believed in the importance of the individual, of 'living man': 'There was in me an instinctive yearning for living man; I wanted to embrace him with the camera, and also to climb inside him, just as Eisenstein had climbed inside the battleship.'[128] His first film was a scientific educational short entitled *Mekhanika golovnogo mozga* (The Mechanics of the Brain),[129] but he felt that the opportunities offered by such films were too limited: 'Finishing the film, I appreciated that the possibilities of the cinema were only beginning to be realised. My encounter with science strengthened my faith in art.'[130]

Pudovkin agreed with Eisenstein about the importance of montage in cinematography: 'Montage is, in essence, a forcible and arbitrary direction of the thought and the associations of the audience.'[131] Nevertheless he was also aware of the significance of the actor as one part of the raw material available to the director who composed and edited the film; hence the heroic characters in Pudovkin's films are individuals, whereas in Eisenstein's films they are symbols of the anonymous mass. Examples of this difference abound: one can compare the character of the son, and the tragic figure of the mother, in Pudovkin's *Mat'* (Mother)[132] with the stereotyped imagery of *Potëmkin*, the characters of *Konets Sankt-Peterburga* (The End of St Petersburg)[133] with the symbols of *Oktyabr'* and the hero of *Potomok Chingis-khana* (The Heir to Genghis-Khan)[134] with the heroine of *Staroe i novoe* (The Old and the New).[135] In Pudovkin's films the characters are individuals, human beings, whereas in Eisenstein's films the heroes are mere symbols, pawns in the tide of history. But Pudovkin did not underestimate the director's importance: his influence was paramount: 'We must remember that there is only the montage image of the actor – otherwise nothing.'[136]

He expanded on this basic statement:

> The image of the actor is only perceived in the future, on the screen, after the director's montage, and what the actor does in front of the screen at any given moment is only the raw material.[137]

and further stated:

The director never sees the actor as a real person, he imagines and sees the future depiction on the screen and carefully selects the material for it, making the actor move one way or another and variously changing the position of the camera in relation to him.[138]

Eisenstein and Pudovkin were, then, agreed on the ultimate importance of the director. They were also agreed on the dangers posed by the conventional sound film to their concept of cinematography and they came together publicly to point this out:

However, an incorrect understanding of the possibilities of the new technical discovery could not only slow down the development and perfection of the cinema as an art but could also threaten to destroy all its contemporary formal achievements.[139]

They saw the principal danger coming from the commercial exploitation of the new invention solely for its novelty value: this would lead to the use of sound for purely narrative purposes and thus to the undermining of the fundamental principle of montage. They therefore proposed that sound should be used as a contrapuntal element in the process of montage:

The first practical experiments with sound should be concentrated in the direction of a sharp contrast between it and the visual images. And only such a 'storm' will convey the necessary sensation, which will lead in consequence to the creation of a new, *contrapuntal orchestration* of visual and sound images.[140]

These points were further elaborated by Pudovkin a year later. He expressed the fear that commercial pressures would not only destroy the concept of montage but would also lead to the re-theatricalisation of the cinema, to a return to the early days of cinematography, before the theories of montage were developed:

In this period the cinema was not considered to be an art form; it was called a poor surrogate for the theatre, and this was right. Now the appearance of sound drives us once more along the line of least resistance towards a surrogate for the theatre.

Already armed with experience and knowledge, we should concentrate all our efforts in the other direction. In any case we must do this to begin with.

We must accept sound as a new material for composition. We should remember that it is not important to us to photograph a crying child in such a way that the viewer simultaneously sees the child, hears his cry, and says 'Ah, how like a real child.'

To us it is important to have the chance of fixing on film and producing in the auditorium the child's cry as a sound impression, evoking definite and exact associations, and then to match this sound with any selected visual impression.

The fact is that the impression received by the cinema audience is built not on the consequence of the frames that are shown, but on their juxtaposition, on their conflict.[141]

These, then, were the agreements and disagreements between the two leading fiction film makers of the Soviet Union during the period under discussion. Of the two, Eisenstein, the experimenter, ran into political trouble in the 1930s; Pudovkin, altogether a more conservative figure, continued to make films until the 1950s.[142] If the contribution of such an important figure in the Soviet cinema can be summed up in a single sentence, it might be said of Pudovkin that he gave to the revolutionary cinema a degree of human warmth that was missing from the films of Eisenstein.

The last major grouping in the Soviet cinema of the 1920s is the least known, but perhaps also the most interesting – FEKS. Shklovsky, writing in 1928, set the scene:

> Petrograd, then not yet Leningrad, was poised between the present and the future, weightless like an object between the Earth and the Moon. This opened the way for experimentation.[143]

Against this background the FEKS manifesto, entitled simply *Ekstsentrizm* (Eccentrism) burst upon an unsuspecting world in the summer of 1922.[144] The Factory of the Eccentric Actor was itself established in Petrograd on 9 July 1922 after the success of the group's first theatrical manifestation *Disput ob ekstsentricheskom teatre* (Dispute on the Eccentric Theatre) on 5 December 1921.[145] FEKS was headed and run by the Depôt of Eccentrics, which comprised the four founder members: Grigori Kozintsev, Leonid Trauberg, Sergei Yutkevich and Georgi Kryzhitsky.[146] Yutkevich and Kozintsev were 17 and 18 years old respectively.[147] They employed the words 'factory' and 'depôt' to describe themselves partly to emphasise their worship of the machine but also because they regarded the word 'studio' as tainted with bourgeois and bohemian associations.[148] When we analyse the views expressed by the Eccentrics, particularly in their manifesto (in as far as it is possible to decipher it!), it is worth remembering the comments made by Kozintsev in his introduction to his memoirs, published in 1971:

> In my lifetime words written about art have surprisingly quickly forfeited their meaning. What we as young men wrote in our 'manifestoes' at the beginning of the twenties soon seemed to us to be rubbish. But much of what grown-up people later wrote about these absurdities now seems no less of a nonsense.
>
> The words have changed, but the work has continued.[149]

The Eccentric manifesto promised 'Salvation in the trousers of the Eccentric,[150] and began:

Four blasts on the whistle:
1 for the actor – from emotion to the machine, from anguish to the trick. The technique – circus. The psychology – head over heels.
2 for the director – a maximum of devices, a record number of inventions, a turbine of rhythms.
3 for the dramatist – the coupler of tricks.
4 for the artist – decoration in jumps.
For the fifth whistle blast – from the public – we are ready.
And remember: the American MARK TWAIN *said: 'Better to be a young pup than an old bird of paradise.'*[151]

The manifesto was printed in a limited edition of a thousand copies; perhaps rather appropriately, three hundred were immediately destroyed by fire, while the remainder were distributed in the street by hand.[152] FEKS demanded the abandonment of the old culture and the old, bourgeois, way of life and its replacement by new cultural forms based on the revolutionary proletarian social order. These forms were to include those that had previously been frowned upon because of their association with the lower orders of society – entertainments such as the fairground, the circus and the music-hall. In fact the manifesto made reference to a mythical Eccentric hero who went by the name of Music-Hall Cinematographovich Pinkertonov.[153] Kozintsev traced the ancestry of Eccentrism:

OUR PARENTS
Parade allez!
In literature – the cabaret-singer, the cry of the auctioneer, street language.
In painting – the circus poster, the jacket of a cheap novel. In music – the jazzband (the commotion of a negro orchestra), circus marches.
In ballet – American song and dance routines.
In theatre – the music-hall, cinema, circus, *café-chantant,* boxing.[154]

He also elaborated on the original statement of the essentials of Eccentrism:

1 THE KEY TO THE FACTS
1 YESTERDAY – comfortable offices. Bald foreheads. People pondered, made decisions, thought things over.
TODAY – a signal. To the machines! Driving belts, chains, wheels, hands, legs, electricity. The rhythm of production.
YESTERDAY – museums, temples, libraries.
TODAY – factories, works, dockyards.
2 YESTERDAY – the culture of Europe.
TODAY –the technology of America.
Industry, production under the Stars and Stripes. Either Americanisation or the undertaker.
3 YESTERDAY – sitting-rooms. Bows. Barons.

TODAY – the shouts of newspaper-sellers, scandals, policemen's truncheons, noise, shouting, stamping, running.

The pace today:

The rhythm of the machine, concentrated by *America,* realised by the *street.*

2 ART WITHOUT A CAPITAL LETTER, A PEDESTAL OR A FIG-LEAF

Life requires art that is

hyperbolically crude, dumbfounding, nerve-wracking, openly utilitarian, mechanically exact, momentary, rapid,

otherwise no-one will hear, see or stop. Everything adds up to this: the art of the 20th century, the art of 1922, the art of this very moment is

Eccentrism.[155]

Yutkevich claimed, 'The aim [of the manifesto] was the final destruction of the bourgeois world.'[156] To celebrate this destruction the Eccentrics re-named Petrograd Eccentropolis for the occasion.[157] The old cultural order was to be swept away and replaced by forms more appropriate to the twentieth century and the age of the machine; as Kozintsev graphically put it:

'We prefer Charlie's arse to Eleonora Duse's hands!'[158]

This proclamation was also intended to underline the rejection of classical art and its replacement by what had hitherto been regarded as 'lower' forms of cultural activity, such as the music-hall, the fairground and the circus. But the contemporary critic, Vladimir Nedobrovo, in his classic study of FEKS published in 1928, specifically denied that the form of Eccentrism to which FEKS adhered had much to do with the Eccentrism of the circus or music-hall:

It is generally thought that Eccentrism means wide check trousers, green hair, a crushed top hat, a negro in a blue tail-coat, the foxtrot or a boxing-match.

This is a vulgarised concept of Eccentrism, although it is not without its grounds. These grounds are infertile and have nurtured only weeds. These weeds have spread further afield...The green hair comes from the music-hall and the variety theatre. By way of Marinetti...

The Eccentrism of the music-hall and the variety theatre starts with the perversion of the realistic form of the object. The object is imbued with caricatured, absurd and unrealistic forms. Even the texture of the object is distorted.

The Eccentrism of the FEKS is not the same as the Eccentrism of the music-hall. Please do not confuse them.

The FEKS see the sense of Eccentrism differently. In as far as their strength and opportunities allow, they attempt to convey this sense to other people.

We cease to notice objects that surround us constantly. We unconsciously perform the usual actions, submerging our ability to think in them.

Repeated sight of an object in a certain context automates our perception of it. I cease to distinguish the objects on my desk and perceive them in overall terms. Some considerable length of time might elapse before I notice that a particular object has been stolen.

To perceive objects we must remove them from this automatic state. We begin to see an object anew if it is in combination with other, unfamiliar objects.[159]

Nedobrovo used the term 'impeded form' to describe the FEKS method of dealing with this phenomenon of automation.[160] This method involved the deliberate alienation of the object from its familiar surroundings so that it became more noticeable: 'The realistic forms of the object remain untouched. But the object acquires new neighbours.'[161] There is one example of this type of impeded form in *Chërtovo koleso* (The Big Wheel):[162] the scene when the love affair develops on the switchback. There is a clearer example in *Pokhozhdeniya Oktyabriny* (The Adventures of Oktyabrina)[163] where a typewriter, inkstand and table are placed on a motorcycle. On the other hand the same film also contains a clear example of the circus and music-hall type of Eccentrism through the distortion of external features in the character of Coolidge Curzonovich Poincaré, although one could perhaps argue, in defence of the Nedobrovo thesis, that this was the first film to be produced by the FEKS group. The concepts of Eccentrism have certain elements in common with the theories of Eisenstein: the fascination for circus and fairground 'attractions', the tempo of the machine, the age of the Revolution, but what distinguished FEKS from Eisenstein above all was the latter's development of the theory of montage. Tempo was important to the Eccentrics, but it was the tempo of an age rather than of a cinema projector. As Kozintsev proclaimed:

The rhythm of the tap-dance. The crackle of the cinema. Pinkerton. The roar of the switchback. The noisy tomfoolery of the clown. The poetics – 'time is money'!

Our rails rush past:

Paris, Berlin, London,
romanticism,
stylisation,
exoticism,
archaism,
reconstruction,
restoration,
the pulpit,
the temple,
the museum!

Only our methods are indivisible and inevitable:

THE AMERICANISATION OF THE THEATRE
in Russian means
ECCENTRISM [164]

The exact rôle of montage for Eccentrism was defined by Shklovsky in 1928:

Perhaps Eccentrism marked a transfer of attention to material with a design. In any case the theory of the montage of attraction of significant moments is connected with the theory of Eccentrism. Eccentrism is based on the selection of memorable moments and on a new, non-automatic connection between them. Eccentrism is a struggle with the monotony of life, a rejection of its traditional conception and presentation.[165]

Kozintsev himself has since written that the FEKS group was perhaps too concerned with the unique qualities of the cinema: 'Like everyone entering the cinema, we started worshipping the lens, the camera, the scissors.'[166] Griffith, and the American cinema in general, were a considerable influence on FEKS, as on Kuleshov,[167] but Russian Eccentrism soon rejected the use of unreal and deformed sets that was so characteristic of German Expressionist cinema.[168] The abnormality of Russian Eccentrism was essentially external to the original film frame: it stemmed from the order in which the frames were organised – in other words, from montage: 'Instead of normal things – the unexpected, always', as a later historian has observed.[169] He compared their technique to that of the early Chaplin and Harold Lloyd,[170] while the Eccentrics themselves referred to the pantomime as their school, although only a school: 'It took some time to appreciate that the pantomime was only a school. To transfer it to the screen was not feasible. In the cinema there are other measures of vitality, its own convention.'[171]

The first FEKS film was *Pokhozhdeniya Oktyabriny*[172] which Kozintsev has described as an 'agitational spectacle on the scale of Nevsky Prospekt'.[173] It created an exaggerated fantasy world and 'used everything in the catalogue of attractions which might amuse and arouse the mind of a normal person'.[174] The principal of these attractions was the farcical character of the villain, Coolidge Curzonovich Poincaré, who was dressed like a tramp wearing the trappings of bourgeois extravagance.[175] His very costume emphasised the underlying sense of incompatibility that was the essence of the concept of 'impeded form', and the extravagance of it was echoed by the appearance of Oktyabrina herself and the Nepman.[176] The manner in which the chase sequence was set and shot on the cupola of St Isaac's Cathedral in Petrograd, although derivative of American films of the period, also represented the concept of 'impeded form', heightening the awareness of the audience by using the unexpected, either in actual content of the frame or in the juxtaposition of frames and images. The latter technique was later employed by the FEKS group in *Chërtovo koleso*,[177] where the love affair develops symbolically but appropriately on a switchback. Here there is a refinement in the technique: the funfair in the background is being used for other reasons, partly to offset and counterpoint the intimacy of the relationship that is developing on the screen, but partly also merely to announce to the world that this is a FEKS film. Similarly in *Bratishka* (Little Brother)[178] the lyrical scenes are set in a car dump and centred on a dilapidated lorry. In both *Shinel'* (The Overcoat),[179] based on Gogol's short story, and *S.V.D.*,[180] a re-creation of the Decembrist Uprising of 1825, the weakness and vulnerability of the individual are shown by placing him against massive stone monuments, cannons or columns of marching soldiers, so that 'impeded form' in these films goes beyond being a mere attraction and imbues the sequence with a deeper meaning.

The last FEKS film, *Novyi Vavilon* (New Babylon),[181] was also the most interesting, partly because of its inherent qualities as a film, but partly because of its position in their work as a whole. If *Po zakonu* could be described by Kuleshov as 'the swansong of our collective',[182] then there can be no doubt that the same could be said of *Novyi Vavilon* and FEKS. The film uses many of the techniques that FEKS had made their own: the mannequin on the barricades of the Paris Commune is a typical touch. But the film contains the first seeds of the rejection of the ideals of machine worship, the first hint that the machine was not automatically the representative of progress. In previous films the machinery had always been a symbol of the progressive element, a force *for* the Revolution, and Yutkevich's first film, *Kruzheva* (Lace),[183] contains some of the most stunning sequences of machine poetry. But in *Novyi Vavilon* the day of reckoning has arrived: the workers defending the barricades of the Commune are brutally mown down, not by the cavalry as in Eisenstein's *Stachka*,[184] but by inhuman forces, the forces of machinery represented by guns, while an old, almost blind, man hammers away on the piano to a theme by Shostakovich which itself, according to Kozintsev, 'poured fat on to the fire' of the film's unfavourable reception.[185] For FEKS as a group the machine became a means rather than an end, and it was a means that they took for granted. Yutkevich's film had been made outside the Factory, in Moscow, even though it realised the atmosphere of the manifesto. In addition the fact that other film makers were preoccupied with poetic machinery was an incentive for the Eccentrics to turn elsewhere. In any event their interest was in the form of machinery – and in particular its rhythm ('Today's tempo is the rhythm of the machine') – and not in its productive capacities. It is this formal rhythm in their films which represents the machine element and which, predictably, led to accusations of Formalism and ideological lassitude. One contemporary critic wrote:

FEKS stand in a false blind alley. Their escape from this blind alley is not only a matter for them but also a matter for the Soviet public. The technical mastery of the FEKS should be placed at the service of the contemporary socially important theme.[186]

And a subsequent historian of the Soviet cinema wrote in the 1950s, 'Their manifestoes and their early works reflect their philistine self-advertisement and openly Formalist essence.'[187]

We have seen that, at the Party Conference on the Cinema in March 1928, the call went out for a closer association between V.A.P.P. and A.R.K.[188] A.R.K. had been established in 1924. A declaration in its name was published in *Pravda* on 27 February 1924[189] and the organisation held its first conference on 13 May 1924.[190] The initiative for the declaration came from a distinguished group of those active in the cinema, and the signatories included N. Lebedev, A. Goldobin, V. Erofeev, A. Anoshchenko, N. Plastinin, Kh. Khersonsky, P. Voevodin, Lev Kuleshov, I. Trainin, and Sergei Eisenstein. The declaration was a strident rallying-cry: 'Seven years after October there is no revolutionary cinema.'[191] Whereas the cinema was being used in the bourgeois countries to lull the working classes into acceptance of the status quo, its immense propaganda potential was being ignored in Soviet Russia: 'The nationalised studios are either idle or working at less than 10 per cent of their capacity.'[192] A.R.K., as an active group of leading film workers, aimed to galvanise the cinema into action. In a sense, therefore, it was acting as the advance guard for O.D.S.K.,[193] which drew its membership from wider sections of the population.[194] In January 1925 A.R.K. started publishing its own journal, *Kinozhurnal A.R.K.*, in which its views were transmitted to a wider public. In April 1926 the name of the journal was changed to *Kino-Front*, to broaden its appeal, and perhaps also to reflect the military terminology of the impending 'cultural revolution'. The journal ceased publication in February 1928, shortly after A.R.K. had come under attack for 'nihilism'.[195] The organisation itself continued until May 1929, when it was re-named A.R.R.K. (Assotsiyatsiya rabotnikov revolyutsionnoi kinematografii – Association of Workers of Revolutionary Cinematography).[196] In this form the association continued into the 1930s. What had started as a relatively small, though influential, pressure group in 1924 was to become the mass organisation for all cinema workers within ten years, and thus also one of the prime weapons for the political coordination of the Soviet cinema. The artistic controversies of the 1920s were rendered irrelevant.

Thus the sequence from *Novyi Vavilon* outlined above, and the rhetorical conclusion that follows it form a key passage not only for FEKS but for Soviet art in general. The pianist, blindly playing on, is shot dead, the Commune defeated, *but* its ideal lives on. In the final analysis therefore art in itself is not enough to carry the Revolution, for the Revolution must have arms as well as ideals. In the troubled years of the 1930s art was certainly an insufficiently effective weapon to preserve the ideals of the October Revolution from the brutal excesses of Stalin's dictatorship, but that is a story that, strictly speaking, does not concern us here.

8. CONCLUSIONS

The cinema, like every art, cannot be apolitical.
Party Conference resolution, 1928.[1]

It was not then until 1928–9 that the Soviet cinema was brought under the effective control of the Party. The 'cultural revolution' that accompanied the First Five Year Plan was to ensure that what Stalin had described as 'the greatest means of mass agitation'[2] was in the 1930s and 1940s to become a mouthpiece for Stalinist orthodoxy.[3] The meaning of the 13th Party Congress resolution of 1924[4] was reinforced in the resolutions of the Party Conference on the Cinema of March 1928:

> The cinema should be a weapon of the proletariat in its struggle for hegemony, leadership and influence in relation to the other classes, it 'should be, in the hands of the Party, the most powerful medium of communist enlightenment and agitation'. . .
>
> In the period of socialist construction the cinema should be the most powerful weapon for the deepening of the class-consciousness of the workers, for the political re-education of all the non-proletarian strata of the population, and above all the peasantry.[5]

That control of the cinema, so that it could be employed as a weapon of political and class warfare, had long been an aim of the Party is undeniable; that that control of the cinema had still not been achieved by the spring of 1928 is perhaps surprising, but the path towards such control had been long and tortuous.

The cinema had grown rapidly after its introduction into the Russian Empire until by 1917 it was the most popular form of entertainment for the urban masses.[6] Despite its popularity, the cinema was never used systematically for propaganda purposes by the Tsar's government. It remained a form of entertainment, rather than a weapon for education, enlightenment or mobilisation. Nevertheless, by the time of the October Revolution the cinema was being taken more seriously as at least a potential weapon for shaping and controlling public opinion.[7] The Russian cinema had grown enormously during the years of the First World War, but the industry was still heavily dependent on imported raw material and equipment. Dwindling supplies of both these commodities caused the first major economic crisis in the development of the cinema in Russia, and this crisis coincided with the political crisis of the *ancien régime*. The leading film producers moved away, taking their staff and their equipment with them. This further impoverished the forces that were left behind. By the time that the Bolsheviks took power in 1917 the conventional industrial structure of the cinema was already disorganised; under the twin pressures of Revolution and Civil War it was to become chaotic.

The Bolsheviks therefore attempted a holding operation. While pursuing a policy of gradual nationalisation of the existing cinema industry and its depleted resources, they also developed a more flexible and mobile system for the transmission of propaganda through the cinema and other means – the agit-trains (and, in the case of the *Krasnaya zvezda*, an agit-steamer). The agit-trains were important for two principal reasons: first, they spread the Bolshevik message into areas that it had not yet reached, using the cinema for the first time as a propaganda weapon, and, second, the simple, direct and essentially visual style of the films that they showed, the *agitki*, had a considerable influence on the distinctive, and dynamic, style of the Soviet films of the later 1920s.

The process of nationalising the cinema industry took longer than anticipated: the decree signed on 27 August 1919[8] had still not been fully enacted by the following spring.[9] And, once the industry had been fully nationalised, it could still not be used as an effective propaganda weapon because of its disorganised state and the shortage of everything from electricity and film stock to trained and experienced personnel at all levels of production, distribution and exhibition. Film production was in a particularly parlous state; studios were unable to meet demand and distribution organisations were therefore forced to import films, particularly from Germany and the United States. These films had entertainment rather than educational or propaganda value for the Bolshevik cause: indeed, some of these imported films were actually considered to be ideologically harmful. But they tided the Bolsheviks over until such time as the Soviet film industry could produce the goods which would make the importation of films unnecessary, and this did not happen until after the 1927–8 season.

The first attempt to organise the nationalised film industry along centralised lines came in December 1922 with the decision to establish Goskino.[10] This attempt failed, partly through lack of planning on the part of Goskino, and partly because the authorities were unwilling or unable to furnish Goskino with sufficient funds to perform the task that it had been set. Goskino was also given very little time in which to succeed: the Mantsev Commission of inquiry was set up in September 1923 and first reported in November.[11] After some delay Sovnarkom finally accepted the Commission's recommendations in April 1924,[12] and Goskino was eventually replaced by Sovkino in December of the same year.[13]

Despite this reorganisation, the Soviet Union continued to be a net importer of films, and the most popular film stars of the 1920s were Charlie Chaplin, Buster Keaton, Douglas Fairbanks and Mary Pickford.[14] The 'pride of the Soviet cinema',[15] *Potëmkin*, was not a success with Soviet audiences even when it was revived after its *succès de scandale* in Berlin.[16] Nevertheless *Potëmkin* did in a sense mark a turning point: it demonstrated what the Soviet film industry was capable of producing in the way of dramatic and revolutionary film propaganda, and it also marked the Soviet cinema's first breakthrough into the world market. Even if Soviet film audiences were not impressed, the film did galvanise at least certain intellectual circles in Western Europe and North America and serve to encourage them in their somewhat utopian views of life in the Soviet Union.[17] It is ironic that, whereas Sovkino was able to take all the credit for the success of *Potëmkin* abroad, the original project, in which Eisenstein's film was to be one of a series entitled *1905 god* (The Year 1905), had begun under the auspices of Goskino before its rather premature burial.[18] Within the Soviet Union *Potëmkin* failed for three reasons: first, it was a 'serious' film and audiences wanted escapism and entertainment; second, Sovkino proved in many ways to be an ineffective distributor for this film, and for several other films on revolutionary themes;[19] and third, the film itself proved, because of its 'dynamic montage' and other largely experimental techniques, to be 'too difficult' for contemporary Soviet audiences, especially when they were still able to see American 'hits' quite easily.[20]

In addition to its general failure to provide a sufficient quantity of ideologically suitable films for the wider Soviet audience, the Soviet cinema also proved itself incapable of providing films appropriate to what were considered to be the three priority areas for Bolshevik propaganda: the peasantry, the workers, and the younger generation. It was once more a problem of inadequate resources: Sovkino was expected not merely to provide the films but also to develop the necessary infrastructure for the distribution and exhibition of these films throughout the Russian

Federation, but it was not given the necessary wherewithal to carry out its tasks.

On another level the lack of centralised control in the Soviet cinema is amply illustrated by the polemics that were conducted between different individual film directors and critics, and between different schools of film-making. These divided the Soviet cinema into the partisans of the documentary film, and the supporters of the fiction film, and within the latter group there were further debates over the respective rôles of editing and acting, over whether the actor should be someone trained as such, someone untrained (a 'real' person), or someone trained to appear as if they had had no training (*naturshchik*), and over whether the hero of a film should be an individual, the mass itself, or an individual representing the mass. These debates were never resolved in their own terms, but dissipated into thin air once the Party had established its 'hegemony, leadership, and influence'.[21]

From the political point of view then the story of the Soviet cinema in the first ten years after the October Revolution is a story of words rather than deeds, of hopes rather than fulfilment. Despite Lenin's remark that, 'Of all the arts for us the cinema is the most important',[22] the cinema was treated in much the same way as the other art forms that the Party could use as vehicles for the transmission of its own propaganda. Indeed, when it came to the 'cultural revolution' that accompanied the first Five Year Plan the cinema was the last of the arts to be accorded the attentions of a Party conference.[23] Nevertheless, no one reading the columns of the Soviet film journals of the 1920s can fail to notice the distinct change in tone, the obvious narrowing of the sphere for discussion, that occurred after the conference in March 1928. The Party may well have arrived late on the scene, but it had certainly arrived.

Why, however, did the Party take more than ten years to exert its control over such an important propaganda medium as the cinema? One reason must be the discrepancy on many fronts between the promises of the Bolsheviks and their realisation. When they took power they had few resources, apart from their control over the commanding heights of the governmental apparatus. This was, of course, one of the reasons why propaganda became so important to them. It was also a reason for the general discrepancy between aspirations and capabilities, promises and fulfilment. It had to be this way if the Russian Empire were ever to become the Soviet Union: the Bolsheviks had to peer beyond what was immediately possible into the realms of what was in the longer term either probable or desirable so that they could offer the hope of a better future to compensate the masses for their present sufferings. It was neither the first nor the last occasion on which this technique of the carrot has been utilised. The cinema was to be one of the government's major weapons in the battle to win over the hearts and minds of the Soviet population in this manner, but the cinema itself became the victim of exaggerated expectations and unrealistic promises. Given the ultimately almost complete reliance of the pre-Revolutionary cinema upon imported resources, the difficulties involved in re-equipping the Soviet cinema after the considerable damage inflicted on it during the Revolution and the Civil War must have been foreseen. The desperate efforts made to acquire supplies from abroad, especially the Cibrario de Goden affair,[24] confirm this view. But, if progress were ever to be made, the theory had to outstrip the reality and the cinema, because of its technical complexity and its chronic dependence on imports, was peculiarly susceptible to this distinction between promise and performance. To a considerable extent then the delays in establishing Party hegemony over the cinema were inherent in the industry itself and in the actual political situation in which it found itself, but this does not mean that the Party can be exonerated from its share of the responsibility.

The Party repeatedly failed to provide the means by which the cinema could be financed and organised as an effective propaganda weapon. The original process of nationalisation was never properly coordinated. The first centralised cinema organisation, Goskino, was never adequately financed, either in terms of capital resources or in terms of taxation relief. It was never given a fair chance to produce the films required of it, although there is admittedly some evidence to show that that chance would probably have been wasted. Then Sovkino was never given the resources to concentrate its efforts on the three key areas: the peasantry, the workers' clubs and the younger generation. Instead it was criticised for producing bourgeois or incomprehensible films and for allowing continued importation of un-Soviet foreign films. It was only when the cinema surrendered its artistic independence in 1928–9 that it received adequate funds in return. But 1928 also marks a watershed in the Party's expectations of the masses. Under the New Economic Policy the masses had merely been required to accept what the Party told them: their rôle had been a passive one. Now, with industrialisation and collectivisation in full swing, the masses were expected to play a more positive and active rôle: they were expected to participate.

In the mobilisation of the masses during the first Five Year Plan the cinema was to play an important part. In the 1920s Soviet film-makers had been able to portray reality as they saw it; in the 1930s they had to portray reality as the Party saw it. Reality as it really was yielded to reality as it ought to be, and that new reality was called 'socialist realism'.

NOTES

Chapter 1 The pre-history of the Soviet cinema

Where no place of publication is given Moscow is the place.

1 A note scribbled in the margin of a police report by Nicholas II in 1913; I. S. Zil'bershtein, 'Nikolai II o kino', *Sovetskii ekran*, 12 April 1927, 10.
2 S. A. Timoshenko, *Iskusstvo kino i montazh fil'ma* (Leningrad, 1926), 9.
3 G. Sadoul, *Histoire générale du cinéma* (2 vols., Paris, 1946), vol. 1, p. 237.
4 This version of the statement is quoted, for example, in Jean-Luc Godard's film *Le Mépris*, made in France in 1963, but the statement should be seen in context: cf. M. Bessy and G. Lo Duca, *Georges Méliès. Mage* (Paris, 1961), 45–6. Georges Méliès, theatre owner and subsequent originator of many aspects of film fantasy, had asked Louis Lumière for permission to use his new invention. The reply was: 'This apparatus is a great secret and I don't want to sell it. I want to exploit it exclusively myself. Thank me, because for you it would mean ruin. It may be exploited for a time as a scientific curiosity. Apart from that it will have no commercial future.'
5 N. A. Lebedev, *Ocherk istorii kino S.S.S.R.* 2nd edn. (1965), 3.
6 S. S. Ginzburg, *Kinematografiya dorevolyutsionnoi Rossii* (1963), 23, Ginzburg is the most reliable historian of the pre-Revolutionary cinema, and I have therefore quoted extensively from his book.
7 Pacatus (pseudonym of Maxim Gorky), 'Beglye zametki', *Nizhegorodskii listok*, 4 July 1896:
8 G. V. Zhurov, *Z minulogo kino na Ukraini 1896–1917* (Kiev, 1959), 9–10.
9 Ginzburg, *Kinematografiya*, p. 38.
10 A. A. Khanzhonkov, *Pervye gody russkoi kinematografii. Vospominaniya* (1937), 12.
11 *Ibid.* p. 11.
12 F. Mesguich, *Tours de manivelle* (Paris, 1933), 22.
13 Timoshenko, p. 12.
14 V. B. Shklovskii, 'Ob Esfiri Shub i eë kinematograficheskom opyte', *Iskusstvo kino*, May 1969, 110.
15 For a survey of similar attitudes towards the cinema in the U.S.A. at the turn of the century, see: 'Omnibus: The Hollywood Image. I. The Silent Era', first transmitted on BBC–1 on 3 May 1970. See also D. J. Wenden, *The birth of the movies* (London, 1975), ch. 1.
16 Khanzhonkov, p. 11.
17 B. S. Likhachëv, *Kino v Rossii (1896–1926)* (Leningrad, 1927), 25.
18 Lebedev, *Ocherk*, p. 9.
19 Likhachëv, *Kino v Rossii*, p. 29.
20 Ginzburg, *Kinematografiya*, p. 40.

21 G. Sadoul, 'Progressivnye techeniya vo frantsuzskom kino (1900–1958)', *Voprosy kinoiskusstva*, 2 (1957), 360–1.
22 Zhurov, pp. 20–1.
23 Ginzburg, *Kinematografiya*, p. 44.
24 Likhachëv, *Kino v Rossii*, p. 40. Further details are to be found in Ginzburg, *Kinematografiya*, p. 46.
25 Ginzburg, *Kinematografiya*, p. 47.
26 *Cine-Fono*, 1907–8, no. 7.
27 Khanzhonkov, p. 22.
28 *Ibid.* p. 19.
29 Ginzburg, *Kinematografiya* p. 51.
30 *Ibid.* p. 47.
31 Skitalets, 'Zhizn' na polotne', *Gazeta-kopeika*, 26 November 1909. This experience also convinced Tolstoy of the value of the cinema. His play, *Zhivoi trup* (The Living Corpse), was written in short episodic scenes that could easily be adapted to the cinema. The play was filmed by Fyodor Otsep in 1926.
32 Ginzburg, *Kinematografiya*, p. 50.
33 K. Chukovskii, *Nat Pinkerton i sovremennaya literatura* (1910), 26.
34 e.g. V. V. Mayakovskii, 'Teatr, kinematograf, futurizm', *Kine-Zhurnal*, 27 July 1913.
35 From a government decree of 1908, quoted in Likhachëv, *Kino v Rossii*, p. 26, n. 1.
36 *Ibid.* p. 34.
37 *Ibid.* p. 27.
38 Khanzhonkov, p. 26.
39 Likhachëv, *Kino v Rossii*, p. 33.
40 A. Serafimovich, 'Mashinnoe nadvigaetsya', *Cine-Fono*, 1911–12, no. 8.
41 Editorial in *Cine-Fono*, 1909, no. 13.
42 Ginzburg, *Kinematografiya*, p. 99.
43 *Ibid.* pp. 100–1.
44 Khanzhonkov, p. 18.
45 See Ginzburg's remarks on Boltyansky and Likhachov in Ginzburg, *Kinematografiya*, p. 55.
46 See above, p. 4.
47 R. Low, *The history of the British film 1906–14* (London, 1948), 87.
48 Ginzburg, *Kinematografiya*, p. 55.
49 *Ibid.* p. 56 and Likhachëv, *Kino v Rossii*, pp. 78–9.
50 Ginzburg, *Kinematografiya*, p. 79n.; Likhachëv, *Kino v Rossii*, p. 79, n. 1.
51 Zhurov, p. 88.
52 Ginzburg, *Kinematografiya*, pp. 74–5.
53 *Ibid.* p. 69.
54 *Ibid.* pp. 70–1. The resolution of the Congress followed a report by G. Fyodorov, entitled 'The cinema as a factor in the development of curricular teaching and extracurricular education' (*Kinematograf, kak faktor v razvitii shkol'nogo obucheniya i vneshkol'nogo obrazovaniya*). Both are contained in the Congress documents published in Moscow in 1911.
55 Ginzburg, *Kinematografiya*, pp. 71–2. Quoting from Charnolusskii, *S"ezdy po narodnomu obrazovaniyu* (1911), 12, he gives the section of the Conference resolution on the cinema in full:
   1 The scientific cinema should be recognised as a method of teaching that enhances the clarity of instruction and the horizons of the student.
   2 Film programmes should be worked out in association with a course and teachers should be encouraged to participate in their preparation.
   3 In view of the technical shortcomings of the cinema, the programmes should not be too long or too frequent.
   4 Central and local stores of well selected films must be

established after the pattern of mobile museums.

5 In view of the ever increasing harmful influence of the street cinemas, we must organise, apart from the school programmes, extracurricular film shows for children and struggle with this influence by instilling in the general public an appreciation of the worthlessness of the existing cinema repertoire.

56 Ginzburg, *Kinematografiya,* p. 72.

57 *Ibid.*

58 Khanzhonkov, p. 68.

59 Ginzburg, *Kinematografiya,* p. 82.

60 See below, pp. 31–5.

61 V. V. Mayakovskii, 'Otnoshenie segodnyashnego teatra i kinematografa k iskusstvu', *Kine-Zhurnal,* 1913, no. 17, reprinted in *Polnoe sobranie sochinenii,* vol. 1 (1955), 273.

62 Likhachëv, *Kino v Rossii,* p. 149. This was to become a familiar pattern in the 1920s.

63 Ginzburg, *Kinematografiya,* p. 155.

64. *Ibid.* p. 156.

65 S. S. Ginzburg, 'Rozhdenie russkogo dokumental'nogo kino', *Voprosy kinoiskusstva,* 4 (1960), 239; cf. Shklovskii, 'Ob Esfiri Shub', p. 110.

66 Ginzburg, *Kinematografiya,* p. 35.

67 Khanzhonkov, p. 75.

68 Ginzburg, *Kinematografiya,* p. 156.

69 *Ibid.*

70 E. G. Lemberg, *Kinopromyshlennost' S.S.S.R. Ekonomika sovetskoi kinematografii* (1930), 11.

71 Ginzburg, *Kinematografiya,* p. 156.

72 *Ibid,* p. 161.

73 *Ibid.* p. 159.

74 *Ibid.* p. 157.

75 *Ibid.* p. 158.

76 E. G. Lemberg, *Ekonomika mirovoi kinopromyshlennosti* (1929) quoted in Ginzburg, *Kinematografiya,* 158.

77 From a report by cinema entrepreneurs to the Minister of Trade and Industry, 7 September 1916, quoted in Ginzburg, *Kinematografiya,* 158.

78 Cf. Ginzburg's arguments, *Kinematografiya,* pp. 158–9.

79 Lebedev, *Ocherk,* p. 41.

80 *Cine-Fono,* 1914, no. 4/5.

81 Khanzhonkov, p. 80.

82 Ginzburg, *Kinematografiya,* p. 181.

83 *Ibid.* pp. 178–9.

84 Skitalets writing in *Gazeta-kopeika,* 30 January 1915.

85 See above, pp. 7–8.

86 Quoted in Khanzhonkov, p. 76.

87 V. M. Dement'ev, *Kinematograf kak pravitel'stvennaya regaliya,* (Petrograd, 1915), 47.

88 Ginzburg, *Kinematografiya,* p. 172.

89 *Ibid.*

90 *Ibid.*

91 *Russkoe slovo,* 5 October 1916.

92 Ginzburg, *Kinematografiya,* p. 175.

93 V. R. Gardin, *Vospominaniya* (2 vols., 1949–52), vol. 1, p. 140.

94 See the series of interviews published in *Teatr* in 1915 under the title *Lyudi iskusstv o kinematografe* (Arts people on the cinema).

95 In an article published in 1914 and reprinted in *Polnoe sobranie sochinenii,* vol. 1, p. 283.

96 Ginzburg, *Kinematografiya,* p. 302.

97 L. Andreev, *Polnoe sobranie sochinenii,* vol. 8 (St Petersburg, 1913), 305–6.

98 *Ibid.* p. 316.

99 Ginzburg, *Kinematografiya,* p. 192.

100 G. M. Kozintsev, 'Narodnoe iskusstvo Charlie Chaplin' in *Sbornik Charles Spencer Chaplin* (1944).

101 Ginzburg, *Kinematografiya,* p. 322.

102 Khanzhonkov, p. 108.
103 Kholodnaya is regarded as the first, and last, Russian 'star' in the Hollywood sense; cf. V. Golovskoi (ed.), *Zvëzdy nemogo kino* (1968), which deals with the 1920s and mentions only foreigners. Kholodnaya died in the 1918 influenza epidemic.
104 Gardin, vol. 1, p. 145.
105 Ginzburg, *Kinematografiya,* p. 319.
106 *Ibid.* p. 321.
107 *Proektor,* 1917, no. 11/12.
108 Ginzburg, *Kinematografiya,* p. 326.
109 e.g. Libken. See above, p. 6 and below, p. 22. Cf. Ginzburg, *Kinematografiya,* p. 327.
110 *Vestnik kinematografii,* 1917, no. 124.
111 See below, p. 22.
112 V. Rosolovskaya, *Russkaya kinematografiya v 1917g. Materialy k istorii* (1937), p. 47.
113 G. M. Boltyanskii, 'Velikaya Oktyabr'skaya sotsialisticheskaya revolyutsiya i rozhdenie sovetskogo kinoiskusstva', *Iz istorii kino,* 2 (1959), 73.
114 His membership of the Union of Patriotic Cinematography strengthened their suspicions.
115 e.g. Ginzburg, *Kinematografiya,* p. 330.
116 *Vestnik kinematografii,* 1917, no. 126.
117 *Proektor,* 1917, no. 11/12.
118 Rosolovskaya, p. 50.
119 Boltyanskii, 'Velikaya Oktyabr'skaya', p. 70.
120 *Proektor,* 1917, no. 11/12.
121 Khanzhonkov, p. 106.
122 From the memoirs of Leskes, a typescript in the archives of V.G.I.K. (Vsesoyuznyi gosudarstvennyi institut kinematografii (All-Union State Institute of Cinematography) quoted in Rosolovskaya, p. 60.
123 In fact censorship was retained for certain categories of material, notably film shot at the front; A. G. Lemberg, 'Iz vospominanii starogo operatora', *Iz istorii kino,* 2 (1959), 122.
124 V. Vishnevskii, 'Fakty i daty iz istorii otechestvennoi kinematografii' *Iz istorii kino,* 1 (1958), 46.
125 *Ibid.* p. 43.
126 See above, p. 18.
127 See above, p. 18.
128 Ginzburg, *Kinematografiya,* p. 353, and L. Pogozheva's introduction in Yu. S. Kalashnikov *et al.* (eds.), *Ocherki istorii sovetskogo kino,* (3 vols., 1956–8), vol. 1, p. 20.
129 e.g. On 12 July at the Ermolev studio. See Rosolovskaya, p. 55.
130 In the longer term this left the Bolsheviks desperately short of resources during the Civil War period when these areas were either occupied or surrounded the White Forces. See below, pp. 46–8.
131 Khanzhonkov, p. 108. The absence of leading film producers from the August conference attracted critical comment in *Proektor,* 1917, no. 15/16.
132 L. Forestier, '*Velikii nemoi*'. (*Vospominaniya kinooperatora*) (Moscow, 1945), p. 94.
133 Yakov Protazanov (1881–1945) directed *Pikovaya dama* (The Queen of Spades) in 1916 and *Otets Sergii* (Father Sergius) in 1918, and after his return from emigration made *Aelita* in 1924 and *Ego prizyv* (His Appeal) in 1925, amongst other films.
134 N. F. Preobrazhenskii, 'Vospominaniya o rabote V.F.K.O.', *Iz istorii kino,* 1 (1958), 86.
135 *Ibid.* 87.
136 Cf. pp. 6–7 above.
137 Vishnevskii, 'Fakty i daty' (1958), p. 45.
138 *Proektor,* 1917, no. 15/16.
139 Rosolovskaya, p. 63, and *Proektor,* 1917, no. 15/16.
140 *Proektor,* 1917, no. 15/16, and see above, p. 17.
141 *Proektor,* 1917, no. 15/16.
142 The decision to impose further

restrictions was taken on the recommendation of the Commission originally established to investigate the Skobelev Committee; see above, p. 21.

143 *Proektor*, 1917, no. 17/18.

Chapter 2 The Bolsheviks, propaganda and the cinema

1 G. M. Boltyanskii, *Lenin i kino* (1925), pp. 16–17, from a conversation between Lenin and Lunacharsky in 1922, recalled by the latter in a letter to Boltyansky. On the same occasion Lenin also remarked, 'You will have to develop production on a wider basis and, in particular, introduce wholesome films to the masses in the city and, to an even greater extent, in the countryside.'

2 S. Fitzpatrick, *The Commissariat of Enlightenment. Soviet organization of education and the arts under Lunacharsky, October 1917–1921* (Cambridge, 1970), ch. 2.

3 V. I. Lenin, *Polnoe sobranie sochinenii*, 5th edn. (55 vols., 1958–65), vol. 35, p. 21.

4 *Ibid.* vol. 44, p. 274: Report to the 2nd All-Russian Congress of Political Education Departments, delivered on 17 October 1921. This theme was reiterated in a poster entitled *Negramotnyi tot-zhe slepoi. Vsyudu ego zhdut neudachi i neschast'ya* (The illiterate man is also blind. Everywhere failure and misfortune await him). The poster depicts a peasant, blindfold, walking over the edge of a cliff; B. S. Butnik-Siverskii, *Sovetskii plakat epokhi grazhdanskoi voiny 1918–1921* (1960), item 3342, p. 494.

5 G. V. Plekhanov, *O zadachakh sotsialistov v bor'be s golodom v Rossii. (Pis'ma k molodym tovarishcham)* (Geneva, 1892), p. 58.

6 Lenin, *Polnoe sobranie sochinenii*, vol. 6, pp. 66–7.

7 *Ibid.* p. 67.

8 See below, pp. 55–7.

9 See below, pp. 95–6 and 102–3, and *Sovetskie khudozhestvennye fil'my. Annotirovannyi katalog* (4 vols., 1961–8), vol. 1, pp. 82–3.

10 Plekhanov, *O zadachakh sotsialistov*, pp. 57–8.

11 *Iskra* nos. 1–51, reprint (Sofia, 1970), *passim*.

12 Ulam states that, 'The historic rôle of *Iskra* lay exactly in the fact that it gave a sense of mission and unity to the isolated groups of intellectuals and advanced workers who constituted Russian Social Democracy of the period.' A. B. Ulam, *Lenin and the Bolsheviks* (London, 1969), p. 214.

13 'Sistema Teilora – Poraboshchenie cheloveka mashinoi' in Lenin, *Polnoe sobranie sochinenii*, vol. 24, pp. 369–70.

14 '"Nauchnaya" sistema vyzhimaniya pota' in Lenin, *Polnoe sobranie sochinenii*, vol. 23, p. 19.

15 See below, p. 56.

16 There is a thorough discussion of these attempts in the following articles from E. A. Speranskaya (ed.), *Agitatsionno-massovoe iskusstvo pervykh let Oktyabrya. Materialy i issledovaniya* (1971): I. Rostovtseva, 'Uchastie khudozhnikov v organizatsii i provedenii prazdnikov 1 Maya i 7 Noyabrya v Petrograde v 1918 godu', pp. 9–66; A Raikhenshtein, 'Materialy prazdnichnogo oformleniya Moskvy 1 Maya 1918 goda', p. 133 and pl. 72–92; E. Speranskaya, 'Materialy k istorii oformleniya pervykh revolyutsionnykh prazdnestv v Saratove i Nizhnem Novgorode', pp. 134–61.

17 B. Thomson, *The premature*

revolution. Russian literature and society 1917–1946 (London, 1972), p. 107.

18 *Ibid.* p. 109.

19 Yu. Annenkov, *Dnevnik moikh vstrech* (2 vols., New York, 1966), vol. 2, pp. 118–26.

20 Butnik-Siverskii; see also G. N. Pavlov, *Sovetskii politicheskii plakat* (Leningrad, 1973); M. O. Malyshev, *Za zemlyu, za mir i volyu 1918–1922* (Leningrad, 1971); V. N. Lyakhov, *Sovetskii reklamnyi plakat 1917–1932* (1972); S. Bojko, *New graphic design in revolutionary Russia* (London, 1972), 32–6; M. Constantine and A. Fern, *Revolutionary Soviet film posters* (London, 1974); F. Mierau, *Links! Links! Links! Eine Chronik in Vers und Plakat* (Berlin, 1970); G. Piltz, *Russland wird rot. Satirische Plakate 1918–1922* (Berlin, 1977).

21 e.g. A. I. Strakhov, *Azbuka revolyutsii*, reprint (Kiev, 1969).

22 Pavlov, *Sovetskii politicheskii plakat, passim.*

23 Mierau, pp. 20–2.

24 Butnik-Siverskii, item 1798, p. 323.

25 J. Darracott and B. Loftus, *First World War posters* (London, 1972), 37.

26 Butnik-Siverskii, item 1762, p. 426.

27 F. Shipulinskii, 'Dusha kino', in *Kinematograf. Sbornik statei* (1919), p. 20.

28 i.e. *velikii nemoi;* hence the title of the volume of memoirs by L. Forestier, '*Velikii nemoi*'. (*Vospominaniya kinooperatora*) (1945). Cf. n. 47 below.

29 This was what was thought at least in the early stages, but obstacles later made themselves felt; cf. n. 46 below and see also p. 90.

30 See above, pp. 6–7.

31 P. Poluyanov, 'Kino i teatr – vragi', *Novyi zritel'*, 19 February 1924, 9–10.

32 P. Poluyanov, *Gibel' teatra i torzhestvo kino* (Nizhny Novgorod, 1925).

33 *Ibid.* p. 1.

34 *Ibid.* p. 6.

35 *Ibid.* pp. 11–12. Poluyanov is quoting from Eichenwald's remarks in the collection *V sporakh o teatre*, published in 1914.

36 Poluyanov, *Gibel'*, p. 12, paraphrasing Eichenwald.

37 *Ibid.* p. 15.

38 *Ibid.* p. 17.

39 *Ibid.* p. 35.

40 *Ibid.* p. 36.

41 A. Voznesenskii, *Iskusstvo ekrana. Rukovodstvo dlya kinoaktërov i rezhissërov* (Kiev, 1924).

42 *Ibid.* p. 7.

43 *Ibid.* p. 10; cf. p. 6 above.

44 *Ibid.* p. 9.

45 *Ibid.* p. 12.

46 *Ibid.* p. 16.

47 e.g. B. N. Eikhenbaum, 'Problemy kino-stilistiki', in Eikhenbaum (ed.), *Poetika kino* (1927), 18–19.

48 P. S. Kogan, 'Kino i literatura', *Sovetskoe kino*, 1925, no. 4/5.

49 Eikhenbaum, p. 24.

50 S. M. Eizenshtein, 'Literatura i kino', *Na literaturnom postu*, 1928, no. 1, p. 72, reprinted in *Izbrannye proizvedeniya* (6 vols., 1964–71), vol. 5, pp. 527–8.

51 O. Brik in 'Mastera o stsenarii (Nasha anketa)', *Kino-Front*, 1926, no. 9/10 (October), 12.

52 B. Arvatov, 'Teatr ili kino ili teatr i kino', *Novyi zritel'*, 26 April 1927, p. 4.

53 K. Samarin, 'Kino ne teatr', *Sovetskoe kino*, 1927, no. 2 (February).

54 N. Ya. Stepanov, *Zametki po iskusstvu kino-ekrana* (Vladivostok, 1928), p. 5.

55 *Ibid.* p. 7.

56 *Ibid.*

57 *Ibid.*

58 S. A. Timoshenko, *Iskusstvo kino i montazh fil'ma* (Leningrad, 1926), p. 13.
59 *Ibid.* p. 14.
60 *Ibid.* p. 19.
61 Eikhenbaum, pp. 38, 49.
62 V. Pudovkin, 'K voprosu zvukovogo nachala v fil'me', *Kino i kul'tura,* 1929, no. 5/6 (May/June), 3.
63 Sadko, 'Kino-"teatr". V paroksizme kinoedstva', *Teatral'naya Moskva,* 13–18 June 1922, 7–8.
64 Voznesenskii, *Iskusstvo ekrana,* pp. 142–3.
65 B. Shapotnikov, 'Futurizm i teatr,' *Maski,* 1912/13, no. 7/8. It is significant that *Maski* was edited by Voznesensky.
66 L. Kuleshov, 'Iskusstvo, sovremennaya zhizn' i kinematografiya', *Kino-Fot,* 25–31 August 1922, 2.
67 *Ibid.*
68 I. Sokolov, 'Skrizhal' veka', *Kino-Fot,* 25–31 August 1922, 3.
69 *Ibid.*
70 G. M. Boltyanskii, 'Iskusstvo budushchego', *Kino,* 1922, no. 1/2, 6–7.
71 *Ibid.* p. 7.
72 See above, nn. 31 and 32.
73 Poluyanov, *Gibel',* p. 37.
74 *Ibid.* p. 38.
75 G. M. Boltyanskii, *Kul'tura kinooperatora* (1927).
76 Cf. W. Benjamin, 'L'oeuvre d'art à l'époque de sa reproduction mécanisée', *Zeitschrift für Sozialforschung,* 1936, no. 1, 40–63.
77 Boltyanskii, *Kul'tura,* p. 7.
78 *Ibid.* p. 4.
79 N. Rovich, 'Bolezni kino', *Novyi zritel',* 12 August 1924, 7–8.
80 *Ibid.* p. 7.
81 *Ibid.* p. 8.
82 B. Arvatov, 'Agit-kino', *Kino-Fot,* 8–15 September 1922, 2.
83 *Ibid.*
84 *Ibid.* R.S.F.S.R. stands for Rossiiskaya sovetskaya federativnaya sotsialisticheskaya respublika – Russian Soviet Federative Socialist Republic.
85 See below, pp. 136–7.
86 Cf. the manifesto published by Marinetti *et al.* in September 1916 under the title 'La cinematografia futurista', reprinted in F. T. Marinetti, *Teoria e invenzione futurista* (Milan, 1968), pp. 118–23, translated in R. W. Flint (ed.), *Marinetti. Selected writings* (London, 1972) 130–4.
87 *Futurismo 1909–1919. Exhibition of Italian Futurism* (Newcastle upon Tyne/Edinburgh, 1972), 91.
88 *Sovetskie khudozhestvennye fil'my,* vol. 1, pp. 42–3.
89 *Kino-Gazeta,* 27 November 1923, 1.
90 V. Mayakovskii, 'Kino i kiko', *Kino-Fot,* 5–12 October 1922, 5.
91 A. Gan, '10-ya Kino-Pravda', *Kino-Fot,* 5–12 October 1922, 4.
92 V. Shklovskii, *Literatura i kinematograf* (Berlin, 1923).
93 *Ibid.* p. 11.
94 *Ibid.* p. 19.
95 *Ibid.* p. 20.
96 *Ibid.* p. 29.
97 A. Lunacharskii, 'O revolyutsionnoi ideologii v kinodele', *Pravda,* 1 April 1924.
98 V. Kirshon, 'Doloi obyvatel'skuyu fil'mu!', *Kino-Front,* 1926, no. 2/3 (no date), 17.
99 See below, ch. 7, *passim.*
100 Lunacharskii, *Pravda,* 1 April 1924.
101 See below, p. 68.
102 O. Beskin, 'Mesto kino', *Sovetskoe kino,* 1927, no. 1/ (January), 1.
103 See below, pp. 124–34.
104 *Kinematograf. Sbornik statei* (1919).
105 A. V. Lunacharskii, 'Zadachi Gosudarstvennogo kino-dela v R.S.F.S.R.', in *Kinematograf. Sbornik statei,* p. 5.
106 V. Kerzhentsev, 'Sotsial'naya bor'ba i ekran', in *Kinematograf. Sbornik statei,* p. 89.

Chapter 3 Revolution and Civil War

1 Lenin, quoted by Clara Zetkin in K. Tsetkin, *Vospominaniya o Lenine*, 1966), 9.

2 G. M. Boltyanskii, 'Velikaya Oktyabr'skaya sotsialisticheskaya revolyutsiya i rozhdenie sovetskogo kinoiskusstva', *Iz istorii kino*, 2 (1959), 85.

3 *Ibid.* p. 79.

4 L. Aksel'rod, 'Dokumenty po istorii natsionalizatsii russkoi kinematografii', *Iz istorii kino*, 1 (1958), 26. The journal *Mir ekrana* reported in highly emotive language on 26 April 1918 the alleged requisitioning of cinemas in Ekaterinburg, Voronezh, Kostroma, Semipalatinsk, Novo-Nikolaevsk, Tyumen, Biysk, Perm, Sarapul, Kustanai, Petropavlovsk, Elabug, and other places. On 19 May it carried stories of wild hooliganism. See also, V. Listov, 'U istokov sovetskogo kino', *Isskusstvo kino*, March 1969, 7.

5 Some sources give the date of the establishment of the Cinema Subsection as January 1918, but December 1917 is more widely accepted.

6 *Vestnik otdela mestnogo upravleniya komissariata vnutrennikh del*, 1918, no. 3, 1.

7 *Mir ekrana*, 26 April 1918, 1.

8 *Proektor*, 1917, no. 17/18 (November), 1, and 1918, no. 1/2 (July), 1.

9 *Vestnik kinematografii*, 1917, no. 123.

10 Aksel'rod, p. 27.

11 *Vechernyaya zhizn'*, 13 April 1918.

12 Aksel'rod, pp. 30–1.

13 *Mir ekrana*, 12 May 1918. This editorial appeared beneath a most un-Soviet still from the film *Caliostro* which, judging from this evidence, depicted one of the more sensual episodes from the decline and fall of the Roman Empire.

14 Despite their precautions the Soviet authorities did become the victims of crooked dealings. The most spectacular involved the Italian-born Jacques Cibrario who in July 1918 was given 220,000 gold roubles and commissioned by Preobrazhensky, then head of the Moscow Cinema Committee, to purchase film equipment in the U.S.A. for export to Soviet Russia. Once in the United States however, Cibrario used the money for his own purposes and the Soviet authorities never saw either their roubles or their equipment. In addition Bruce Lockhart is alleged to have attempted to smuggle out the master copies of the *Tsarskaya khronika* (The Tsar's Chronicle), the Tsar's family films, to Great Britain. See particularly, Boltyanskii, 'Velikaya Oktyabr'skaya', pp. 81–2; and N. F. Preobrazhenskii, 'Vospominaniya o rabote V.F.K.O.', *Iz istorii kino*, 1 (1958), 89 and n. 1.

15 See above, pp. 10–12.

16 S. Ginzburg, *Kinematografiya dorevolyutsionnoi Rossii* (1963), 156. See above, p. 11.

17 Taldykin is one example. See, L. Forestier, '*Velikii nemoi*'. (*Vospominaniya kinooperatora*) (1945), 98, and Preobrazhenskii, p. 88.

18 Ivan Mosjoukine the actor, Vladimir Starevich the animator, and Yakov Protazanov the director were among those who went to Paris. Vladimir Sokoloff became a prominent actor in German silent films and Rouben Mamoulian became a leading Hollywood director. Of these, only Protazanov returned to

Russia, in 1923, to make films like *Aelita* in 1924, *Ego prizyv* (His Appeal) in 1925 and *Sorok pervyi* (The Forty-first) in 1927: M. N. Aleinikov (ed.), *Yakov Protazanov* (1957).

19 *Sovetskie khudozhestvennye fil'my. Annotirovannyi katalog* (4 vols., 1961–8), vol. 1, pp. 5–26.

20 *Kinogazeta*, 1918, no. 3, and E. G. Lemberg, *Kinopromyshlennost' S.S.S.R. Ekonomika sovetskoi kinematografii* (1930), 15–16.

21 *Kinogazeta*, 1918, no. 5.

22 N. A. Lebedev, *Ocherk istorii kino S.S.S.R.*, 2nd edn. (1965), 141.

23 Listov, 'U istokov sovetskogo kino', p. 14, and V. Vishnevskii, 'Fakty i daty iz istorii otechestvennoi kinematografii', *Iz istorii kino*, 1 (1958), 66–9. A similar calculation had earlier been published in *Proektor*, 1917, no. 17/18 (November), 1.

24 H. Carter, *The new theatre and cinema of Soviet Russia* (London, 1924), 240.

25 Quoted in Listov, 'U istokov sovetskogo kino', p. 13.

26 *Izvestiya V.Ts.I.K.*, 19 August 1918. Cf. Aksel'rod, pp. 27, 33.

27 Customs controls over the movement of equipment and materials out of the city of Moscow were introduced on 4 June 1918; Listov 'U istokov sovetskogo kino', p. 32.

28 *Proektor*, 1918, no. 1/2 (July), gives the full text. In October 1918 the Committee published *Kino-Byulleten'*, giving reasons for the censorship of 174 films. There is some evidence that censorship of sorts had been introduced in Moscow as early as March 1918; *Izvestiya Moskvy i Moskovskoi oblasti*, 1918, no. 40 (288).

29 *Proektor*, 1918, no. 1/2 (July).

30 Aksel'rod, pp. 32–3. See also n. 14 above.

31 *Ibid.* p. 34.

32 See below, pp. 55–7.

33 *Narodnyi komissariat po prosveshcheniyu. 1917 – Oktyabr' – 1920. (Kratkii otchët)* (1920), 87.

34 *Narodnoe prosveshchenie*, 1919, no. 30.

35 Listov, 'U istokov sovetskogo kino', p. 6.

36 *Ibid.* pp. 14–15.

37 *Narodnoe prosveshchenie*, 1918, no. 23/5.

38 *Vos'moi s"ezd R.K.P.(b). Mart 1919 goda. Protokoly* (1959), 433.

39 *Izvestiya V.Ts.I.K.*, 2 September 1919.

40 *Izvestiya V.Ts.I.K.*, 18 September 1919.

41 e.g. Boltyanskii, 'Velikaya Oktyabr'skaya', p. 95.

42 A. M. Gak (ed.), *Samoe vazhnoe iz vsekh iskusstv. Lenin o kino*, 2nd edn. (1973), 52.

43 Boltyanskii, 'Velikaya Oktyabr'skaya', p. 95.

44 *Ibid.*

45 A. G. Lemberg, 'Iz vospominanii starogo operatora', *Iz istorii kino*, 2 (1959), 126.

46 Aksel'rod, p. 36.

47 e.g. the FEKS group; G. M. Kozintsev, *Glubokii ekran* (1971), 6.

48 V. R. Gardin, *Vospominaniya* (2 vols., Moscow, 1949–52), vol. 1, pp. 167–70, and also Vishnevskii, 'Fakty i daty' (1958), p. 71, and 'V.G.I.K. – 50. Tsifry i fakty', *Sovetskoe kino*, 1969, no. 41 (352).

49 'Vysshaya kinoshkola strany. Beseda s A. N. Groshevym', *Iskusstvo kino*, October 1969, 41.

50 *Ibid.*

51 See below, pp. 135–6.

52 M. Astaf'eva, 'Dekret, prochitannyi arkhitektorom', *Iskusstvo kino*, March 1969, 16, 18.

53 See above, pp. 2–3.

54 F. Mesguich, *Tours de manivelle* (Paris, 1933), *passim*, and A. A. Khanzhonkov, *Pervye gody russkoi kinematografii. Vospominaniya* (1937), *passim*.

55 Khanzhonkov, p. 12.
56 Ya. Burov, 'Vozniknovenie, apparat i rabota agitparpoezdov V.Ts.I.K.' in V. Karpinskii (ed.), *Agitparpoezda V.Ts.I.K. Ikh istoriya, apparat, metody i formy raboty* (1920), 5.
57 The main fleet of agit-trains and the steamer *Krasnaya zvezda* (Red Star) were controlled from the centre, but smaller operations, such as the seven agit-lorries used in Petrograd in 1919, were run by local soviets; R. Marchand and P. Weinstein, *L'art dans la Russie nouvelle: le cinéma* (Paris, 1927), 40. Where appropriate, agit-sledges were used in difficult terrain; *Iz istorii Grazhdanskoi voiny v S.S.S.R. Sbornik dokumentov*, vol. 3 (1961), 686.
58 Burov, p. 6. Cf. *Iskusstvo kino*, October 1968, pp. 114–17.
59 Burov, p. 6.
60 *Ibid.*
61 V. Karpinskii, 'Metody i formy raboty agitparpoezdov V.Ts.I.K.' in Karpinskii (ed.), *Agitparpoezda V.Ts.I.K.*, p. 26.
62 Burov, p. 7. Cf. P. Voevodin, 'Agitpoezd *Oktyabr'skaya Revolyutsiya*', *Partiinaya zhizn'*, 1957, no. 5 (May), 73–4.
63 Karpinskii, 'Metody i formy', p. 26.
64 Cf. note 35.
65 Lenin was shot on 30 August 1918 and the film *Lenin na progulke v Kremle posle vyzdorovleniya* (Lenin Walking in the Kremlin after his Recovery) was made on 23 September: A. A. Lebedev (ed.), *Kinokamera pishet istoriyu* (1971), 34–5; M. L. Polyanovskii, *My vidim Il'icha* (1969), 13–17; A. M. Gak *et al.* (eds.), *Lenin. Sobranie fotografii i kinokadrov* (2 vols., 1970-2), vol. 2, pp. 18–97.
66 Burov, p. 11. This somewhat half-hearted attitude towards the project by many at the centre was also reflected in the lack of political leadership in the initial stages from some of the People's Commissariats.
67 E. A. Speranskaya (ed.), *Agitatsionno-massovoe iskusstvo pervykh let Oktyabrya* (1971), pl. 113–30.
68 e.g. *ibid.* pl. 114, 115.
69 e.g. *ibid.* pl. 123–6.
70 Issued in forty-three numbers by the Cinema Committee of Narkompros between 1 June 1918 and 24 December 1919.
71 S. Drobashenko (ed.), *Dziga Vertov. Stat'i, dnevniki, zamysly* (1966), 317.
72 Based on information in *Sovetskie khudozhestvennye fil'my*, vol. 1, pp. 5–26.
73 A. M. Gak, 'Lenin i kino. Poiski novykh dokumentov', *Iz istorii kino*, 7 (1968), 12, and G. M. Boltyanskii, *Lenin i kino* (1925), 27–32.
74 Lemberg, 'Iz vospominanii starogo operatora', pp. 127–9.
75 V. Listov, 'Nachalo', *Iskusstvo kino*, August 1970, 31.
76 N. A. Lebedev, 'Boevye dvadtsatye gody', *Iskusstvo kino*, December 1968, 85. The plan had affinities with Gorky's project for a publishing house for world literature.
77 The information that follows is based on Karpinskii.
78 L. V. Maksakova *Agitpoezd 'Oktyabr'skaya Revolyutsiya' (1919–20gg)* (1956), 11.
79 *Ibid.* pp. 27–33.
80 *Ibid.* p. 62.
81 *Istoricheskii zhurnal*, 1940, no. 3, 32.
82 Ts. Gofman, 'K istorii pervogo agitparokhoda V.Ts.I.K. "Krasnaya zvezda"', *Voprosy istorii*, 1948, no. 9, 64.
83 N. K. Krupskaya, 'Po gradam i vesyam sovetskoi respubliki', *Novyi mir*, 1960, no. 11, 113–30.
84 *Ibid.* p. 115.
85 *Ibid.*

86 *Ibid.* p. 122.
87 N. K. Krupskaya, *Pedagogicheskie sochineniya*, vol. 11 (1963), 191.
88 Gofman, pp. 65–6.
89 For a recent examination on film of similar problems encountered in Kirghizia, see Andrei Mikhalkov-Konchalovsky's *Pervyi uchitel'* (The First Teacher), a Kirgizfilm/Mosfilm co-production, made in 1965 and based on a story by Chingiz Aitmatov.
90 E. Kubelikov, *Kinoiskusstvo Azerbaidzhana* (Baku, 1960), 9. Cf. Maxim Gorky's first reactions to the cinema, p. 2 above.
91 Maksakova, p. 11.
92 N. K. Krupskaya, *Politprosvetrabota* (1932), 175–6. A partial text was published in Karpinskii, p. 60, and a full text in Gak, *Samoe vazhnoe*, pp. 22–3; cf. Gak, p. 68.
93 *Devyatyi s"ezd R.K.P.(b). Mart – aprel' 1920 goda. Protokoly* (1960), 405.
94 Maksakova, p. 13.

Chapter 4 The disorganisation of organisation: the early twenties

1 *Trinadtsatyi s"ezd R.K.P.(b). 23–31 maya 1924 goda. Stenograficheskii otchët* (1924), 132.
2 *Kino*, 1923, no. 1/5 (January).
3 See above, pp. 49–50.
4 On 19 June 1923 the back page of *Pravda* carried an advertisement for the American film *Sodom and Gomorrah*: 'A poem of human passions in two parts and fourteen reels. In the principal rôle the famous artiste Lucy Dorney. In the richness of its settings and in its techniques the picture surpasses everything seen hitherto on the screen.'
5 See above, p. 51, for the manner in which the Bolsheviks attempted to deal with this problem. Cf. N. A. Lebedev, 'Kino', *Pravda*, 3 January 1923.
6 Lunacharsky was himself the originator of a screenplay dedicated to Mary Pickford and entitled *Potselui Meri Pickford* (The Kiss from Mary Pickford). The film was a comedy involving newsreel shots of Mary Pickford and Douglas Fairbanks and was released in September 1927: *Sovetskie khudozhestvennye fil'my. Annotirovannyi katalog* (4 vols., 1961–8), vol. 1, p. 219.
7 As late as 1927 the Soviet public was still kept informed of the intimate details of Chaplin's private life. When his wife started divorce proceedings against him in the American courts Lunacharsky was again moved to write. On this occasion he penned an article entitled 'Pokhod protiv Charli Chaplina' (The Campaign against Charlie Chaplin) in *Vechernyaya Moskva*, 7 March 1927. Even *Pravda* reviewed Chaplin's films, e.g. on 12 January 1923.
8 In 1926–7 income from the distribution of Soviet films within the U.S.S.R. was 2,991,064 roubles less than the income accruing from the distribution of foreign films. In 1927–8 income from Soviet films exceeded that from foreign films for the first time, by 627,829 roubles: E. G. Lemberg, *Kinopromyshlennost' S.S.S.R. Ekonomika sovetskoi kinematografii* (1930), 71.
9 See above, p. 46.
10 See above, p. 29, and below, p. 88.
11 L. Trotskii, 'Vodka, tserkov' i kinematograf', *Pravda*, 12 July 1923, reprinted in *Voprosy byta. Epokha 'kul'turnichestva' i eë zadachi* (1923). The English translation is from chapter 3,

'Vodka, the Church and the Cinema', of *Problems of life* (London, 1924), 37–9, reprinted as *Problems of everyday life* (New York, 1973), 31–5. Alcoholism became an increasing problem throughout the 1920s. In 1928 *Kul'turnyi front,* no. 718, 33, published the following table showing alcoholics as a percentage of the inpatients of Soviet mental hospitals:

1921	2.2%	1924	6.0%
1925	9.9%	1926	25.0%
1927	42.0%		

See also the discussion in M. Rafail, *Za novogo cheloveka* (Leningrad, 1928).

12 Trotskii, *Problems of everyday life*, p. 33.

13 *Ibid.*

14 L. M. Sukharebskii, *Nauchnoe kino* (1926), 11.

15 'Dukh Banko' [i.e. 'Banquo's Ghost'), '"Velikii" glukhonemoi', *Zhizn' iskusstva,* 18 December 1923, 21.

16 *Sed'moi ekstrennyi s"ezd R.K.P.(b). Mart 1918 goda. Stenograficheskii otchët* (1962).

17 *Vos'moi s"ezd R.K.P.(b). Mart 1919 goda. Protokoly* (1959).

18 *Devyatyi s"ezd R.K.P.(b). Mart – aprel' 1920 goda. Protokoly* (Moscow, 1960), 405. See above, p. 62.

19 *Desyatyi s"ezd Rossiiskoi Kommunisticheskoi Partii: Stenograficheskii otchët. (8–16 marta 1921g.)* (1921), 74ff., 320.

20 *Odinnadtsatyi s"ezd R.K.P.(b). Mart – aprel' 1922 goda. Stenograficheskii otchët* (1961), 424.

21 *Ibid.*

22 Between 1917 and 1921 *Pravda* published no articles on the cinema: N. A. Lebedev, 'O Proletkino', *Pravda,* 8 May 1923, and 'Boevye dvadtsatye gody', *Iskusstvo kino,* December 1968, 90. Cinema information and film reviews were published under the general heading 'Theatre and Music'; the first article to appear under the separate heading 'Cinema' was published on 9 September 1923.

23 V. I. Lenin, *Polnoe sobranie sochinenii,* vol. 44 (Moscow, 1964), 360–1. This formula became known as the 'Leninist proportion' and was construed by Dziga Vertov, among others, as implying that 75 per cent of Soviet films should be entertainment fiction, while the remaining 25 per cent should be newsreels or documentaries. Goebbels pursued a similar formula, quoting the Soviet example, and in particular Eisenstein's *Battleship Potemkin* in his speech to German film workers on 28 March 1933: E. Leiser, *Deutschland, erwache! Propaganda im Film des Dritten Reiches* (Reinbek bei Hamburg, 1968), 10. Goebbels' comparisons eventually drew a protest from Eisenstein in the form of an open letter published in *Literaturnaya gazeta,* 22 March 1934, translated in *Film Art,* 5 (Winter 1934), 7–11.

24 Lenin, *Polnoe sobranie sochinenii, ibid.*

25 *X Vserossiiskii s"ezd Sovetov rabochikh, krest'yanskikh, krasnoarmeiskikh i kazach'ikh deputatov R.S.F.S.R. (23–27 dekabrya 1922g.), Stenograficheskii otchët s prilozheniyami* (1923), 87.

26 *Ibid.* The decree mentioned by Lunacharsky is the Sovnarkom decree of 19 December 1922 establishing Goskino. See below, p. 71.

27 *X Vserossiiskii s"ezd Sovetov,* p. 87.

28 *Ibid.* p. 203.

29 On 25 March, 28 September and 28 October, according to V. Vishnevskii, 'Fakty i daty iz istorii otechestvennoi kinematografii (1921–1924)', *Iz istorii kino,* 3 (1960), 127–9.

30 *Ibid.* p. 130.

31 Cf. E. H. Carr, *A history of*

Soviet Russia, vol. 2 (Harmondsworth, 1966), p. 304, and A. M. Gak, 'K istorii sozdaniya Sovkino', *Iz istorii kino,* 5 (1962), 132.

32 A. M. Gak (ed.), *Samoe vazhnoe iz vsekh iskusstv. Lenin o kino,* 2nd edn. (1973), 35–8.

33 *Ibid.* p. 37.

34 A. M. Gak, 'Lenin i kino. Poiski novykh dokumentov', *Iz istorii kino,* 7 (1968), 12–13.

35 Gak, *Samoe vazhnoe,* pp. 217–18, n. 60.

36 G. M. Boltyanskii, *Lenin i kino* (1925), 21–2.

37 Gak, 'Lenin i kino', p. 13.

38 Vishnevskii, 'Fakty i daty' (1960), p. 138.

39 See above, p. 69.

40 *Deyatel'nost' Goskino – Tsentral'nogo Gosudarstvennogo organa Narkomprosa R.S.F.S.R. Okt. 1923 – Okt. 1924* (1925), 1.

41 Kh. Abul-Kasymova *et al.* (eds.), *Istoriya sovetskogo kino 1917–1967,* vol. 1 (1969), 23.

42 See below, p. 74.

43 e.g. Sevzapkino opened an office in Moscow and sent filming expeditions to Siberia, the Caucasus, Central Asia and China.

44 Gak, 'K istorii', p. 131.

45 See above, pp. 10–11.

46 See above, ch. 3, n. 14.

47 It was headed by Clara Zetkin, Willi Münzenberg and Francesco Misiano.

48 Yu. A. Fridman, 'Dvizhenie pomoshchi mezhdunarodnogo proletariata Sovetskoi Rossii v 1921–1922 godakh', *Voprosy istorii,* 1958, no. 1, 100.

49 W. Münzenberg, *Fünf Jahre internationale Arbeiterhilfe* (Berlin, 1926), 43.

50 The importance of this outlet was not lost on Soviet cinema enthusiasts, e.g.: N. Kadisheva, 'Kinopropaganda na zapade', in I. N. Bursak (ed.), *Kino* (1925), 96–8. Their general attitude is well expressed by Huntly Carter: 'Russia would like to export revolutionary films, but the English government does not want them', in H. Carter, *The new theatre and cinema of Soviet Russia* (London, 1924), 237. The exportation of Soviet films through Germany explains the often sensational change of title: for example, *Oktyabr'* became *Zehn Tage, die die Welt erschütterten* and hence *Ten Days That Shook the World,* while *Potomok Chingis-khana* (The Heir to Genghis Khan) became *Sturm über Asien* and *Storm over Asia.*

51 *Pravda,* 18 March 1923.

52 *Ibid.*

53 Yu. L'vunin and I. Polyanskii (eds.), 'Blagodarya lichnomu sodeistviyu V. I. Lenina. . .Novye dokumenty rasskazyvayut', *Iskusstvo kino,* January 1970, p. 8. Cf. *Kino-Gazeta,* 1923, no. 13.

54 L'vunin and Polyanskii, p. 11.

55 *Sovetskie khudozhestvennye fil'my,* pp. 50–1.

56 *Ibid.* p. 168.

57 *Ibid.* p. 193.

58 *Ibid.* p. 157.

59 *Ibid.* p. 147.

60 *Ibid.* pp. 202–3.

61 *Ibid.* pp. 285–6 and see above, n. 50.

62 *Sovetskie khudozhestvennye fil'my,* p. 219, and see above, n. 6.

63 Münzenberg, pp. 169–74.

64 See above, n. 8.

65 Lebedev, 'Kino', *Pravda,* 3 January 1923.

66 Gak, 'K istorii', p. 133.

67 *Ibid.* pp. 134–5.

68 *Deyatel'nost' Goskino,* pp. 6–7. Cf. Gak, 'K istorii', p. 134.

69 *Ibid.* p. 136.

70 *Pravda,* 14 January 1923.

71 *Sovetskoe kino,* 1925, no. 1.

72 Gak, 'K istorii', p. 134.

73 V. Shentyapin, 'Moskovskaya kinokonferentsiya', *Pravda,* 14 July 1923.

74 *Ibid.*

75 Gak, 'K istorii', p. 136.

76 *Ibid.* pp. 140–1. Cf *Deyatel'nost' Goskino*, p. 3.
77 *Zhizn' iskusstva*, 11 September 1923, 22.
78 'O kinostroitel'stve', *Pravda*, 22 August 1923.
79 V. Erofeev, 'K organizatsii kinoproizvodstva', *Pravda*, 13 September 1923.
80 *Ibid.*
81 V. Erofeev, 'Ne kino-arkhiv a kino-gazeta', *Pravda*, 21 September 1923.
82 Gak, 'K istorii', p. 141.
83 *Ibid.*
84 *Deyatel'nost' Goskino*, p. 4.
85 N. Plastinin, 'Da dokole zhe?', *Pravda*, 16 February 1924.
86 'Dela kinematograficheskie', *Pravda*, 16 February 1924.
87 *Ibid.*
88 *Ibid.*
89 N. Plastinin, 'Chego zhdët sovetskaya kinematografiya?', *Pravda*, 16 March 1924.
90 A. Goldobin, 'Chto delaetsya dlya sovetskoi kinematografii', *Pravda*, 26 March 1924.
91 Reported in *Pravda*, 1 and 2 April 1924, and in *Deyatel'nost' Goskino*, pp. 4–5.
92 *Pravda*, 1 April 1924. But cf. nn. 6 and 7 above.
93 See above, ch. 3, *passim*.
94 *Pravda*, 1 April 1924.
95 Gak, 'K istorii', p. 142.
96 *Pravda*, 2 April 1924.
97 Gak, 'K istorii', 142. The gist of the recommendations was published in *Kinonedelya*, 15 April 1924.
98 See above, n. 1.
99 *Trinadtsatyi s"ezd R.K.P.(b).* pp. 702–3, and *Pravda*, 4 June 1924.
100 *Pravda*, 15 June 1924.
101 *Deyatel'nost' Goskino*, p. 6.
102 *Pravda*, 30 July 1924.
103 Gak, 'K istorii', pp. 143–4.
104 A. L'vov, 'Dokole zhe?', *Pravda*, 10 January 1924. Cf. n. 85 above.
105 A. L'vov, *Kinematograficheskaya yazva izlechima* (1924). The title may be translated as 'The Cinema's Ulcer can be Cured'.
106 *Ibid.* p. 3.
107 *Ibid.*
108 *Ibid.* p. 8.
109 *Ibid.*
110 *Ibid.* p. 9.
111 *Ibid.* p. 13.
112 *Pravda*, 7 September 1923 and 2 October 1923. Cf. L'vov, *Kinematograficheskaya yazva*, pp. 11–13.
113 *Ibid.* p. 9.
114 *Ibid.*
115 A. Goldobin, 'Opyt Goskino v bor'be na kino-fronte', *Zhizn' iskusstva*, 8 July 1924, 13–14.
116 *Ibid.*
117 A. Goldobin (ed.), *Kino na territorii S.S.S.R. (Po materialam provintsial'noi pressy)* (1924).
118 *Ibid.* pp. 5–6.
119 *Ibid.* p. 6.
120 *Ibid.* p. 3, n. 1.
121 *Ibid.* pp. 52–3.
122 *Ural'skii rabochii*, 3 July 1924, quoted in Goldobin, *Kino na territorii S.S.S.R.*, p. 58.
123 *Ural'skii rabochii*, 25 July 1924, quoted in Goldobin, *Kino na territorii S.S.S.R.*, p. 19.
124 *Nefterabochii*, 19 July 1924, quoted in Goldobin, *Kino na territorii S.S.S.R.*, p. 11.
125 See, for example, *Vyatskaya Pravda*, 2 July 1924, quoted in Goldobin, *Kino na territorii S.S.S.R.*, p. 13.
126 Goldobin, *Kino na territorii S.S.S.R.*, p. 7.
127 See above, n. 60.
128 *Deyatel'nost' Goskino*, pp. 7–9, and n.
129 *Ibid.* pp. 9–10.

Chapter 5 The organisation of disorganisation: the later twenties

1 *Pskovskii nabat*, 3 July 1924, quoted in A. Goldobin, *Kino na territorii S.S.S.R.* (*Po material-am provintsial'noi pressy*) (1924), 64.
2 *Kino*, 1924, no. 4 (June/September).
3 See above, p. 8.
4 See above, ch. 3.
5 Lenin, *Polnoe sobranie sochinenii*, vol. 44 (1964), 361. See above p. 68. Cf. A. I. Katsigras (ed.), *Kino-rabota v derevne* (1925), *passim*.
6 *Krasnoe znamya* (Krasnodar), 12 July 1924, quoted in Goldobin, *Kino na territorii S.S.S.R.*, p. 70. Cf. I. L. Kosmatov and Yu. Saltanov, 'Chto takoe kinematograf?', in A. I. Katsigras (ed.), *Kino-rabota v derevne* (1925), 9. E. Kuste, *Kino i ego chudesa* (Leningrad, 1925), 99; *Kino*, 1924, no. 4 (June/September).
7 Although written in 1919 the account was first published as: N. K. Krupskaya, 'Po gradam i vesyam sovetskoi respubliki', *Novyi mir*, 1960, no. 11 (November), 113–30. See above, pp. 59–60.
8 I. Trainin, *Kino-promyshlennost' i Sovkino* (1925), 21.
9 V. Vainshtok and D. Yakobzon, *Kino i molodëzh'* (Leningrad, 1926), 57.
10 *Ibid.* A. I. Katsigras, 'Kak organizovat' kinoperedvizhku v derevne', in Katsigras (ed.), *Kino-rabota*, p. 83, provides illustrated evidence of the amazed reactions of the peasantry to the cinema.
11 *Zhizn' iskusstva*, 20 January 1925, in its editorial (p. 1) acclaimed the cinema's rôle in affirming 'the necessity of a closer union [*smychka*] between the town and the countryside'.
12 E. G. Lemberg, *Kino – derevne. Kak ustroit' kino v derevne* (1929), 3.
13 See above, p. 3.
14 A. I. Katsigras, 'K voprosu o kino dlya derevni', *Zhizn' iskusstva*, 19 August 1924, 18.
15 Goldobin, *Kino na territorii S.S.S.R.*, p. 64.
16 P. S. Radetskii, *Peredvizhnoi kinematograf* (Leningrad, 1926), *passim*. Cf. the introductory remarks in Katsigras (ed.), *Kino-rabota*, p. 4.
17 KOK was the Cyrillic transliteration of the French word 'COQ' (cockerel), the trade mark of Pathé, who had dominated the Russian market before 1914, and the name of their mobile projector. Cf. G. M. Boltyanskii, 'Kino v derevne', in I. N. Bursak (ed.), *Kino* (1925), 33.
18 R. Marchand and P. Weinstein, *L'art dans la Russie nouvelle: le cinéma* (Paris, 1927), 110.
19 Radetskii, *passim* and N. Spiridovskii (ed.), *Gibel' fil'my. Porcha fil'my i mery preduprezhdeniya* (1927).
20 Boltyanskii, 'Kino v derevne', p. 33.
21 Katsigras, 'K voprosu', p. 18.
22 'Kinofikatsiya derevni', *Zhizn' iskusstva*, 11 May 1926. 1.
23 'K voprosu o kinofikatsii derevni', *Sovetskoe kino*, January 1925, 51; N. Yudin, 'Za derevenskii prokat "Sovkino"', *Zhizn' iskusstva*, 27 July 1926, 14; 'Kinofikatsiya derevni', 1.
24 Boltyanskii, 'Kino v derevne', p. 33.
25 Yudin, p. 14. Cf. S. Syrtsov and A. Kurs (eds.), *Sovetskoe kino na pod"ëme* (1926), 5.
26 *Ibid.*
27 Katsigras (ed.), *Kino-rabota*, p. 44.
28 G. M. Boltyanskii, *Kinokhronika i kak eë snimat'* (1926), 4, quotes a Communist Party resolution of

late 1925. See also: Lemberg, *Kino – derevne*, pp. 21–2, and 'Kinofikatsiya derevni', 1.

29 B. Gorn, 'Kino v derevne', *Novyi zritel'*, 21 June 1927, 3.

30 See ch. 6, n. 51 and pp. 119–23.

31 'Kinofikatsiya derevni', 1, and Lemberg, *Kino – derevne*, p. 21.

32 E. G. Lemberg, *Kinopromyshlennost' S.S.S.R. Ekonomika sovetskoi kinematografii* (1930), 164.

33 *Ibid.* p. 165. See also: 'Bol'noe mesto nashego kino-dela', *Zhizn' iskusstva*, 13 October 1925, 1, and I. Davydov, 'O tsentralizatsii kino-seti', *Novyi zritel'*, 15 August 1927, 8.

34 A. Gak, 'K istorii sozdaniya Sovkino', *Iz istorii kino*, 5 (1962), 141. See above, p. 81.

35 V. Il'inskii, *Byudzhet rabochikh S.S.S.R. v 1922–1926 godakh* (1928), 100. The figures are for November 1925.

36 *Novyi zritel'*, 29 September 1929, 8. Cf. above, p. 66.

37 Lemberg, *Kinopromyshlennost'*, pp. 202, 207.

38 B. Filippov, *Kino v rabochem klube* (1926), 29. As far as workers' clubs were concerned, Sovkino reached an agreement with V.Ts.S.P.S. (Vsesoyuznyi Tsentral'nyi Sovet Professional'nykh Soyuzov, the trade union organisation), on preferential tariff rates. See below, p. 92.

39 V. V. Mayakovskii, *Teatr i kino*, vol. 2 (1954), 441.

40 K. Shvedchikov, 'Sovkino', in Syrtsov and Kurs, pp. 16–45; Trainin, *Kino-promyshlennost'*, pp. 14, 17, 21.

41 S. Vyvodtsov, 'Kino v Uzbekistane', *Sovetskii ekran*, 30 August 1927, 14.

42 Vainshtok and Yakobzon, p. 62.

43 G. Chakhir'yan, 'Ocherk istorii kino Armenii' in Chakhir'yan (ed.), *Kinematografiya Armenii* (1962), 9–12.

44 K. D. Tsereteli, *Yunost' ekrana* (Tbilisi, 1965), 11.

45 M. Z. Rzaeva, *Dokumental'noe kino Azerbaidzhana* (Baku, 1971), 6–7.

46 *Ibid.* p. 17.

47 D. Teshabaev, *Kinoiskusstvo sovetskogo Uzbekistana* (1968), 3.

48 Vainshtok and Yakobzon, p. 60.

49 Filippov, *Kino v rabochem klube*, p. 6.

50 *Ibid.* pp. 12–13.

51 *Ibid.*

52 Lemberg, *Kinopromyshlennost'*, p. 93.

53 *Ibid.*

54 See above, p. 90.

55 K. Mal'tsev (ed.), *Sovetskoe kino pered litsom obshchestvennosti* (1928), 146.

56 Lemberg, *Kinopromyshlennost'*, p. 202.

57 Syrtsov and Kurs, pp. 71–6; Marchand and Weinstein, pp. 71–4.

58 *Proletkino*, 1923, no. 1/2 (May/June), 4.

59 *Proletarskoe kino*, 1 February 1925, 3.

60 A. Goldobin, 'Nashe kino i ego zritel'', *Novyi zritel'*, 10 February 1925, 6.

61 *Ibid.*

62 'Krizis nashego kinoproizvodstva', *Zhizn' iskusstva*, 10 August 1926, 1.

63 G. M. Boltyanskii, 'K fil'movomu golodu v predstoyashchem sezone', *Pravda*, 13 August 1926.

64 'Krizis nashego proizvodstva', 1.

65 Boltyanskii, *Pravda*, 13 August 1926.

66 I. Trainin, 'Nuzhno peresmotret' vospros', *Pravda*, 11 March 1926.

67 'Novye vekhi', *Sovetskii ekran*, 21 June 1927.

68 Trainin, *Kino-promyshlennost'*, p. 26; Lemberg, *Kinopromyshlennost'*, p. 34.

69 V. I., 'O nashem kinoprokate', *Pravda*, 11 September 1926.

70 V. Nedobrovo, 'Devyatimesyachnyi balans kino-ekrana', *Zhizn' iskusstva*, 7 July 1925, 10–11.

71 'Kino-propaganda', *Zhizn' iskusstva*, 3 November 1925, 1.

72 *Pravda*, 4 February 1926.
73 *Pravda*, 17 January 1926.
74 N. I. Kleiman and K. B. Levina (eds.), *Bronenosets Potëmkin* (1969), 1.
75 *Kino-gazeta*, 16 February 1926.
76 *Pravda*, 8 January 1926.
77 *Pravda*, 3 January 1926.
78 *Pravda*, 19 January 1926.
79 *Pravda*, 16 February 1926.
80 *Ibid.*
81 *Pravda*, 2 February 1926.
82 Kleiman and Levina, pp. 223–48.
83 *Pravda*, 12 May 1926. On 9 May *Pravda* reported that a special showing of the film had been arranged in Berlin for Douglas Fairbanks and Mary Pickford. Fairbanks had declared that *Potëmkin* was the 'most powerful film he had even seen', while his wife expressed herself 'profoundly moved by what she had seen'. Cf. A. Lagorno, 'Meri Pikford i Duglas Ferbenks o *Potëmkine*', *Sovetskii ekran*, 8 June 1928, 7.
84 See above, p. 94.
85 Kh. Khersonskii, 'Kinointerventsiya', *Pravda*, 2 June 1926. Cf. Lemberg, *Kinopromyshlennost'*, p. 82.
86 *Pravda*, 15 June 1926.
87 *Pravda*, 29 June 1926.
88 *Pravda*, 6 July 1926.
89 e.g. *Pravda*, 9 March 1926.
90 e.g. *Ibid.* It is particularly amusing to note that at this period the cinema advertisements in *Pravda* were placed next to those for private clinics for the treatment of venereal disease.
91 e.g. *Pravda*, 22 May 1926.
92 *Shagai, Sovet!* was reviewed in *Pravda* on 12 March 1926 but a correspondent complained on 16 May 1926 that it had still not been released. In the article cited in note 85 Khersonsky complained that, instead of re-releasing films like *Stachka* (Strike) or Vertov's *Kino-Glaz* (Cine-Eye), 'Our cinema screens, in summer even more than in winter, are hired out to the French bourgeoisie, to Italian beauties, to Piels, the tears of Veidt and other "trash".'
93 Lemberg, *Kinopromyshlennost'*, pp. 49–51.
94 *Ibid.* p. 39.
95 *Ibid.* p. 71.
96 e.g. V. Nedobrovo, 'K itogam kino-sezona', *Zhizn' iskusstva*, 15 June 1926, 19–20; K. Denisov, 'Meshchanstvo v kino', *Sovetskii ekran*, 29 January 1927, 3; A. Kayurov, 'Politika prokata Sovkino', *Novyi zritel'*, 8 February 1927, 13; N. Yakovlev, 'Sootnoshenie chastei', *Sovetskii ekran*, 12 February 1927, 3.
97 Lemberg, *Kinopromyshlennost'*, p. 85.
98 V. Nedobrovo, 'Pochemu net geroya v sovetskom kino?', *Zhizn' iskusstva*, 16 August 1927, 8.
99 V. Nedobrovo, 'Romantika byta v kino', *Zhizn' iskusstva*, 14 December 1926, 5.
100 *Sovetskie khudozhestvennye fil'my. Annotirovannyi katalog* (4 vols., 1961–8), vol. 1, p. 82.
101 *Ibid.* p. 215.
102 *Ibid.* pp. 202–3.
103 E. I. Shub, *Zhizn' moya – kinematograf* (1972), 470.
104 *Sovetskie khudozhestvennye fil'my*, p. 312.
105 *Ibid.* pp. 124–5.
106 *Ibid.* p. 147.
107 *Ibid.* pp. 285–6. See ch. 4, n. 50.
108 *Ibid.* pp. 224–5.
109 *Ibid.* p. 333.
110 *Ibid.* pp. 339–40.
111 *Ibid.* p. 408.
112 *Ibid.* pp. 246–7.
113 *Ibid.* p. 345.
114 *Ibid.* pp. 373–4.
115 *Ibid.* pp. 333–4.
116 *Ibid.* p. 230.
117 *Ibid.* p. 270–1.
118 N. P. Abramov, *Dziga Vertov* (1962), 165.

119 *Ibid.*
120 Shub, *Zhizn' moya*, pp. 249–50, 470.
121 *Kinoslovar'* (2 vols., 1966–70), vol. 2, p. 679.
122 N. Sats, 'Deti i kinematograf', *Novyi zritel'*, 14 October 1924, 6–8.
123 Continuation of same article in *Novyi zritel'*, 4 November 1924, 8.
124 N. Sats, 'Deti zhdut svoyu fil'mu', *Zhizn' iskusstva*, 9 March 1926, 3.
125 Vainshtok and Yakobzon, pp. 8–9.
126 *Ibid.* p. 44.
127 *Ibid.* p. 19.
128 *Ibid.* p. 10.
129 *Ibid.* The quotation in the last sentence is a reference to the resolution of the 13th Party Congress: N. A. Lebedev (ed.), *Partiya o kino* (1939), 67.
130 Vainshtok and Yakobzon, p. 11, show that 61.8 per cent of the Kharkov survey sample preferred the cinema to other forms of entertainment. The theatre came a poor second with 20.9 per cent.
131 *Ibid.* p. 12.
132 *Ibid.* p. 21.
133 *Ibid.* p. 22.
134 See below, pp. 124–51.
135 B. S. Ol'khovyi (ed.), *Puti kino. Pervoe Vsesoyuznoe partiinoe soveshchanie po kinematografii* (1929), 50.
136 L. M. Sukharebskii, *Nauchnoe kino* (1926), 45.
137 Trainin, *Kino-promyshlennost'*, p. 31.
138 Yu. S. Kalashnikov *et al.* (eds.), *Ocherki istorii sovetskogo kino* (3 vols., 1956–8), vol. 1, p. 78.
139 Quoted in the obituary for Dzerzhinsky published in *Novyi zritel'*, 27 July 1926, 5.
140 K. Yukov, 'K voprosu ob organizatsii kinematografistov', in Mal'tsev, *Sovetskoe kino*, p. 173. Cf. below, p. 150.
141 K. Mal'tsev, *Na pomoshch' sovetskomu kino* (1927), 3.
142 *Ibid.* p. 6.
143 *Ibid.*
144 *Ibid.* pp. 7, 11, 13; I. Potëmkin, 'O blizhaishchikh zadachakh O.D.S.K.', *Zhizn' iskusstva*, 6 April 1926, 5.
145 Mal'tsev, *Na pomoshch'*, p. 14; G. M. Boltyanskiii, 'Kino i sovetskaya obshchestvennost'', *Zhizn' iskusstva*, 7/10 November 1925, 15.
146 Mal'tsev, *Na pomoshch'*, pp. 15, 20–2.
147 *Ibid.* pp. 24–5. In the countryside O.D.S.K. was also expected to report back to the centre on the reception of films among rural audiences; Lemberg, *Kino–derevne*, p. 58.
148 i.e. Members of the Komsomol.
149 Gorn, p. 3.
150 *Ibid.* See above, p. 58.
151 Boltyanskii, 'Kino i sovetskaya obshchestvennost'', p. 15.

Chapter 6 The Party takes control

1 'K predstoyashchemu kinosoveshchaniyu', *Zhizn' iskusstva*, 27 September 1927, 1.
2 N. A. Lebedev, *Ocherk istorii kino S.S.S.R.*, 2nd edn. (1965), 261.
3 For an excellent introduction to this phenomenon see S. Fitzpatrick, 'Cultural Revolution in Russia, 1928–32', *Journal of Contemporary History*, 9 (1974), no. 1, pp. 33–52.
4 Lebedev, *Ocherk*, p. 263.
5 The conference was originally announced in *Pravda*, 6 January 1928, for 20 to 27 February, but on 10 January 1928 the paper announced, without explanation, a postponement until 10 March. The further postponement of the

opening session until 15 March was neither announced nor explained. It merely became apparent from the reports in *Pravda* on 15 March 1928.

6 The proceedings of the conference were published in B. S. Ol'khovyi (ed.), *Puti kino. Pervoe Vsesoyuznoe partiinoe soveshchanie po kinematografii* (1929), subsequently referred to as *Puti kino*.

7 *Sovetskii ekran*, 27 July 1926, 5.

8 The Russian word *obyvatel'* has two senses: 'man in the street' and 'philistine'. Here the word is obviously intended to be ambiguous.

9 Here again there is a play on words: '*potëmki*' in this phrase may be translated as 'mystery', but there is an obvious allusion to the title of the film *Potëmkin*.

10 See above, pp. 95–6

11 K. Denisov, 'Meshchanstvo v kino', *Sovetskii ekran*, 29 January 1927, 3.

12 A. Kayurov, 'Politika prokata Sovkino', *Novyi zritel'*, 8 February 1927, 13.

13 N. Yakovlev, 'Sootnoshenie chastei', *Sovetskii ekran*, 12 February 1927, 3.

14 *Novyi zritel'*, 13 September 1927, 14.

15 'K predstoyashchemu', 1.

16 F. Grinfel'd, 'K partsoveshchaniyu o kino-rabote', *Zhizn' iskusstva*, 6 December 1927, 5.

17 *Ibid.*

18 A. Piotrovskii, 'Budem maksimalistami!', *Zhizn' iskusstva*, 13 December 1927, 4.

19 *Ibid.*

20 P. Blyakhin, 'K partsoveshchaniyu', *Novyi zritel'*, 13 December 1927, 4.

21 B. Filippov, 'Zagadki Sovkino', *Zhizn' iskusstva*, 20 December 1927, 4–5.

22 A. Piotrovskii, 'Ob "ideologii" i "kommertsii"', *Zhizn' iskusstva*, 27 December 1927, 5.

23 A. Piotrovskii, 'Kino i pisateli', *Zhizn' iskusstva*, 17 January 1928, 6.

24 *Pyatnadtsatyi s"ezd V.K.P.(b). Dekabr' 1927 goda. Stenograficheskii otchët.* (1962), vol. 2, p. 1467.

25 *Pyatnadtsatyi s"ezd V.K.P. (b). Stenograficheskii otchët* (1928), 60.

26 e.g. by L. Vaks and N. Yudin, 'V bor'be s vodkoi', *Novyi zritel'*, 29 September 1929, 8–9.

27 *Ibid.*

28 'Tov. Lunacharskii o kino', *Zhizn' iskusstva*, 24 January 1928, 2.

29 *Ibid.*

30 See above, ch. 4, nn. 6 and 7.

31 M. Efremov, 'Organizatsionnye voprosy kino', *Zhizn' iskusstva*, 21 February 1928, 2.

32 M. Gartsman, 'U poroga kinostroitel'stva', *Zhizn' iskusstva*, 31 January 1928, 7.

33 *Trinadtsatyi s"ezd R.K.P.(b). 23–31 maya 1924 goda. Stenograficheskii otchët* (1924), 132. See above, p. 64.

34 *Puti kino*, p. 6.

35 *Ibid.* p. 9.

36 *Ibid.* pp. 9–10.

37 *Ibid.* p. 11.

38 *Ibid.*

39 *Ibid.* p. 19.

40 *Ibid.*

41 *Ibid.*

42 *Ibid.* p. 25.

43 *Ibid.* p. 28.

44 *Ibid.* p. 25.

45 *Ibid.* p. 26.

46 *Ibid.* p. 27.

47 *Ibid.* p. 29.

48 *Ibid.* p. 40.

49 *Ibid.*

50 *Ibid.* p. 37.

51 Shortly after the conference, one critic described Eisenstein's *Oktyabr'* as 'not easily accessible': T. Rokotov, 'Pochemu malodostupen *Oktyabr'*?', *Zhizn' iskusstva*, 10 April 1928, 16–17. Leonid Trauberg used Krinitsky's expression to mock Sovkino

in 'Eksperiment, ponyatnyi millionam', *Zhizn' iskusstva,* 1 January 1929, 14, while Eisenstein and Alexandrov used the same title to defend themselves against criticisms of their film *General'naya liniya* (The General Line) in *Sovetskii ekran,* 5 February 1929, 6–7.

52 *Puti kino,* p. 41.
53 *Ibid.* pp. 43–4.
54 *Ibid.* pp. 41–2. See above, p. 105.
55 *Puti kino,* p. 42.
56 *Ibid.* p. 32.
57 *Ibid.* p. 34.
58 *Ibid.* p. 31.
59 Savitsky, the delegate from G.T.K. (Gosudarstvennyi tekhnikum kinematografii, the state film school), also emphasised the need for active ideological guidance from the workers and peasants and alleged that there was a surfeit of aliens in the film industry; as evidence of this he cited seventeen recent arrests in the Mezhrabpom studios. *Ibid.* pp. 92–3.
60 *Ibid.* p. 69.
61 *Ibid.* p. 74.
62 Also known as *Tret'ya Meshchanskaya* (Third Meshchanskaya Street). See above, ch. 5, n. 116.
63 *Puti kino,* pp. 49–50.
64 *Ibid.* p. 66.
65 *Ibid.* p. 65.
66 *Ibid.*
67 *Ibid.* p. 139.
68 *Ibid.* p. 142.
69 *Ibid.* p. 144.
70 *Ibid.* p. 103.
71 e.g. Rafes, *Puti kino,* pp. 65–6; Trainin, *ibid.* pp. 137–8; and Shvedchikov, *ibid.* p. 157.
72 *Puti kino,* p. 161.
73 *Ibid.* p. 163.
74 *Ibid.* p. 188.
75 *Ibid.* p. 190.
76 *Ibid.* p. 209.
77 *Ibid.* p. 214.
78 *Ibid.* p. 216.
79 *Ibid.* p. 219.
80 *Ibid.* p. 222. Hence perhaps the riposte from Eisenstein cited in n. 51.
81 *Ibid.* p. 226.
82 See above, p. 109.
83 *Puti kino,* p. 227.
84 By Krinitsky in his report, *ibid.* p. 42; see above, p. 109.
85 *Puti kino,* p. 240.
86 *Ibid.* pp. 233–4.
87 *Ibid.* p. 235.
88 *Ibid.* p. 240.
89 *Ibid.* p. 254.
90 *Ibid.* pp. 241–2.
91 *Ibid.* p. 250.
92 *Ibid.* pp. 255–68.
93 *Ibid.* p. 256.
94 *Ibid.* p. 258.
95 *Ibid.*
96 *Ibid.* p. 259.
97 *Ibid.* p. 260.
98 *Ibid.* p. 275.
99 *Ibid.*
100 See above, p. 99.
101 *Ibid.* p. 281.
102 *Ibid.* pp. 381–93.
103 *Ibid.* p. 347.
104 *Ibid.* p. 348.
105 *Ibid.* p. 318.
106 *Ibid.* p. 319.
107 *Ibid.* p. 381.
108 *Ibid.* pp. 381–2.
109 *Ibid.* pp. 382–4.
110 *Ibid.* pp. 384–6.
111 *Ibid.* p. 388.
112 *Ibid.* pp. 389–90. See above, pp. 150–1.
113 *Puti kino,* pp. 389–90.
114 *Ibid.* p. 393.
115 *Ibid.* pp. 394–407.
116 *Ibid.* p. 395.
117 *Ibid.* p. 404.
118 *Ibid.* p. 405.
119 *Ibid.* p. 399.
120 Review by V. Muskin in *Sovetskii ekran,* 16 April 1926.
121 *Puti kino,* p. 400.
122 *Ibid.* p. 402.
123 *Ibid.* p. 401. Smirnov went on to assert that, as far as *Kino* was concerned, 'There is no countryside': *ibid.* p. 404.
124 *Ibid.* pp. 405–6.
125 *Ibid.* pp. 408–9.
126 *Ibid.* p. 412.

127 *Ibid.* p. 430.
128 *Ibid.* pp. 430–1.
129 *Ibid.* p. 430.
130 *Ibid.* p. 432.
131 *Ibid.* pp. 453–8.
132 *Ibid.* pp. 459–66.
133 *Ibid.* p. 453, n. 1; p. 459, n. 1.
134 *Ibid.* pp. 445–52.
135 *Ibid.* p. 445.
136 *Ibid.* p. 449.
137 See above, p. 94.
138 *Puti kino*, p. 445.
139 *Ibid.* pp. 447–8.
140 *Ibid.* p. 444.
141 *Ibid.* p. 431.
142 R. Pikel', 'Ot khvostizma k chëtkoi klassovoi linii', *Zhizn' iskusstva,* 3 April 1928, 2–3.
143 *Ibid.* p. 2.
144 *Ibid.*
145 *Ibid.*
146 *Ibid.* p. 3.
147 *Ibid.* Cf. Krinitsky's actual remarks in *Puti kino*, p. 229: 'The cinema now stands under the public gaze and the several cinema workers and other comrades are mistaken when they say that we are passing resolutions that will turn out to be mere scraps of paper, useless scraps that will be forgotten. It seems to me that we are all, without exception, united by a single thought: all Party organisations will systematically supervise and ensure in reality the fulfilment by cinema workers of these resolutions – what they are to do, how they are to fulfil the tasks that the Party has laid before the cinema.'
148 'Partiya i kino', *Kommunisticheskaya revolyutsiya*, 1928, no. 7 (April), 3.
149 *Ibid.* p. 6.
150 *Puti kino*, p. 260; see above, p. 113.
151 'Partiya i kino', pp. 8–9.
152 *Puti kino,* pp. 399–400; see above, p. 116.
153 'Sovetskaya kinematografiya – edinyi organizm', *Sovetskii ekran*, 3 April 1928, 3.
154 'Doloi!', *Sovetskii ekran*, 26 June 1928, 3.
155 V. Timofeev, 'Kinofikatsiya derevni', *Zhizn' iskusstva,* 10 April 1928, 3; 'Kinofikatsiya Leningradskoi oblasti', *Zhizn' iskusstva,* 29 July 1928, 1.
156 V. Timofeev, 'Za sovetskuyu kinoproektsionnuyu tekhniku', *Zhizn' iskusstva,* 14 October 1928, 1.
157 A. Piotrovskii, 'Detskoe kino pered novoi opasnost'yu', *Zhizn' iskusstva,* 14 October 1928, 6–7.
158 A. Piotrovskii, 'Kino 1928 goda', *Zhizn' iskusstva,* 4 November 1928, 9.
159 A. Piotrovskii, 'Est' li krizis v sovetskoi kinematografii?', *Zhizn' iskusstva,* 25 November 1928, 7.
160 *Potomok Chingis-khana*: see above, ch. 4, n. 50, and *Sovetskie khudozhestvennye fil'my. Annotirovannyi katalog* (4 vols., 1961–8), vol. 1, pp. 285–6.
161 *Novyi Vavilon*; *Sovetskie khudozhestvennye fil'my*, p. 333.
162 *Vesëlaya kanareika*; *Sovetskie khudozhestvennye fil'my*, p. 317.
163 *Prividenie, kotoroe ne vozvrashchaetsya*; *Sovetskie khudozhestvennye fil'my,* pp. 339–40.
164 Piotrovskii, 'Est' li', p. 6. Kozintsev, whom Piotrovsky attaches to the older generation, was only 24 when *Novyi Vavilon* was completed in 1929!
165 'Ob ukreplenii kadrov kino', in N. A. Lebedev (ed.), *Partiya o kino* (1939), 82–5.
166 *Ibid.* p. 82.
167 Lebedev, *Ocherk*, pp. 268–9.
168 Yu. S. Kalashnikov *et al.* (eds.), *Ocherki istorii sovetskogo kino* (3 vols., 1956–8), vol. 1, p. 228.
169 'Novyi kurs Sovkino', *Sovetskii ekran*, 8 January 1929, 6.
170 *Ibid.* p. 5.
171 P. Blyakhin, 'K itogam kinosezona 1927–8 goda', *Kino i kul'tura*, 1929, no. 2 (February), 4.
172 'Za sovetskii stsenarii', *Zhizn' iskusstva*, 24 March 1929, 1.
173 e.g. M. Gor'kii (ed.), *Belomorsko-*

Bal'tiiskii kanal imeni Stalina, cited in R. Hare, *Maxim Gorky: Romantic Realist and Conservative Revolutionary* (London, 1962), 219–21.
174 *Sovetskie khudozhestvennye fil'my,* pp. 75–6.
175 *Ibid.* pp. 82–3.
176 *Ibid.* pp. 215–16.
177 *Ibid.* p. 147.
178 *Ibid.* pp. 202–3.
179 *Ibid.* p. 333.
180 *Ibid.* pp. 195–6.
181 *Ibid.* p. 312.
182 P. Petrov-Bytov, 'U nas net sovetskoi kinematografii', *Zhizn' iskusstva,* 21 April 1929, 8.
183 *Ibid.*
184 *Ibid.*
185 *Ibid.*
186 A. Piotrovskii, 'Platforma Petrov-Bytova i sovetskaya kinematografiya', *Zhizn' iskusstva,* 12 May 1929, 4.
187 A. Piotrovskii, 'Zapadnichestvo v nashem kino', *Zhizn' iskusstva,* 30 June 1929, 7.
188 S. Podol'skii, 'Puti sovetskogo kino', *Zhizn' iskusstva,* 19 May 1929, 2.
189 I. Sollertinskii, 'Kino pod znakom rekonstruktsii', *Zhizn' iskusstva,* 4 November 1929, 9.
190 *XIV Vserossiiskii s"ezd sovetov. Stenograficheskii otchët* (1929), part 12, p. 11.
191 V. Vishnevskii, *25 let sovetskogo kino v khronologicheskikh datakh* (1945), 44, and V. Vishnevskii and P. Fionov, *Sovetskoe kino v datakh i faktakh* (1973), 58.

Chapter 7 Theory and film

1 T. Glebova, 'Dal'neishee', *Kino-Fot,* 10 December 1922, 3.
2 Lenin, *Polnoe sobranie sochinenii,* 5th edn, vol. 44 (1964), pp. 360–1. See above, p. 68.
3 *Leninskii sbornik,* vol. 35 (1945), p. 176.
4 Lenin also concerned himself with the use of instructional films for production purposes. Apart from *Gidrotorf* (see above, ch. 3, n. 72), he mentioned this aspect of the cinema in both 1920: *Polnoe sobranie sochinenii,* vol. 42 (1963), 16, and 1921: vol. 52 (1965), 136–7).
5 D. Vertov, 'My. Variant manifesta', *Kino-Fot,* 25–31 August 1922, 11–12.
6 D. Vertov, 'Kinoki. Perevorot', *Lef,* 1923, no. 3 (June/July), 135–43.
7 Vertov, 'My', p. 11.
8 *Ibid.*
9 *Ibid.*
10 *Ibid.*
11 *Ibid.* pp. 11–12.
12 *Ibid.*
13 *Ibid.*
14 A. Gan, 'Kinematograf i kinematografiya', *Kino-Fot,* 25–31 August 1922, 1.
15 Vertov, 'Kinoki', p. 137.
16 *Ibid.* pp. 140–1.
17 *Ibid.* p. 141.
18 *Ibid.* p. 143.
19 *Ibid.*
20 D. Vertov, 'Otvet na pyat' voprosov', *Kino-Gazeta,* 21 October 1924.
21 *Ibid.*
22 S. Drobashenko (ed.), *Dziga Vertov. Stati'i, dnevniki, zamysly* (Moscow, 1966), 317. The alternative title of the film was in fact *Zhizn' vrasplokh.*
23 V. Erofeev, 'Kino-glaz', *Kino-Gazeta,* 21 October 1924.
24 Drobashenko, p. 317.
25 I. V. Sokolov, '*Shestaya chast' mira*', *Kino-Front,* 1927, no. 2 (1 February), 9.
26 T. F. Seleznëva, *Kinomysl' 1920–kh. godov* (Leningrad, 1972), 42.
27 O. Brik, 'Protivokinoyadie', *Novyi Lef,* 1927, no. 2 (February), 28.
28 Vertov, 'Otvet'.

29 D. Vertov, 'Kino-glaz', in *Na putyakh iskusstva* (1925), 220.
30 Vertov, quoted in A. Belenson, *Kino segodnya. Ocherki sovetskogo kinoiskusstva.* (*Kuleshov – Vertov – Eizenshtein*) (1925), 36.
31 D. Vertov, 'Kino-glaz', *Pravda*, 19 July 1924.
32 Drobashenko, p. 317.
33 'Fil'me grozit opasnost'. Beseda s Dzigoi Vertovym', *Novyi zritel'*, 27 January 1929, 13.
34 D. Vertov, 'On i ya', *Kino-Fot*, 8–15 September 1922, 9–10.
35 D. Vertov, 'Kino-Pravda', *Kino-Fot*, 8 January 1923, 13.
36 A. Fevral'skii, 'Tendentsii iskusstva i "Radio-Glaz"', *Molodaya gvardiya*, 1925, no. 7 (July), 167.
37 O. Oten, 'Kinokam', *Kino-Fot*, 19–25 September 1922, 9.
38 N. Kaufman, 'Kinoki', *Sovetskii ekran*, 18 January 1929, 8–9.
39 G. M. Boltyanskii, *Kinokhronika i kak eë snimat'* (1926), 3.
40 Belenson, p. 11.
41 V. B. Shklovskii, 'Semantika kino', *Kinozhurnal A.R.K.*, 1925, no. 8 (August), 5.
42 *Ibid.*
43 *Ibid.*
44 *Ibid.*
45 V. B. Shklovskii, 'Kuda shagaet Dziga Vertov?', *Sovetskii ekran*, 10 August 1926, 4.
46 *Ibid.* Shklovsky reiterated this view in the booklet *Ikh nastoyashchee* (1927), 67.
47 V. B. Shklovskii, 'Sergei Eizenshtein i "neigrovaya fil'ma"', *Novyi Lef*, 1927, no. 4 (April), 34.
48 *Ibid.*
49 *Ibid.*
50 A. Anoshchenko, 'Kinokoki', *Kinonedelya*, 19 February 1924, 2.
51 G. M. Boltyanskii, 'Teoriya i praktika kinokov', *Sovetskoe kino*, 1926, no. 4/5.
52 E. I. Shub, 'Dokumental'noe kino. Dela i lyudi', from 'Krupnym planom', reprinted in *Zhizn' moya – kinematograf* (1972), p. 206. Cf. 'Pervye gody v kinematografe (1922–1930)', in *Zhizn' moya*, p. 83.
53 Seleznëva, *Kinomysl'*, p. 49.
54 Shub and Eisenstein re-edited the two parts of Fritz Lang's *Dr Mabuse der Spieler* (Dr Mabuse the Gambler) into a single film for distribution in Soviet Union.
55 V. B. Shklovskii, 'Ob Esfiri Shub i eë kinematograficheskom opyte', *Iskusstvo kino*, May 1969, 110.
56 *Ibid.* p. 115.
57 *Ibid.* p. 116.
58 Seleznëva, p. 49.
59 Seleznëva cites as an example the shot in *Velikii put'* (The Great Way) of Rockefeller, which Shub was unable to authenticate. *Ibid.* p. 51.
60 V. Pertsov, '"Igra" i demonstratsiya', *Novyi Lef*, 1927, no. 11/12 (November/December), 35.
61 Shub, 'Pervye gody', p. 85.
62 Shub, *Zhizn' moya*, p. 470.
63 See above, p. 68.
64 V. Pertsov, 'Sotsial'noe znachenie kartiny *Po zakonu*', *Kino-Front*, 1926, no. 9/10 (no date), 27.
65 Pudovkin's introduction to L. V. Kuleshov, *Iskusstvo kino* (1929), 3–4.
66 *Sovetskie khudozhestvennye fil'my. Annotirovannyi katalog* (4 vols., 1961–8), vol. 1, pp. 157–8. The film was released in the West under the title *Dura Lex.*
67 Arsen, 'Sotsial'noe znachenie kartiny *Po zakonu*', *Kino-Front*, 1926, no. 9/10 (no date), 31.
68 L. V. Kuleshov, 'Iskusstvo svetotvorchestva', *Kino*, 1918, no. 12.
69 L. V. Kuleshov, 'Kamernaya kinematografiya', *Kino-Fot*, 8–15 September 1922, 3.
70 V. I. Pudovkin, 'Masterskaya Kuleshova', *Iskusstvo kino*, January/February 1940, 85.
71 Belenson, pp. 19–20.

72 Kuleshov, *Iskusstvo kino,* p. 16.
73 *Ibid.* pp. 12–13.
74 Kuleshov, 'Kamernaya kinematografiya', p. 3.
75 Kuleshov, *Iskusstvo kino,* p. 20.
76 *Ibid.* p. 15.
77 L. V. Kuleshov, 'Amerikanshchina', *Kino-Fot,* 25–31 August 1922, 14–15.
78 Kuleshov, *Iskusstvo kino,* pp. 44–5.
79 A. Piotrovskii, *Khudozhestvennye techeniya v sovetskom kino* (Leningrad, 1930), 20.
80 L. Kuleshov, 'Pryamoi put'', *Kino-Gazeta,* 25 November 1924.
81 M. Levidov, *Chelovek i kino* (1927), 62–3.
82 L. V. Kuleshov, 'Chto nado delat'?', *Kino-Gazeta,* 26 September 1923.
83 *Sovetskie khudozhestvennye fil'my,* pp. 65–6.
84 M. Levidov, *Lev Kuleshov* (1927), 10–11.
85 Belenson, p. 24.
86 Kuleshov, *Iskusstvo kino,* p. 46.
87 *Ibid.*
88 Shklovskii, *Ikh nastoyashchee,* p. 7.
89 O. Rakhmanova, 'O metode vospitaniya aktëra', *Kinozhurnal A.R.K.,* 1925, no. 6/7 (June/July), 11.
90 *Ibid.*
91 *Ibid.*
92 *Ibid.*
93 Kuleshov, *Iskusstvo kino,* pp. 46–7.
94 L. V. Kuleshov, 'Chto nado delat'', *Kino i kul'tura,* 1930, no. 11/12 (November/December), 9.
95 *Ibid.* p. 12.
96 B. M. Eikenbaum (ed.), *Poetika kino* (1927).
97 S. M. Eizenshtein, *Izbrannye proizvedeniya* (6 vols., 1964–71), vol. 2, p. 277.
98 S. M. Eizenshtein, 'Chto govoryat o *Bronenostse Potëmkine*', *Sovetskii ekran,* 1926, no. 2, 10.
99 Seleznëva, p. 105.
100 *Sovetskie khudozhestvennye fil'my,* pp. 82–3.
101 *Ibid.* p. 345.
102 Eikhenbaum, p. 73.
103 Eizenshtein, *Izbrannye proizvedeniya,* vol. 2, p. 291.
104 Belenson, p. 54.
105 M. Seton, *Sergei M. Eisenstein* (London, 1952), 84.
106 S. M. Eizenshtein, 'Dva cherepa Aleksandra Makedonskogo', *Novyi zritel',* 31 August 1926, 10.
107 *Ibid.*
108 A. Gvozdev, 'Novaya pobeda sovetskogo kino. (*Bronenosets Potëmkin* i *Teatral'naya Oktyabr'*)', *Zhizn' iskusstva,* 26 January 1926, 8.
109 *Ibid.* pp. 7–8.
110 Piotrovskii, *Khudozhestvennye techeniya,* p. 24.
111 S. M. Eizenshtein, 'Perspektivy', *Iskusstvo,* 1928, no. 1/2 (January/February).
112 i.e. Moskovskii khudozhestvennyi akademicheskii teatr (Moscow Arts Theatre), associated above all with Stanislavsky.
113 Eizenshtein, 'Perspektivy'.
114 B. Balázs, *Der sichtbare Mensch oder die Kultur des Films* (Vienna, 1924).
115 S. Eizenshtein, 'Bela zabyvaet nozhnitsu', *Kino,* 6 June 1926.
116 *Ibid.*
117 Seleznëva, p. 141.
118 Belenson, pp. 63, 68; Shklovskii, *Ikh nastoyashchee,* p. 88; Piotrovskii, *Khudozhestvennye techeniya,* p. 30.
119 *Sovetskie khudozhestvennye fil'my,* pp. 215–16.
120 N. A. Lebedev, *Ocherk istorii kino S.S.S.R.,* 2nd edn. (1965), p. 323.
121 T. Rokotov, 'Pochemu malodostupen *Oktyabr'*?', *Zhizn' iskusstva,* 10 April 1928, 16.
122 Kh. Khersonskii, 'Ot *Stachki* k *Potëmkinu*', *Kinozhurnal A.R.K.,* 1926, no. 2 (February), 5.

123 *Sovetskie khudozhestvennye fil'my*, pp. 75–6.
124 'Preduprezhdenie', *Kinozhurnal A.R.K.*, 1925, no. 10 (October), 1–2.
125 N. K. Krupskaya, 'O fil'me *Oktyabr'*', *Pravda*, 9 February 1928.
126 L. Moussinac, *Le cinéma soviétique* (Paris, 1928), 161.
127 Quoted in Yu. Annenkov, *Dnevnik moikh vstrech. Tsikl tragedii* (2 vols., New York, 1966), vol. 1, p. 102.
128 *Ibid.* p. 103.
129 A. Karaganov, *Vsevolod Pudovkin* (Moscow, 1973), 24.
130 V. I. Pudovkin, 'Kak ya stal rezhissërom', reprinted in *Izbrannye stat'i* (1955), 41.
131 V. I. Pudovkin, *Kinostsenarii* (1926), 57.
132 *Sovetskie khudozhestvennye fil'my*, p. 147.
133 *Ibid.* pp. 202–3.
134 *Sovetskie khudozhestvennye fil'my*, pp. 285–6. See above, ch. 4, n. 50.
135 See above, n. 101.
136 V. Pudovkin, *Kinorezhissër i kinomaterial* (1926), 66.
137 *Ibid.* p. 62.
138 *Ibid.* p. 71.
139 S. M. Eizenshtein, V. I. Pudovkin, G. M. Aleksandrov, 'Zayavka', *Zhizn' iskusstva*, 5 August 1928, 4.
140 *Ibid.* p. 5.
141 V. I. Pudovkin, 'K voprosu zvukovogo nachala v fil'me', *Kino i kul'tura*, 1929, no. 5/6 (May/June), 3.
142 Karaganov, pp. 230–2.
143 V. B. Shklovskii, 'O rozhdenii i zhizni FEKS'ov', in V. Nedobrovo, *FEKS, Grigorii Kozintsov. Leonid Trauberg* (1928), 4.
144 *Ekstsentrizm. Sbornik statei* (Petrograd, 1922).
145 V. Nedobrovo, 'Ekstsentrizm FEKS'ov', in *Ekstsentrizm*, p. 7.
146 *Ibid.*
147 Kh. Khersonskii, *Stranitsy yunosti kino. Zapiski kritika* (1965), 17.
148 E. Dobin, *Kozintsev i Trauberg* (Leningrad, 1963), 14.
149 G. Kozintsev, *Glubokii ekran* (1971), 6.
150 *Ekstsentrizm*, p. 2.
151 *Ibid.*
152 Shklovskii in Nedobrovo, *FEKS*, p. 3.
153 *Ekstsentrizm*, p. 3.
154 *Ibid.* p. 4.
155 *Ibid.* pp. 3–4.
156 Khersonskii, *Stranitsy*, p. 115.
157 *Ekstsentrizm*, p. 1.
158 *Ibid.* p. 4.
159 Nedobrovo, *FEKS*, pp. 7–8.
160 *Ibid.* p. 9.
161 *Ibid.*
162 *Sovetskie khudozhestvennye fil'my*, p. 174.
163 *Ibid.* pp. 70–1.
164 *Ekstsentrizm*, p. 5.
165 Shklovskii in Nedobrovo, pp. 5–6.
166 Kozintsev, *Glubokii ekran*, p. 45.
167 *Ibid.* p. 52.
168 Shklovskii in Nedobrovo, p. 5.
169 Dobin, p. 21.
170 *Ibid.* p. 23.
171 Kozintsev, p. 97.
172 See above, n. 163.
173 Kozintsev, *Glubokii ekran*, p. 45.
174 S. A. Gerasimov, 'Fabrika ekstsentricheskogo aktëra', *Iskusstvo kino*, January/February 1940, 96–7.
175 Dobin, pp. 264–6.
176 *Ibid.* p. 267.
177 See above, n. 162.
178 *Sovetskie khudozhestvennye fil'my*, p. 124.
179 *Ibid.* pp. 175–6.
180 *Ibid.* pp. 224–5, and see above, p. 97.
181 *Ibid.* p. 333.
182 See above, n. 94.
183 *Sovetskie khudozhestvennye fil'my*, pp. 270–1.
184 *Ibid.* pp. 75–6.
185 Kozintsev, *Glubokii ekran*, p. 103.

186 B. Alpers, 'Put' FEKS'ov', *Kino i zhizn'*, 20 December 1929.
187 R. N. Yurenev in Yu. Kalashnikov *et al.* (eds.), *Ocherki istorii sovetskogo kino* (3 vols., 1956–8), vol. 1, p. 119.
188 See above, p. 115.
189 'Deklaratsiya Assotsiatsii revolyutsionnoi kinematografii', *Pravda*, 27 February 1924.
190 B. Gusman, 'Godovshchina Assotsiatsii revolyutsionnoi kinematografii', *Novyi zritel'*, 19 May 1925, 12.
191 'Deklaratsiya'.
192 *Ibid.*
193 Gusman, 'Godovshchina', p. 12.
194 See above, pp. 99–101.
195 N. Yakovlev, 'Nigilisty iz A.R.K.'a', *Sovetskii ekran*, 17 January 1928, 3.
196 I.K.S., 'Pyatiletie A.R.R.K. (1924–29 god)', *Novyi zritel'*, 26 May 1929, 14.

Chapter 8 Conclusions

1 B. S. Ol'khovyi (ed.), *Puti kino. Pervoe Vsesoyuznoe partiinoe soveshchanie po kinematografii* (1929), 430–1.
2 *Trinadtsatyi s"ezd R.K.P.(b). 23–31 maya 1924 goda. Stenograficheskii otchët* (1924), 132.
3 See, for instance, Marc Ferro's analysis of *Chapaev* (Chapayev), 'The fiction film and historical analysis', in P. Smith (ed.), *The historian and film* (Cambridge, 1976), 80–94.
4 *Trinadtsatyi s"ezd R.K.P.(b).*, pp. 702–3.
5 *Puti kino*, p. 431.
6 See above, p. 14.
7 See above, pp. 13–14.
8 *Izvestiya V.Ts.I.K.*, 2 September 1919.
9 A. M. Gak (ed.), *Samoe vazhnoe iz vsekh iskusstv. Lenin o kino*, 2nd edn. (1973), 52.
10 See above, pp. 70–2.
11 See above, pp. 77–82.
12 A. M. Gak, 'K istorii sozdaniya Sovkino', *Iz istorii kino*, 5 (1962), 131.
13 *Ibid.* pp. 143–4.
14 Fairbanks and Pickford were so popular that Soviet publications resorted to their opinions in order to boost *Potëmkin*: *Pravda*, 9 May 1926, and A. Lagorno, 'Meri Pikford i Duglas Ferbenks o *Potëmkine*', *Sovetskii ekran*, 8 June 1928, 7.
15 *Pravda*, 4 February 1926.
16 See above, pp. 95–6.
17 Winifred Bryher advised her readers to circumvent the British censorship by travelling abroad to see Soviet films: 'Don't "See England First", but make for the Ursulines, the Vingt Huit or Berlin next holiday. Judge for yourself what the censor considers unfitted for you. Then come back and decide whether this humiliating position accords with the traditions of England, which they proclaim they are keeping in surety.' Bryher, *Film problems of Soviet Russia* (Territet (Switzerland), 1929), 133.
18 A. Agadzhanova, '1905 god', *Sovetskii ekran*, 6 October 1925, 3–5.
19 Kh. Khersonskii, 'Kinointerventsiya', *Pravda*, 2 June 1926.
20 See above, pp. 96–7.
21 *Puti kino*, p. 431.
22 G. M. Boltyanskii, *Lenin i kino* (1925), 16–17. See above, ch. 2, n. 1.
23 See above, p. 102.
24 See above, ch. 3, n. 13.

BIBLIOGRAPHY

This bibliography contains details of the books, articles and other sources used the system of transliteration outlined on p. xiii. In the final section I below. Where no place of publication is given Moscow is the place. I have used the system of transliteration outlined on p. xiii. In the final section I have given page references to articles in periodicals but not in newspapers.

OFFICIAL DOCUMENTS

Party Congresses and Conferences
Congresses of Soviets
Other official or semi-official documents

BIBLIOGRAPHIES AND WORKS OF REFERENCE

UNPUBLISHED DISSERTATIONS AND THESES

BOOKS AND ARTICLES IN BOOKS

NEWSPAPERS AND PERIODICALS

OFFICIAL DOCUMENTS

Runs systematically examined
Articles specifically consulted

OFFICIAL DOCUMENTS

Party Congresses and Conferences

Sed'moi ekstrennyi s"ezd R.K.P.(b). Mart 1918 goda. Stenograficheskii otchët, 1962.

Vos'moi s"ezd R.K.P.(b). Mart 1919 goda. Protokoly. 1959.

Vos'maya konferentsiya R.K.P.(b). Dekabr' 1919 goda. Protokoly. 1961.

Devyatyi s"ezd R.K.P.(b). Mart – aprel' 1920 goda. Protokoly. 1960.

Desyatyi s"ezd Rossiiskoi Kommunisticheskoi Partii: Stenograficheskii otchët. (8–16 marta 1921g.). 1921.

Odinnadtsatyi s"ezd R.K.P.(b). Stenograficheskii otchët (27 marta–2 aprelya 1922g.). 1922.

Odinnadtsatyi s"ezd R.K.P.(b). Mart – aprel' 1922 goda. Stenograficheskii otchët. 1961.

Dvenadtsatyi s"ezd R.K.P.(b). 17–25 *aprelya 1923 goda. Stenograficheskii otchët.* 1968.

Trinadtsatyi s"ezd R.K.P.(b). 23–31 maya 1924 goda. Stenograficheskii otchët. 1924.

Trinadtsatyi s"ezd R.K.P.(b). Mai 1924 goda. Stenograficheskii otchët. 1963.

XIV S"ezd Vsesoyuznoi kommunisticheskoi partii (bol'shevikov), 18–31 dekabrya 1925g. Stenograficheskii otchët. 1926.

Pyatnadtsatyi s"ezd V.K.P.(b). Stenograficheskii otchët. 1928.

XV S"ezd Vsesoyuznoi kommunisticheskoi partii (bol'shevikov), 2 dekabrya – 19 dekabrya 1927 g. Stenograficheskii otchët, 2 vols. 1935.

Pyatnadtsatyi s"ezd V.K.P.(b). Dekabr' 1927 goda. Stenograficheskii otchët. 2 vols. 1961–2.
Shestnadtsataya konferentsiya V.K.P. (b). Aprel' 1929 goda. Stenograficheskii otchët. 1962.

Congresses of Soviets

S"ezdy sovetov R.S.F.S.R. v postanovleniyakh i resheniyakh. 1939.
1-i S"ezd Sovetov S.S.S.R. Stenograficheskii otchët s prilozheniyami. 1923.
Postanovleniya 1-ogo S"ezda Sovetov S.S.S.R. 1923.
II S"ezd Sovetov S.S.S.R. Stenograficheskii otchët. 1924.
Postanovleniya II S"ezda Sovetov S.S.S.R. 1924.
III S"ezd Sovetov S.S.S.R. Stenograficheskii otchët. 1925.
Postanovleniya III S"ezda Sovetov S.S.S.R. 1925.
IV S"ezd Sovetov S.S.S.R. Stenograficheskii otchët. 1927.
Postanovleniya IV S"ezda Sovetov S.S.S.R. 1927.
X Vserossiiskii s"ezd Sovetov rabochikh, krest'yanskikh, krasnoarmeiskikh i kazach'ikh deputatov R.S.F.S.R. (23–27 *dekabrya 1922 g.*). *Stenograficheskii otchët s prilozheniyami.* 1923.
XIV Vserossiiskii s"ezd sovetov. Stenograficheskii otchët. 1929.

Other official or semi-official documents

Deyatel'nost' Goskino – Tsentral'nogo Gosudarstvennogo organa Narkomprosa R.S.F.S.R. Okt. 1923–Okt. 1924. 1925.
Deyatel'nost' Vserossiiskogo kinematograficheskogo aktsionernogo obshchestva Sovetskoe kino 'Sovkino' s 1go. marta 1925g. po 1omu. oktyabrya 1927g. 1928.
Goskino. Obzor deyatel'nosti ot 1. oktyabrya 1923g. do 1. oktyabrya 1924g. 1925.
Narodnyi kommissariat po prosveshcheniyu. 1917 – Oktyabr' – 1920. (*Kratkii otchët*). 1920.
Otchët Vserossiiskogo Tsentral'nogo Soveta Professional'nykh Soyuzov za 1919 god. 1920.
Partiino-politicheskaya rabota v Krasnoi Armii. (*Aprel' 1918 – fevral' 1919*). *Dokumenty.* 1961.
Partiino-politicheskaya rabota v Krasnoi Armii. (*Mart 1919 – 1920gg.*). *Dokumenty.* 1964.
Puti kino. Pervoe Vsesoyuznoe partiinoe soveshchanie po kinematografii. (ed. B. S. Ol'khovyi). 1929.
Sbornik dekretov i postanovlenii raboche-krest'yanskogo pravitel'stva po narodnomu prosveshcheniyu. Vypusk vtoroi (*s 7. noyabrya 1918g. po 7. noyabrya 1919g.*). 1920.

BIBLIOGRAPHIES AND WORKS OF REFERENCE

Bøger om film. Copenhagen, 1961.
Boltyanskii, G. M. (ed.) *Kinospravochnik na 1926 god.* 1926.
Boltyanskii, G. M. (ed.) *Kino-spravochnik na 1927 god.* 1927.
Boltyanskii, G. M. (ed.) *Kinospravochnik na 1929 god.* 1929.
Dvadtsat' rezhissërskikh biografii. 1971.
Il'inskii, V. *Byudzhet rabochikh S.S.S.R. v. 1922–1926 godakh.* 1928.
Itogi desyatiletiya sovetskoi vlasti v tsifrakh 1917–1927. 1927.

Kinoletopis'. Annotirovannyi katalog kinozhurnalov i dokumental'nykh fil'mov ukrainskikh studii (1923–1941). Kiev, 1969.
Kinoslovar'. 2 vols. 1966–70.
Knigi o kino (1917–1960): Annotirovannaya bibliografiya. 1962.
Nadezhda Konstantinovna Krupskaya. Bibliografiya trudov i literatury o zhizni i deyatel'nosti. 1969.
Periodicheskaya pechat' S.S.S.R. *1917–1949g. Bibliograficheskii ukazatel'.* 8 vols. 1955–63.
Piliver, I. S. and Dorogokupets, V. G. *Sistema deistvuyushchego kino-zakonodatel'stva R.S.F.S.R.* 1929.
Propaganda i agitatsiya v resheniyakh i dokumentakh V.K.P.(b). 1947.
Répertoire mondiale des périodiques cinématographiques. Brussels, 1960.
Sovetskie khudozhestvennye fil'my. Annotirovannyi katalog. 4 vols. 1961–8.
Stsenaristy sovetskogo khudozhestvennogo kino, 1917–1967. Spravochnik. 1972.
Vishnevskii, V. *25 let sovetskogo kino v khronologicheskikh datak.* 1945.
Vishnevskii, V., and Fionov, P. *Sovetskoe kino v datakh i faktakh.* 1973.
Vsya kinematografiya. Nastol'naya adresnaya i spravochnaya kniga 1916g. 1916.

UNPUBLISHED DISSERTATIONS AND THESES

Bruce, S. (née Fitzpatrick) *The Commissariat of Enlightenment under Lunacharsky (1917–1921).* Oxford, 1969 (D.Phil. thesis).
Cohen, L. H. *The cultural–political traditions and developments of the Soviet cinema from 1917–1962.* Berkeley (California), 1973 (University of Southern California Ph.D. dissertation).
Durham, F. G. *Content and its control in the Russian and Soviet film.* Cambridge (Mass.), 1963 (M.A. dissertation).
Leaming, B. D. *Engineers of human souls: The transition to socialist realism in the Soviet cinema of the 1930s.* New York, 1976 (New York University Ph.D. dissertation).
Tait, A. L. *The literary works of A. V. Lunačarskij (1875–1933).* Cambridge, 1971 (Ph.D. thesis).

BOOKS AND ARTICLES IN BOOKS

Abramov, N. P. *Dziga Vertov.* 1962.
Abul-Kasymova, Kh. *et al.* (eds.). *Istoriya sovetskogo kino 1917–1967.* 4 vols. 1969–76.
Agel, H. *Les grands cinéastes que je propose.* Paris, 1967.
Akhrorov, A. *Tadzhikskoe kino (1929–1969).* Dushanbe, 1971.
Akimova, A. A. (ed.) *Adrian Piotrovskii. Teatr, kino, zhizn'.* Leningrad, 1969.
Aktëry sovetskogo kino. Vypusk 4-i. Leningrad, 1968.
Aleinikov, M. N. (ed.) *Yakov Protazanov.* 1957.
Aleinikov, M., and Ermol'ev, I. *Prakticheskoe rukovodstvo po kinematografii.* 1916.
Altenloh, E. *Zur Soziologie des Kino.* Jena, 1914.
Amengual, B. *V. I. Poudovkine.* Paris, 1968.
Andersen, T. *Vladimir Tatlin. Moderna Museets katalog nr 75.* Stockholm, 1968.
Andreev, L. 'Pis'mo o teatre', in *Polnoe sobranie sochinenii,* vol. 8. St Petersburg, 1913.

Andreeva, M. F. *Perepiska. Vospominaniya. Stat'i. Dokumenty. Vospominaniya o M. F. Andreevoi.* 1968.
Andreeva, M. S. *Kommunisticheskaya partiya – organizator kul'turno-prosvetitel'noi raboty v S.S.S.R. (1917–1933gg.).* 1963.
Annenkov, Yu. *Dnevnik moikh vstrech. Tsikl tragedii.* 2 vols. New York, 1966.
Anoshchenko, N. D. *Zvuchashchaya fil'ma v S.S.S.R. i za granitsei.* 1930.
Ardov, V. *Krupnym planom.* 1926.
Ardov, V. *Na stsene i – ryadom. Yumoristicheskie rasskazy i fel'etony o teatre i drugikh isskusstvakh.* 1962.
Aristarco, G. *Istorya teorii kino.* 1968.
Arlazorov, M. S. *Protazanov.* 1973.
Arossev, A. (ed.) *Soviet Cinema.* 1935.
Arts Council of Great Britain. *Art in Revolution. Catalogue.* London, 1971.
Artsybashev, V. *Fotokino Leningrad. Illyustrirovannyi spravochnik.* Leningrad, 1924.
Babel', I. *Bluzhdayushchie Zvëzdy.* 1926.
Babitsky, P. and Lutich, M. *The Soviet Movie Industry – Two Studies.* New York, 1953.
Babitsky, P. and Rimberg, J. *The Soviet Film Industry.* New York, 1955.
Bakun, V. A. and Sepman, I. V. (eds.) *Fridrikh Ermler. Dokumenty, stat'i, vospominaniya.* Leningrad, 1974.
Balázs, B. *Der Film. Werden und Wesen einer neuen Kunst.* Vienna, 1961.
Balázs, B. *Der sichtbare Mensch oder die Kultur des Films.* Vienna, 1924.
Bann, S. (ed.) *The Tradition of Constructivism.* London, 1974.
Barabash, Yu. Ya. *Dovzhenko. Nekotorye voprosy estetiki i poetiki.* 1968.
Barna, Y. *Eisenstein.* London, 1973.
Barshak, O. *Kino v derevne.* Leningrad, 1929.
Batalov, N. P. *Stat'i, vospominaniya, pis'ma.* 1971.
Belenson, A. *Kino segodnya. Ocherki sovetskogo kinoiskusstva. (Kuleshov – Vertov – Eizenshtein).* 1925.
Berest, B. *Istoriya ukrainskogo kina.* New York, 1962.
Bessy, M., and Lo Duca, G. *Georges Méliès. Mage.* Paris, 1961.
Birman, S. G. *Sud'boi darovannye vstrechi.* 1971.
Bleiman, M. Yu. *Pravda revolyutsii – pravda iskusstva.* 1961.
Bogdanov, A. A. *Elementy proletarskoi kul'tury v razvitii rabochego klassa.* 1920.
Bogdanov, A. A. *O proletarskoi kul'ture.* 1924.
Boitler, M. *Kino-teatr. Organizatsiya i upravlenie.* 1926.
Boitler, M. *Reklama i kino-reklama.* 1926.
Bojko, S. *New graphic design in revolutionary Russia.* London, 1972.
Boltyanskii, G. M. 'Kino v derevne', in I. N. Bursak (ed.), *Kino* (Moscow, 1925), p. 33.
Boltyanskii, G. M. *Kinokhronika i kak eë snimat'.* 1926.
Boltyanskii, G. M. *Kul'tura kinooperatora.* 1927.
Boltyanskii, G. M. *Lenin i kino.* 1925.
Borland, H. *Soviet literary theory and practice during the first Five-Year Plan, 1928–32.* New York, 1950.
Bratolyubov, S. *Na zare sovetskoi kinematografii. Iz istorii kinoorganizatsii Petrograda – Leningrada 1918–1925 godov.* Leningrad, 1976.
Breitburg, S. *Dooktyabr'skaya 'Pravda' ob iskusstve i literature.* 1937.
Brikhnichev, I. *Metody i formy agitatsii v oblasti likvidatsii bezgramotnosti.* 1920.

Brodskii, N. L., L'vov-Rogachevskii, V., and Sidorov, N. P. (eds.) *Literaturnye manifesty. (Ot simvolizma do 'Oktyabrya'). Sbornik materialov.* 1929.
Brodskii, N. L., and Sidorov, N. P. (eds.) *Ot simvolizma do 'Oktyabrya'.* 1924.
Brown, E. J. *The proletarian episode in Russian literature 1928–32.* New York, 1953.
Bryher, W. *Film problems of Soviet Russia.* Territet (Switzerland), 1929.
Burov, Ya. 'Voznikovnovenie, apparat i rabota agitparpoezdov V.Ts.I.K.' in V. Karpinskii (ed.), *Agitparpoezda V.Ts.I.K. Ikh istoriya, apparat, metody i formy raboty* (1920), p. 5.
Bursak, I. N. (ed.) *Kino: Sovetskaya kinematografiya.* 1925.
Butnik-Siverskii, B. S. *Sovetskii plakat epokhi grazhdanskoi voiny 1918–1921.* 1960.
Bychkova, N., and Lebedev, A. *Pervyi Narkom prosveshcheniya. (O A. V. Lunacharskom).* 1960.
Carr, E. H. *A history of Soviet Russia.* Harmondsworth, 1966–
Carter, H. *The new spirit in the cinema.* London, 1930.
Carter, H. *The new spirit in the Russian theatre 1917–28.* London, 1929.
Carter, H. *The new theatre and cinema of Soviet Russia.* London, 1924.
Carter, H. 'The Soviet cinema and the people: Their social unity', in Griffith, H. (ed.) *Playtime in Russia.* London, 1935.
Cervoni, A. *Marc Donskoï.* Paris, 1966.
Chaikovskii, V. *Mladencheskie gody russkogo kino.* 1928.
Chakhir'yan, G. (ed.) *Kinematografiya Armenii.* 1962.
Chipp, H. B. *Theories of modern art.* Berkeley (California), 1968.
Chukovskii, K. *Iz vospominanii.* 1958.
Chukovskii, K. *Nat Pinkerton i sovremennaya literatura.* 1910.
Cinémathèque Royale de Belgique. *Le film muët soviétique.* Brussels, 1965.
Constantine, M., and Fern, A. *Revolutionary Soviet film posters.* London, 1974.
Darracott, J., and Loftus, B., *First World War posters.* London, 1972.
Dement'ev, V. M. *Kinematograf kak pravitel'stvennaya regaliya.* Petrograd, 1915.
Diaz, P. *Asta Nielsen – eine Biographie.* Berlin, 1920.
Dickinson, T., and De La Roche, C. *Soviet cinema.* London, 1948.
Dobin, E. *Kozintsev i Trauberg.* Leningrad, 1963.
Doloi negramotnost'. Bukvar' dlya vzroslykh. 1920.
Dovzhenko, A. P. *Dovzhenkovi dumi.* Kiev, 1968.
Dovzhenko, A. P. *Sobranie sochinenii.* 4 vols. 1966–9.
Dovzhenko, A. P. *Tvori.* 3 vols. Kiev, 1958–60.
Dovzhenko, A. P. *'Ya prinadlezhu k lageryu poeticheskomu. . .' Stat'i, vystupleniya, zametki.* 1967.
Dovzhenko, A. P. *Život i delo. Zbornik članaka.* Belgrade, 1964.
Drobashenko, S. (ed.) *Dziga Vertov. Stat'i, dnevniki, zamysly.* 1966.
Dzidziguri, A., and Papava, A. *Cinematographic art in Soviet Georgia.* Tbilisi, 1976.
Eastman, M. *Artists in uniform.* London, 1934.
Eikhenbaum, B. M. (ed.) *Poetika kino.* 1927.
Eizenshtein, S. M. (Eisenstein, S. M.) *The Battleship Potemkin.* London, 1968.
Eizenshtein, S. M. (Eisenstein, S. M.) *The film sense.* London, 1968.
Eizenshtein, S. M. *Izbrannye proizvedeniya.* 6 vols. 1964–71. (ed. S. I. Yutkevich *et al.*)

Eizenshtein, S. M. *Izbrannye stat'i*. 1956.
Eizenshtein, S. M. (Eisenstein, S. M.) *Notes of a film director*. London, 1959.
Eizenshtein, S. M. and Yutkevich, S. I. *Materialy po istorii mirovogo kino-iskusstva – Griffit*. 1944.
Ekstsentrizm. Sbornik statei. Petrograd, 1922.
Elagin, Yu. *Ukroshchenie iskusstv*. New York, 1952.
Elkin, A. S. *Lunacharskii*. 1967.
El'kina, D. (ed.) *Likvidatoram negramotnosti. Prakticheskoe rukovodstvo*. 1921.
Eremin, D. *30 let sovetskoi kinematografii*. 1950.
Erenburg, I. *Fabrika snov*. Berlin, 1931. (Also published in German as: *Die Traumfabrik. Chronik des Films*. Berlin, 1931.)
Erenburg, I. *Materializatsiya fantastiki*. 1927.
Ermolaev, H. *Soviet literary theories, 1917–1934. The genesis of socialist realism*. Berkeley (California), 1963.
Fernandez, D. *Eisenstein*. Paris, 1975.
Filippov, B. *Kino v rabochem klube*. 1926.
Fitzpatrick, S. (ed.) *Cultural revolution in Russia, 1928–1931*. Bloomington (Indiana), 1978.
Fitzpatrick, S. *The Commissariat of Enlightenment. Soviet organization of education and the arts under Lunacharsky, October 1917–1921*. Cambridge, 1970. (See also: Bruce, S., thesis.)
Flint, R. W. (ed.) *Marinetti. Selected writings*. London, 1972.
Forestier, L. (Forest'e, L.) *'Velikii nemoi'. (Vospominaniya kinooperatora)*. 1945.
Freeman, J., Kunitz, J., and Lozowick, L. *Voices of October: Art and literature in Soviet Russia*. New York, 1930.
Fülöp-Miller, R. *Geist und Gesicht des Bolschewismus*. Vienna, 1926. Translated as *The Mind and Face of Bolshevism* (New York, 1927).
Futurismo 1909–1919. Exhibition of Italian Futurism. Newcastle upon Tyne/ Edinburgh, 1972.
Gabrilovich, E. I. *O tom, chto proshlo*. 1967.
Gafurova, K. A. *Bor'ba za internatsional'noe splochenie trudyashchikhsya Srednei Azii i Kazakhstana, 1917–1924gg*. 1972.
Gak, A. M. (ed.) *Samoe vazhnoe iz vsekh iskusstv. Lenin o kino*. 2nd edn. 1973.
Gak, A.M., and Glagoleva, N. A. (ed.) *Lunacharskii o kino*. 1965.
Gak, A. M. *et al.* (eds.) *Lenin. Sobranie fotografii i kinokadrov*. 2 vols.: *I. Fotografii. 1874–1923*. 1970. *II. Kinokadry. 1918–1922*. 1972.
Gardin, V. R. *Vospominaniya*. 2 vols. 1949–52.
Gavryushin, K. L. *Molodëzhi o kino*. 1930.
Gavryushin, K. L. (ed.) *Sovetskie kinoshkoly. Spravochnik dlya postupayushchikh v kinoshkoly S.S.S.R.* 1929.
Gavryushin, K. L. (ed.) *Spravochnik dlya postupayushchikh v kinotekhnikumy, -shkoly, -studii v 1926/27 uchebnom godu na osnovanii ofitsial'nykh dannykh kinouchebnykh zavedenii*. 1926.
Gerasimov, S. A. *Zhizn', fil'my, spory*. 1971.
Gibian, G., and Tjalsma, H. W. (eds.) *Russian Modernism. Culture and the avant-garde, 1900–1930*. Ithaca (N.Y.), 1976.
Ginzburg, S. S. *Kinematografiya dorevolyutsionnoi Rossii*. 1963.
Glagoleva, N. A. (ed.) *Mat'*. 1975.
Glagoleva, N. A. *Vsevolod Pudovkin*. 1968.
Gogolev, L. D. (ed.) *Kriz' kinoob"ektiv chasu. Spogadi veteraniv ukrains'kogo kino*. Kiev, 1970.

Goldobin, A. (ed.) *Kino na territorii S.S.S.R. (Po materialam provintsial'noi pressy).* 1924.

Golovnya, A. D. *Ekran – moya palitra.* 1971.

Golovskoi, V. (ed.) *Zvëzdy nemogo kino. Sbornik.* 1968.

Gorchakov, N. A. *The theater in Soviet Russia.* New York, 1957.

Gornitskaya, N. S. (ed.) *Iz istorii Lenfil'ma. Stat'i, vospominaniya, dokumenty. 1920-e gody. Vypusk I.* Leningrad, 1968.

Gornitskaya, N. S. (ed.) *Iz istorii Lenfil'ma. Stat'i, vospominaniya, dokumenty. 1920-e gody. Vypusk II.* Leningrad, 1970.

Gornitskaya, N. S. (ed.) *Iz istorii Lenfil'ma. Stat'i, vospominaniya, dokumenty. 1920-e – 1930-e gody. Vypusk III.* Leningrad, 1973.

Griffith, H. (ed.) *Playtime in Russia.* London, 1935.

Hare, R. *Maxim Gorky: Romantic Realist and Conservative Revolutionary.* London, 1962.

Herlinghaus, H. (ed.) *Der sowjetische Revolutionsfilm: Zwanziger und dreissiger Jahre. Eine Dokumentation.* Berlin (G.D.R.), 1967.

Huaco, G. A. *The sociology of film art.* New York, 1965.

Iezuitov, N. *Aktëry M.Kh.A.T.'a v kino.* 1938.

Iezuitov, N. *Gardin.* 1940.

Iezuitov, N. *Pudovkin. Puti tvorchestva.* 1937.

Inkeles, A. *Public opinion in Soviet Russia.* Cambridge (Mass.), 1950.

Ivanovskii, A. V. *Vospominaniya kinorezhissëra.* 1967.

Iz istorii Grazhdanskoi voiny v S.S.S.R. Sbornik dokumentov. Vol. 3. 1961.

Iz istorii sovetskoi esteticheskoi mysli. Sbornik statei. 1967.

Iz istorii stroitel'stva sovetskoi kul'tury. Moskva 1917–1918gg. 1964.

Kalashnikov, Yu. S., Lebedev, N. A., Pogozheva, L. P., and Yurenev, R. N. (eds.) *Ocherki istorii sovetskogo kino.* 3 vols. 1956–8.

Karaganov, A. *Vsevolod Pudovkin.* 1973.

Karpinskii, V. (ed.) *Agitparpoezda V.Ts.I.K. Ikh istoriya, apparat, metody i formy raboty. Sbornik statei.* 1920.

Katsigras, A. I. *Chto takoe kino. Pochemu figury dvizhutsya na ekrane.* 1926.

Katsigras, A. I. (ed.) *Kino-rabota v derevne.* 1925.

Kerr, A. *Russische Filmkunst.* Berlin, 1927.

Kerzhentsev, P. M. *K novoi kul'ture.* Petrograd, 1921.

Kerzhentsev, P. M. *Kul'tura i sovetskaya vlast'.* 1919.

Kerzhentsev, P. M. *Revolyutsiya i teatr.* 1918.

Khaichenko, G. A. *Igor' Il'inskii.* 1962.

Khanzhonkov, A. A. *Pervye gody russkoi kinematografii. Vospominaniya.* 1937.

Kheifits, I. *O kino.* Leningrad, 1966.

Khersonskii, Kh. *Stranitsy yunosti kino. Zapiski kritika.* 1965.

Kinematograf. Sbornik statei. 1919.

Kinooperator Andrei Moskvin. Sbornik. Leningrad, 1971.

Klaue, W., and Lichtenstein, M. (eds.) *Sowjetischer Dokumentarfilm.* Berlin (G.D.R.), 1967.

Kleiman, N. I., and Levina, K. B. (eds.) *Bronenosets Potëmkin.* 1969.

Kogan, P. S. *Proletarskaya literatura.* Ivanovo-Voznesensk, 1926.

Kol'tsov, A. V. *Kul'turnoe stroitel'stvo v R.S.F.S.R. v gody pervoi pyatiletki (1928–1932).* 1960.

Konlechner, P., and Kubelka, P. (eds.) *Sergej Michaelowitsch Eisenstein. Eine Übersicht.* Vienna, 1964.

Kozintsev, G. M. *Glubokii ekran.* 1971.

Kozintsev, G. M. *Rasskaz o tvorcheskom puti.* 1967.

Krasinskii, A. V. *Yurii Tarich.* Minsk, 1971.

Kravchenko, G. *Mozaika proshlogo.* 1971.
Krinitskii, A. I. *Zadachi sovetskogo kino.* 1929.
Krupskaya, N. K. *Na tret'em fronte.* 1927.
Krupskaya, N. K. *Pedagogicheskie sochineniya*, vol. 11, 1963.
Krupskaya, N. K. *Politprosvetrabota.* 1932.
Krupskaya, N. K. *Vospominaniya o Lenine.* 1957.
Kryuchechnikov, N. V. *Slovo v fil'me.* 1964.
Kubelikov, E. *Kinoiskusstvo Azerbaidzhana.* Baku, 1960.
Kühn, G., Tümmler, K., and Wimmer, W. *Film und revolutionäre Arbeiterbewegung in Deutschland 1918–1932.* 2 vols. Berlin (G.D.R.), 1975.
Kuleshov, L. V. *Azbuka kinorezhissury.* 1968.
Kuleshov, L. V. *Iskusstvo kino.* 1929.
Kuleshov, L. V. *Repetitsionnyi metod v kino.* 1935.
Kuleshov, L. V. 'Volya. Uporstvo. Glaz', in *Eizenshtein. 'Bronenosets Potëmkin'.* 1926.
Kumanev, V. A. *Sotsializm i vsenarodnaya gramotnost'.* 1967.
Kurbatov, Ya. *Svet nad barkhanami. (Sem' rasskazov o kinoiskusstve Sovetskogo Turkmenistana).* 1972.
Kurs, A. *Samoe mogushchestvennoe.* 1927.
Kuste, E. *Kino i ego chudesa. Sovremennyi kinematograf, ego dostizheniya i tekhnika.* Leningrad, 1925.
Kutasov, I. Ya. *Nagladnaya agitatsiya.* 1962.
Kuznetsov, I. V., and Fingerit, E. M. *Gazetnyi mir Sovetskogo Soyuza 1917–1970gg.* Vol. 1. 1972.
Lazaris, G. V. *Kino na sluzhbu uchebe.* 1930.
Lebedev, A. A. (ed.) *Kinokamera pishet istoriyu.* 1971.
Lebedev, N. A. *K voprosu o spetsifike kino.* 1935.
Lebedev, N. A. *Kinematograf v dorevolyutsionnoi Rossii. (Konspekty lektsii).* 1958.
Lebedev, N. A. *Kino i zritel'. (Zametki kinoveda).* 1969.
Lebedev, N. A. (ed.) *Lenin, Stalin, partiya o kino.* 1938.
Lebedev, N. A. *Ocherk istorii kino S.S.S.R. Nemoe kino (1918–1934).* 2nd edn. 1965.
Lebedev, N. A. (ed.) *Partiya o kino.* 1939.
Lebedev, N. A. *Stanovlenie sovetskogo kinoiskusstva (1921–1925). (Konspekty lektsii).* 1960.
Lebedev, N. A. *Vnimanie: kinematograf!* 1974.
Lebedev, N. A. *Vozniknovenie sovetskogo kino (1918–1921). (Konspekty lektsii).* 1959.
Lebedev, S. S. *Lenta pamyati. Vospominaniya kinooperatora.* 1974.
Lemberg, E. G. *Kino – derevne. Kak ustroit' kino v derevne.* 1929.
Lemberg, E. G. *Kinopromyshlennost' S.S.S.R. Ekonomika sovetskoi kinematografii.* 1930.
Lenin, V. I. *Polnoe sobranie sochinenii.* 5th edn. 55 vols. 1958–65.
Lenin and Stalin on propaganda. Little Lenin Library, vol. 24. London, 1942.
Lenin o kino. See: Gak. A. M.
Lenin o kul'ture i iskusstve. 1956. See also: Lifshits, M. I.
Lenin o literature i iskusstve. 1960.
Lenin o propagande i agitatsii. 1957.
Lenin on culture and cultural revolution. 1970.
Lenin, revolyutsiya, teatr. Dokumenty i vospominaniya. Leningrad, 1970.
Lenin über Agitation und Propaganda. Berlin (G.D.R.), 1974.
Leninskii sbornik, vol. 35, 1945.

Levaco, R. (ed.) *Kuleshov on film. Writings by L. Kuleshov*. London, 1974.
Levidov, M. *Chelovek i kino: estetiko–sotsiologicheskii etyud*. 1927.
Levidov, M. *Lev Kuleshov. Ocherk kino–rezhissërskoi raboty*. 1927.
Levitskii, A. A. *Rasskazy o kinematografe*. 1964.
Leyda, J. *Films beget films*. London, 1964.
Leyda, J. *Kino. A history of the Russian and Soviet film*. London, 1960.
Lifshits, M. I. (ed.) *Lenin o kul'ture i iskusstve*. 1938.
Likhachëv, B. S. *Kino v Rossii (1896–1926). Materialy k istorii russkogo kino. Chast' 1: 1896–1913*. Leningrad, 1927.
Lintsbakh, Ya. *Printsipy filosofskogo yazyka. Opyt tochnogo yazykoznaniya*. Petrograd, 1916.
Listov, V. *Istoriya smotrit v ob"ektiv*. 1974.
London, K. *The seven Soviet arts*. London, 1937.
Lorenz, R. (ed.) *Proletarische Kulturrevolution in Sowjetrussland (1917–1921)*. Munich, 1969.
Low, R., and Manvell, R. *The history of the British film 1896–1906*. London, 1948.
Low, R., and Manvell, R. *The history of the British film 1906–1914*. London, 1948.
Low, R. *The history of the British film 1914–1918*. London, 1948.
Low, R. *The history of the British film 1918–1929*. London, 1971.
Lüdecke, W. *Der Film in Agitation und Propaganda der revolutionären deutschen Arbeiterbewegung (1919–1933)*. Berlin, 1973.
Lukács, G. *Schriften zur Literatursoziologie*. Neuwied, 1961.
Lunacharskaya-Rozenel', N. A. *Pamyat' serdtsa*. 1965.
Lunacharskii, A. V. (Lunatscharsky, A. W.) *Der russische Revolutionsfilm*. Zurich, 1929.
Lunacharskii, A. V. *Kino na zapade i u nas*. Leningrad, 1928.
Lunacharskii, A. V. *Neizdannye materialy*. Literaturnoe nasledstvo, vol. 82. 1970.
Lunacharskii o kino. See: Gak, A. M.
Lunacharskii, A. V. *Stat'i o sovetskoi literature*. 1971.
Lunacharskii, A. V. *Stat'i, vyskazyvaniya, stsenarii, dokumenty*. 1965.
L'vov, A. *Kinematograficheskaya yazva izlechima*, 1924.
Lyakhov, V. N. *Sovetskii reklamnyi plakat 1917–1932*. 1972.
Maksakova, L. V. *Agitpoezd 'Oktyabr'skaya Revolyutsiya' (1919–20gg.)*. 1956.
Mal'tsev, K. *Na pomoshch' sovetskomu kino*. 1927.
Mal'tsev, K. (ed.) *Sovetskoe kino pered litsom obshchestvennosti. Sbornik diskussionnykh statei*. 1928.
Malyshev, M. O. *Za zemlyu, za mir i volyu 1918–1922*. Leningrad, 1971.
Marchand, R., and Weinstein, P. *L'art dans la Russie nouvelle: le cinéma*. Paris, 1927.
Marinetti, F. T. *Teoria e invenzione futurista*. Milan, 1968.
Markov, V. *Russian Futurism*. London, 1969.
Marshall, H. *Soviet cinema*. London, 1945.
Mayakovskii, V. V. *Kino*. 1940.
Mayakovskii, V. V. *Teatr i kino*. 2 vols. 1954.
Mazaev, A. I. *Kontseptsiya 'proizvodstvennogo iskusstva' 20-kh. godov*. 1975.
Meierkhol'd, V. E. *O teatre*. St Petersburg, 1913.
Meierkhol'd, V. E. *Stat'i, pis'ma, rechi, besedy*. 2 vols. 1968.
Mesguich, F. *Tours de manivelle: Souvenirs d'un chasseur d'images*. Paris, 1933.

Mierau, F. *Links! Links! Links! Eine Chronik in Vers und Plakat 1917–1921.* Berlin (G.D.R.), 1970.
Mitry, J. *Ivan Mosjoukine 1889–1939*. Paris, 1969.
Mitry, J. *S. M. Eisenstein*. Paris, 1961.
Mogilëvskii, A. I., Filippov, V., and Rodionov, A. M. *Treaty Moskvy 1917–1927gg.* 1928.
Moholy-Nagy, L. *Painting, photography, film*. London, 1969.
Moldavskii, D. *S Mayakovskim v teatre i kino. Kniga o Sergee Yutkeviche.* 1975.
Monaco, P. *Cinema and Society. France and Germany during the Twenties.* New York, 1976.
Montagu, I. *With Eisenstein in Hollywood.* Berlin (G.D.R.), 1968.
Moussinac, L. *Le cinéma soviétique*. Paris, 1928.
Moussinac, L. *Sergei Eisenstein*. New York, 1970.
Münzenberg, W. *Fünf Jahre Internationale Arbeiterhilfe*. Berlin, 1926.
Mur, L. *Fabrika serykh tenei. (Den' kino-fabriki)*. 1927.
Muratov, L. G. *Aleksandr Ivanov*. Leningrad, 1968.
Na putyakh iskusstva. 1925.
Nazarov, A. V. *Kino*. 1925.
Nedobrovo, V. *FEKS. Grigorii Kozintsov, Leonid Trauberg*. 1928.
Nesterovich, O. T. *Zhizn' v kino. Veterany o sebe i svoikh tovarishchakh.* 1971.
Nestrikh, M., *Kino i obshchedostupnost' lektsii*. 1924.
Nilsen, V. *The cinema as graphic art*. London, 1937.
Novozhilova, L. I. *Sotsiologiya iskusstva. (Iz istorii sovetskoi estetiki 20-kh. godov)*. Leningrad, 1968.
Oms, M. *Grigori Kozintsev*. Paris, 1976.
Ozerov, I. Kh. *Na novyi put'! K ekonomicheskomu osvobozhdeniyu Rossii.* 1915.
Pavlov, G. N. *Sovetskii politicheskii plakat*. Leningrad, 1973.
Pazhitnova, L. I. *Mark Donskoi. Sbornik*. 1973.
Piltz, G. *Russland wird rot. Satirische Plakate 1918–1922*. Berlin (G.D.R.), 1977.
Piotrovskii, A. *Khudozhestvennye techeniya v sovetskom kino*. Leningrad, 1930.
Pisarevskii, D. S. *Iskusstvo millionov*. 1958.
Plachinda, S. P. *Oleksandr Dovzhenko: Zhittya i tvorchist'*. Kiev, 1964.
Plekhanov, G. V. *Iskusstvo i literatura*. 1948.
Plekhanov, G. V. *O zadachakh sotsialistov v bor'be s golodom v Rossii. (Pis'ma k molodym tovarishcham)*. Geneva, 1892.
Pogozheva, L. P. *Mikhail Romm*. 1967.
Poluyanov, P. *Gibel' teatra i torzhestvo kino*. Nizhny Novgorod, 1925.
Polyanovskii, M. L. *My vidim Il'icha*. 1969.
Polyanovskii, M. L. *Poet na ekrane. (Mayakovskii – kinoaktër)*. 1958.
Poznanskaya, L. (ed.) *Iz istorii kino*. 1967.
Pudovkin, V. I. *Aktër v fil'me*. Leningrad, 1934.
Pudovkin, V. I. *Film technique and film acting*. London, 1929.
Pudovkin, V. I. *Izbrannye stat'i*. 1955.
Pudovkin, V. I. *Kak ya stal rezhissërom*. 1946.
Pudovkin, V. I. *Kinorezhissër i kinomaterial*. 1926.
Pudovkin, V. I. *Kinostsenarii*. 1926.
Pudovkin, V. I. *On film technique*. London, 1929.
Pudovkin, V. I. *Sobranie sochinenii*. 3 vols. 1974–6.
Rachuk, I. A. *Oleksandr Dovzhenko*. Kiev, 1964.

Rachuk, I. A. *Poetika Dovzhenko.* 1964.
Radetskii, P. S. *Peredvizhnoi kinematograf.* Leningrad, 1926.
Rafail, M. *Za novogo cheloveka.* Leningrad, 1928.
Romanov, A. V. *Kinoiskusstvo i sovremennost'.* 1968.
Romanov, A. V. *Nemerknushchii ekran. Zapiski zhurnalista.* 1973.
Romm, M. I. *Besedy o kino.* 1964.
Roshal', G. L. *Kinolenta zhizni.* 1974.
Roshal', L. M. *Mir i igra.* 1973.
Rosolovskaya, V. *Russkaya kinematografiya v 1917g. Materialy k istorii.* 1937.
Rostovtsev, I. G. *Bronenosets 'Potëmkin'.* 1962.
Rotha, P. *The film till now.* London, 1967.
Rotha, P. *et al. Eisenstein 1898–1948.* London, 1948.
Rozen, S. G. *Grigorii Roshal'.* 1965.
Rühle, J. *Literature and revolution. A critical study of the writer and communism in the twentieth century.* London, 1969.
Rybakova, O. *Komissarzhevskaya.* Leningrad, 1971.
Rye, J. *Futurism.* London, 1972.
Rynin, N. A. *Kinematografiya.* Leningrad, 1924.
Rzaeva, N. Z. *Dokumental'noe kino Azerbaidzhana.* Baku, 1971.
Sadoul, G. *Histoire du cinéma mondial des origines à nos jours.* Paris, 1949.
Sadoul, G. *Histoire générale du cinéma. I. L'invention du cinéma, 1832–1897.* Paris, 1946.
Schlemmer, O., Moholy-Nagy, L., and Molnar, F. *The theater of the Bauhaus.* Middletown (Conn.), 1961.
Schnitzer, L. and J. *Alexandre Dovjenko.* Paris, 1966.
Schnitzer, L. and J. *Le cinéma soviétique par ceux qui l'ont fait.* Paris, 1966. Translated as: *Cinema in revolution.* London, 1973.
Schnitzer, L. and J. *Vsevolod Poudovkine.* Paris, 1966.
Seleznëva, T. F. *Kinomysl' 1920-kh. godov.* Leningrad, 1972.
Seton, M. *Sergei M. Eisenstein.* London, 1952. 2nd edn. London, 1978.
Shaporenko, T. P. *Chetyre vstrechi.* 1962.
Shcherbak, V. M. *Bol'shevistskaya agitatsiya i propaganda (Oktyabr' 1917 – mart 1919gg.).* 1969.
Shchukin, B. V. *Stat'i, vospominaniya, materialy.* 1965.
Shklovskii, V. B. *Chaplin,* Berlin, 1923.
Shklovskii, V. B. 'Eizenshtein', in *Eizenshtein. 'Bronenosets Potëmkin'.* 1926.
Shklovskii, V. B. *Eizenshtein.* 1973.
Shklovskii, V. B. *Kak pisat' stsenarii.* 1931.
Shklovskii, V. B. *Ikh nastoyashchee.* 1927.
Shklovskii, V. B. *Literatura i kinematograf.* Berlin, 1923.
Shklovskii, V. B. *Motalka. O kino-remesle. Knizhka ne dlya kinematografistov.* 1927.
Shklovskii, V. B. 'O rozhdenii i zhizni FEKS'ov', in V. Nedobrovo, *FEKS, Grigorii Kozintsov. Leonid Trauberg* (1928), 3–6.
Shklovskii, V. B. *O teorii prozy.* 1929.
Shklovskii, V. B. *Puteshestvie v stranu kino.* 1926.
Shklovskii, V. B. *Room. Zhizn' i rabota.* 1929.
Shklovskii, V. B. (Schklowskij, V. B.) *Schriften zum Film.* Frankfurt am Main, 1966.
Shklovskii, V. B. *Tetiva. O neskhodstve skhodnogo.* 1970.
Shklovskii, V. B. *Tret'ya fabrika.* 1926.
Shklovskii, V. B. *Za sorok let.* 1965.
Shklovskii, V. B. *Zhili – byli.* 1966.

Shklovskii, V. B., and Eizenshtein, S. M. A. *Khokhlova*. 1926.
Shub, E. I. *Zhizn' moya – kinematograf*. 1972.
Shub, E. I. 'Pervye gody v kinematografe (1922–1930)' in *Zhizn' moya*, pp. 66–105.
Shutko, K. I. (ed.) *Kul'turfil'ma*. 1929.
Smirnov, A. S. *Agitatsiya i propaganda bol'shevikov v derevne v period podgotovki Oktyabr'skoi Revolyutsii (Mart-Oktyabr' 1917g.)*. 1957.
Smirnov, I. S. *Lenin i sovetskaya kul'tura. Gosudarstvennaya deyatel'nost' V. I. Lenina v oblasti kul'turnogo stroitel'stva (oktyabr' 1917g. – leto 1918g.)*. 1960.
Smith, P. (ed.) *The historian and film*. Cambridge, 1976.
Sobolëv, R. P. *Lyudi i fil'my russkogo dorevolyutsionnogo kino*. 1961.
Sobolëv, R. P. *Yurii Zhelyabuzhskii*. 1963.
Socialist Realism in literature and art. 1971.
Sokolov, I. V. (ed.) *Istoriya sovetskogo kinoiskusstva zvukovogo perioda*. 2 vols. 1946.
Solntseva, Yu. I. *Aleksandr Dovzhenko. Kinorezhissër, pisatel', khudozhnik*. 1972.
Solntseva, Yu. I., and Mar'yamov, G. A. *Dovzhenko. 'Zemlya'. Kniga – fil'm*. 1966.
Solntseva, Yu. I., and Pazhitnova, L. I. (eds.) *Arsenal*. 1977.
Sorlin, P., and Ropars-Wuilleumier, M.-C. *Octobre. Ecriture et idéologie. I. Analyse filmique*. Paris, 1976.
Speranskaya, E. A. (ed.) *Agitatsionno-massovoe iskusstvo pervykh let Oktyabrya. Materialy i issledovaniya*. 1971.
Spiridovskii, N. (ed.) *Gibel' fil'my. Porcha fil'my i mery preduprezhdeniya*. 1927.
Stalin, J. V. *Sochineniya*. 13 vols. 1946–51.
Stepanov, N. Ya. *Zametki po iskusstvu kino-ekrana*. Vladivostok, 1928.
Strakhov, A. I. *Azbuka revolyutsii*. Kiev, 1969.
Sudendorf, W. *Sergej M. Eisenstein. Materialien zu Leben und Werk*. Munich, 1975.
Sukharebskii, L. M. *Nauchnoe kino*. 1926.
Swallow, N. *Eisenstein. A documentary portrait*. London, 1976.
Syrtsov, S., and Kurs, A. (eds.) *Sovetskoe kino na pod"ëme*. 1926.
Tairov, A. *Zapiski rezhissëra*. 1921.
Teshabaev, D. *Kinoiskusstvo sovetskogo Uzbekistana*. 1968.
Thomson, B. *The premature revolution. Russian literature and society 1917–1946*. London, 1972.
Timoshenko, S. A. *Iskusstvo kino i montazh fil'ma*. Leningrad, 1926.
Tisse, E. 'Tekhnika s"ëmki 'Bronenostsa Potëmkina'', in *Eizenshtein. 'Bronenosets Potëmkin'*. 1926.
Trainin, I. *Kino-promyshlennost' i Sovkino*. 1925.
Trotskii, L. (Trotsky, L.) *Problems of life*. London, 1924. Reprinted as *Problems of everyday life*. New York, 1973.
Trotskii, L. *Voprosy byta. Epokha 'kul'turnichestva' i eë zadachi*. 1923.
Tsereteli, K. D. *Yunost' ekrana*. Tbilisi, 1965.
Tsetkin, K. *Vospominaniya o Lenine*. 1966.
Tsimbal, S. *Raznye teatral'nye vremena*. Leningrad, 1969.
Tudor, A. *Theories of film*. London, 1974.
Turkin, V. K. *Iskusstvo kino i ego dramaturgiya*. 1958.
Ulam, A. B. *Lenin and the Bolsheviks*. London, 1969.
Uspenskii, V. *O.D.S.K. Organizatsiya i rabota yacheek i kruzhkov*. 1926.
Vainshtok, V., and Yakobzon, D. *Kino i molodëzh'*. Leningrad, 1926.

Velekhova, N. *Okhlopkov*. 1970.
Vendrovskaya, L. D. (ed.) *Vstrechi s Meierkhol'dom. Sbornik vospominanii*. 1967.
Verdone, M., and Amengual, B. *La FEKS*. Premier plan, no. 54, Paris, 1970.
Vertov, D. 'Kino-glaz', in *Na putyakh iskusstva*. 1925.
Vertova-Svilova, E. I., and Vinogradova, A. L. (eds.) *Dziga Vertov v vospominaniyakh sovremennikov*. 1976.
Vishnevskii, V. *Khudozhestvennye fil'my dorevolyutsonnoi Rossii*. 1945.
Volkov-Lannit, L. F. (ed.) *Aleksandr Rodchenko risuet, fotografiruet, sporit*. 1968.
Voznesenskii, A. *Iskusstvo ekrana. Rukovodstvo dlya kino-aktërov i rezhissërov*. Kiev, 1924.
Vygotskii, L. S. *Psikhologiya iskusstva*. 1968.
Wenden, D. J. *The birth of the movies*. London, 1975.
Woroszylski, W. *The life of Mayakovsky*. London, 1971.
Yurenev, R. N. *Alexandr Dovzhenko*. 1959.
Yurenev, R. N. '*Bronenosets Potëmkin*' *Sergeya Eizenshteina*. 1965.
Yurenev, R. N. (ed.) *Eizenshtein v vospominaniyakh sovremennikov*. 1974.
Yutkevich, S. I. *Kino – eto pravda 24 kadra v sekundu*. 1974.
Yutkevich, S. I. *Kontrapunkt rezhissëra*. 1960.
Yutkevich, S. I. *O kinoiskusstve. Izbrannoe*. 1962.
Yutkevich, S. I. *Razgadka poeziei*. 1968.
Zak, M. E. *Mikhail Romm i traditsii sovetskoi kinorezhissury*. 1975.
Zakhava, B. E. *Sovremenniki*. 1969.
Zetkin, C. *See* Tsetkin, K.
Zharov, M. *Zhizn', teatr, kino*. 1967.
Zhdan, V. N. (ed.) *Kratkaya istoriya sovetskogo kino*. 1969.
Zhurov, G. V. *Z minulogo kino na Ukraini 1896–1917*. Kiev, 1959.
Zorkaya, N. M. *Sovetskii istoriko–revolyutsionnyi fil'm*. 1962.

NEWSPAPERS AND PERIODICALS

Runs systematically examined

Apollon. St Petersburg/Petrograd, 1909–17.
Cine-Fono. 1907–18.
Ekran. 1921–2.
Ekran. 1923–30.
Ekran Kinogazety. 1925 (continued as *Sovetskii ekran* and subsequently as *Kino i zhizn'*, q.v.).
Ezhegodnik kino. 1956 onwards.
Iskusstvo. Kiev, 1922.
Iskusstvo. 1923–8.
Iskusstvo kino. 1936–41; 1945 onwards (formerly *Proletarskoe kino* and *Sovetskoe kino*, q.v.).
Iz istorii kino. 1958 onwards.
Khudozhestvennaya zhizn'. 1919–20.
Kino. 1922–3.
Kino. Leningrad, 1925.
Kino. 1926–41 (formerly *Kino-Gazeta*, q.v.).
Kino i kul'tura. 1929–30.
Kino i zhizn'. 1929–30 (formerly *Ekran Kinogazety* and *Sovetskii ekran*, q.v.).
Kino, teatr, sport. Petrograd, 1923.
Kino-Byulleten'. 1918.
Kino-Fot. 1922–3.

Kino-Front. 1926–8 (formerly *Kinozhurnal A.R.K.*, q.v.).
Kino-Gazeta. 1923–6 (continued as *Kino*, q.v.).
Kino-Gruzii. Tiflis, 1925.
Kinonedelya. Leningrad, 1924–5 (published simultaneously in Moscow and Berlin).
Kino-teatr. 1918–19.
Kinoteatral'nyi vestnik po Ekaterinoslavu. Ekaterinoslav, 1925.
Kino-zhizn'. 1922–3.
Kinozhurnal A.R.K. 1925–6 (continued as *Kino-Front*, q.v.).
Kommunisticheskaya revolyutsiya. 1920–35 (formerly *Vestnik agitatsii i propagandy*, q.v.).
Krasnyi arkhiv. 1922–41.
Kul'turnyi front. 1924–30.
Lef. 1923–5.
Makhovik. Zlatoust, 1923–6.
Mir ekrana. 1918.
Molodaya gvardiya. 1922–41.
Novyi Lef. 1927–8.
Novyi zritel'. 1924–9.
Politrabotnik. 1920–4.
Pravda. 1917–30.
Proektor. 1915–18.
Proletarskaya kul'tura. 1918–19.
Proletarskoe kino. 1925 (formerly *Proletkino*, q.v.).
Proletarskoe kino. 1931–2 (continued as *Sovetskoe kino* and *Iskusstvo kino*, q.v.).
Proletkino. 1923–4 (continued as *Proletarskoe kino*, q.v.).
Proletkino Povolzh'ya. Saratov, 1923.
Prozhektor. 1923–5.
Sovetskii ekran. 1925–9 (formerly *Ekran Kinogazety*, and continued as *Kino i zhizn'*, q.v.).
Sovetskoe kino. 1925–8.
Sovetskoe kino. 1933–5 (formerly *Proletarskoe kino*, and continued as *Iskusstvo kino*, q.v.).
Teatr. issues for 1915 only.
Teatral'naya Moskva. 1921–2.
Teatral'naya prodagitatsiya. 1920.
Vestnik agitatsii i propagandy. 1920–1 (continued as *Kommunisticheskaya revolyutsiya*, q.v.).
Vestnik kinematografii. 1917.
Vestnik kinematografov v S. Peterburge. St Petersburg, 1908.
Voprosy kinoiskusstva. 1956 onwards.
Zhizn' iskusstva. Petrograd/Leningrad, 1918–29.
Zrelishcha. 1922–4.
Zrelishcha. Sverdlovsk, 1925–6.
Zrelishcha Samary. Teatr, kino, muzyka. Samara, 1927.

Articles specifically consulted

Agadzhanova, A. '1905 god', *Sovetskii ekran*, 6 October 1925, 3–5.
'Agitpoezdki M. I. Kalinina v gody grazhdanskoi voiny', *Krasnyi arkhiv*, 1938, no. 1 (86), 93–168.
Aksel'rod, L. 'Dokumenty po istorii natsionalizatsii russkoi kinematografii', *Iz istorii kino*, 1 (1958), 25–37.

Aksënov, I. A. '*Stachka*', *Zhizn' iskusstva*, 23 April 1925, 15.
Alpers, B. 'Put' FEKS'ov', *Kino i zhizn'*, 20 December 1929.
Anoshchenko, A. 'Kinokoki', *Kinonedelya*, 19 February 1924, 2.
Anoshchenko, A. 'Kinomonopoliya, sindikat i regulirovanie kino', *Zhizn' iskusstva*, 11 September 1923, 22.
Antokol'skii, P. 'O kino i teatre', *Novyi zritel'*, 15 January 1924, 11.
Aranovich, D. 'Sovremennyi kinoplakat', *Sovetskii ekran*, 12 July 1927, 13–14.
Ardov, V. 'O kino-patriotizme i kino-teoal'yanse', *Novyi zritel'*, 2 September 1924, 9.
Arkovets, 'A.R.R.K. nuzhno reorganizovat'', *Kino i zhizn'*, 1 February 1930.
Arsen, A. 'Sotsial'noe znachenie kartiny *Po zakonu*', *Kino-Front*, 1926, no. 9/10 (no date), 28–31.
Arvatov, B. 'Agit-kino', *Kino-Fot*, 8–15 September 1922, 2.
Arvatov, B. 'Teatr ili kino ili teatr i kino', *Novyi zritel'*, 26 April 1927, 4–5.
Aseev, N. '*Bronenosets Potëmkin*', *Sovetskii ekran*, 5 January 1928, 4.
Astaf'eva, M. 'Dekret, prochitannyi arkhitektorom', *Iskusstvo kino*, March 1969, 16–19.
Aumont, J. 'Un rêve soviétique', *Cahiers du cinéma*, 271 (November 1976), 26–44.
Aumont, J., Bonitzer, P., Narboni, J., and Oudart, J.-P. '*La Nouvelle Babylone*. La metaphore "commune"', *Cahiers du cinéma*, 230 (July 1971), 15–21, and 232 (October 1971), 43–51.
Babishkin, O. 'Nasha *Zemlya*', *Novini kinoekranu*, May 1970, 11.
Balázs, B. 'O budushchem fil'my', *Kino*, 6 June 1926, 3.
Barale, F. 'Groupes et classes sociales en Russie soviétique de 1917 à 1925 à travers les films de l'époque', *Cahiers du monde russe et soviétique*, XVII (1976), no. 2/3 (April/September), 249–85.
Barshak, O. 'O perspektivakh A.R.K.', *Kinozhurnal A.R.K.*, 1925, no. 9 (September), 32.
Barthes, R. 'Le troisième sens. Notes de recherche sur quelques photogrammes de S. M. Eisenstein', *Cahiers du cinéma*, 222 (July 1970), 12–19.
Belyaev, V. 'Kinofikatsiya muzyki', *Zhizn' iskusstva*, 10 March 1929, 3.
Benjamin, W. 'L'oeuvre d'art à l'époque de sa reproduction mécanisée', *Zeitschrift für Sozialforschung* (Paris), 1936, no. 1, 40–63.
Beskin, O. 'Mesto kino', *Sovetskoe kino*, 1927, no. 1 (January), 1.
Blyakhin, P. 'K itogam kino-sezona 1927–28 goda', *Kino i kul'tura*, 1929, no. 2 (February), 3–4.
Blyakhin, P. 'K partsoveshchaniyu', *Novyi zritel'*, 13 December 1927, 14.
Blyum, V. 'O "prirode" kino', *Zhizn' iskusstva*, 28 December 1926, 9–10.
Blyum, V. 'Protiv "teatra durakov" – za kino', *Zhizn' iskusstva*, 28 October 1924, 3–4.
'Bol'noe mesto nashego kino-dela', *Zhizn' iskusstva*, 13 October 1925, 1.
Boltyanskii, G. M. 'Iskusstvo budushchego', *Kino*, 1922, no. 1/2, 6–7.
Boltyanskii, G. M. 'K fil'movomu golodu v predstoyashchem sezone', *Pravda*, 13 August 1926.
Boltyanskii, G. M. 'Kino i sovetskaya obshchestvennost'', *Zhizn' iskusstva*, 7/10 November 1925, 15.
Boltyanskii, G. M. 'Kino-khronika', *Pravda*, 15 August 1923.
Boltyanskii, G. M. 'Na puti k industrial'nomu kino-VUZu', *Zhizn' iskusstva*, 26 April 1927, 3.
Boltyanskii, G. M. 'Teoriya i pratika kinokov', *Sovetskoe kino*, 1926, no. 4/5.

Boltyanskii, G. M. 'Velikaya Oktyabr'skaya sotsialisticheskaya revolyutsiya i rozhdenie sovetskogo kinoiskusstva', *Iz istorii kino*, 2 (1959), 63–116.

Boltyanskii, G. M. 'Vozrozhdenie kinematografii i eë "spasiteli"', *Ekran*, 25 April 1922, 11.

Boltyanskii, G. M. 'Vsemirnyi sprut', *Ekran*, 28 March 1922, 11.

Boltyanskii, G. M. 'Zadachi kinokhroniki i formy rabot', *Pravda*, 4 August 1923.

Bonch-Bruevich, V. 'Lenin i kino – Po lichnym vospominaniyam', *Kino-Front*, 1927, no. 13/14 (no date), 2–5.

Bonitzer, P. 'Les machines e(x)tatiques', *Cahiers du cinéma*, 271 (November 1976), 22–5.

Brik, O. 'Protivokinoyadie', *Novyi Lef*, 1927, no. 2 (February), 28.

Cahiers du cinéma. Special numbers: 'Russie: Années vingt', 220/221 (May/June 1970); 'S. M. Eisenstein', 226/227 (January/February 1971).

Chaikovskii, V. 'Kak ya byl izdatelem pervoi kino-gazety', *Sovetskii ekran*, 11 December 1927, 5.

'*Le cuirassé Potemkine*', *L'avant-scène du cinéma*, no. 11, 15 January 1962, 1–25.

Davydov, I. 'O tsentralizatsii kino-seti', *Novyi zritel'*, 15 August 1927, 8.

'Deklaratsiya Assotsiatsii revolyutsionnoi kinematografii', *Pravda*, 27 February 1924.

'Dela kinematograficheskie', *Pravda*, 16 February 1924.

Denisov, K. 'Meshchanstvo v kino', *Sovetskii ekran*, 29 January 1927, 3.

Dmitriev, V. 'Teatr i kino', *Novyi zritel'*, 14 July 1925, 3.

'Doloi!', *Sovetskii ekran*, 26 June 1928, 3.

Drozdowski, B. 'Historia rewolucji i legenda rewolucji', *Kino* (Warsaw), 1972, no. 7 (July), 38–43.

'Dukh Banko', '"Velikii" glukhonemoi', *Zhizn' iskusstva*, 18 December 1923, 21.

Dymov, S. 'Sovetizatsiya kino', *Zhizn' iskusstva*, 8 March 1927, 9.

Efremov, M. 'Organizatsionnye voprosy kino', *Zhizn' iskusstva*, 21 February 1928, 2.

Eizenshtein, S. M. 'Bela zabyvaet nozhnitsu', *Kino*, 6 June 1926.

Eizenshtein, S. M. 'Chto govoryat o *Bronenostse Potëmkine*', *Sovetskii ekran*, 1926, no. 2, 10.

Eizenshtein, S. M. 'Daësh' Gosplan', *Kino-Front*, 1927, no. 13/14 (no date), 6–8.

Eizenshtein, S. M. 'Dva cherepa Aleksandra Makedonskogo', *Novyi zritel'*, 31 August 1926, 10.

Eizenshtein, S. M. 'K voprosu o materialisticheskom podkhode k forme', *Kinozhurnal A.R.K.*, 1925, no. 4/5 (April/May), 5–8.

Eizenshtein, S. M. 'Literatura i kino', *Na literaturnom postu*, 1928, no. 1 (January), 71–3.

Eizenshtein, S. M. 'Montazh attraktsionov', *Lef*, 1923, no. 3 (June/July), 70–5.

Eizenshtein, S. M. 'Perspektivy', *Iskusstvo*, 1928, no. 1/2 (January/February).

Eizenshtein, S. M., and Aleksandrov, G. M. 'Eksperiment, ponyatnyi millionam', *Sovetskii ekran*, 5 February 1929, 6–7.

Eizenshtein, S. M., Pudovkin, V. I., and Aleksandrov, G. M. 'Zayavka', *Zhizn' iskusstva*, 5 August 1928, 4–5.

Erofeev, V. 'K organizatsii kino-proizvodstva', *Pravda*, 13 September 1923.

Erofeev, V. 'Kino-glaz', *Kino-gazeta*, 21 October 1924.

Erofeev, V. 'Ne kino-arkhiv a kino-gazeta', *Pravda*, 21 September 1923.

Fel'dman, K. *'Arsenal', Sovetskii ekran,* 12 March 1929, 5.
Ferro, M. '1917: History and cinema', *Journal of Contemporary History,* 3 (1968), no. 4, 45–61.
Fevral'skii, A. 'Rabochii klub na ekrane', *Pravda,* 28 February 1927.
Fevral'skii, A. 'Tendentsii iskusstva i "Radio-Glaz"', *Molodaya gvardiya,* 1925, no. 7 (July), 166–8.
Filippov, B. 'Nashi prakticheskie zadachi', *Kino-nedelya,* 1924, no. 13, 8.
Filippov, B. 'Zagadki Sovkino', *Zhizn' iskusstva,* 20 December 1927, 4–5.
'Fil'me grozit opasnost'. Beseda s Dzigoi Vertovym', *Novyi zritel',* 27 January 1929, 13.
Fitzpatrick, S. 'Cultural Revolution in Russia, 1928–32', *Journal of Contemporary History,* 9 (1974), no. 1, 33–52.
Freilikh, S. 'Zhazhda eposa', *Iskusstvo kino,* September 1974, 39–49.
Fridman, Yu. A. 'Dvizhenie pomoshchi mezhdunarodnogo proletariata Sovetskoi Rossii v 1921–1922 godakh', *Voprosy istorii,* 1958, no. 1 (January), 85–101.
Gak, A. M. 'K istorii sozdaniya Sovkino', *Iz istorii kino,* 5 (1962), 131–44.
Gak, A. M. 'Kinoorganizatsii Petrograda v 1918–1925gg.', *Iz istorii kino,* 4 (1961), 56–83.
Gak, A. M. 'Lenin i kino. Poiski novykh dokumentov', *Iz istorii kino,* 7 (1968), 7–20.
Gan, A. '10-ya Kino-Pravda', *Kino-Fot,* 5–12 October 1922, 4.
Gan, A. 'Kinematograf i kinematografiya', *Kino-Fot,* 25–31 August 1922, 1.
Gan, A. 'Priznanie Kinokov', *Zrelishcha,* 1924, no. 77, 12.
Gartsman, M. 'U poroga kino-stroitel'stva', *Zhizn' iskusstva,* 31 January 1928, 7.
Gerasimov, S. A. 'Fabrika ekstsentricheskogo aktëra', *Iskusstvo kino,* January/February 1940, 96–7.
Gets, S. 'Ukrainskaya kinematografiya na perelome', *Zhizn' iskusstva,* 7 April 1929, 18–19.
Giercke, C. 'Dziga Vertov', *Afterimage* (London), April 1970, no p. nos.
Ginzburg, S. S. 'Rozhdenie russkogo dokumental'nogo kino', *Voprosy kinoiskusstva,* 4 (1960), 238–75.
Glebova, T. 'Dal'neishee', *Kino-Fot,* 10 December 1922, 3.
Gofman, Ts. 'K istorii pervogo agitparokhoda V.Ts.I.K. "Krasnaya zvezda"', *Voprosy istorii,* 1948, no. 9 (September), 63–70.
Goldobin, A. 'Blizhaishie zadachi kino', *Proletarskoe kino,* 1 February 1925, 4.
Goldobin, A. 'Chto delaetsya dlya sovetskoi kinematografii', *Pravda,* 26 March 1924.
Goldobin, A. 'Nashe kino i ego zritel'', *Novyi zritel',* 10 February 1925, 5–6.
Goldobin, A. 'O polozhenii kinematografii', *Pravda,* 1 April 1924.
Goldobin, A. 'Opyt Goskino v bor'be na kino-fronte', *Zhizn' iskusstva,* 8 July 1924, 13–14.
Gordin, Yu. 'Perspektivy kino-sezona', *Zhizn' iskusstva,* 15 September 1929, 12–13.
Gor'kii, M. (Pacatus), 'Beglye zametki', *Nizhegorodskii listok,* 4 July 1896.
Gorn, B. 'Kino v derevne', *Novyi zritel',* 21 June 1927, 3.
Goslavskaya, S. 'So stranitsy 293-i (iz memuarov)', *Iskusstvo kino,* May 1969, 136–45.
Grinfel'd, F. 'K partsoveshchaniyu o kino-rabote', *Zhizn' iskusstva,* 6 December 1927, 5.
Groshev, A. N. 'Vysshaya kinoshkola strany', *Iskusstvo kino,* October 1969, 41–4.

Gusman, B. 'Godovshchina Assotsiatsii Revolyutsionnoi Kinematografii', *Novyi zritel'*, 19 May 1925, 12.

Gusman, B. 'O kino-glaze', *Pravda*, 15 October 1924.

Gusman, B. 'Pervye podarki kul'turnogo Zapada', *Pravda*, 24 December 1922.

Gvozdev, A. 'Novaya pobeda sovetskogo kino. (*Bronenosets Potëmkin* i *Teatral'naya Oktyabr'*)', *Zhizn' iskusstva*, 26 January 1926, 7–8.

Habryn, A. 'Przed Wiertowem. O narodzinach radzieckej publicystiki filmowej', *Kino* (Warsaw), 1973, no. 11 (November).

Iezuitov, N. 'Kinoiskusstvo dorevolyutsionnoi Rossii', *Voprosy kinoiskusstva*, 2 (1957), 252–307.

I.K.S. 'Pyatiletie A.R.R.K. (1924–29 god)', *Novyi zritel'*, 26 May 1929, 14.

Ionov, I. 'Rabochie, bud'te agitatorami za kino!', *Zhizn' iskusstva*, 7–10 November 1925, 8–10.

'K predstoyashchemu kino-soveshchaniyu', *Zhizn' iskusstva*, 27 September 1927, 1.

'K 50-letiyu Leninskogo dekreta o kino', *Iskusstvo kino*, August 1969, 141–56.

'K voprosu o kinofikatsii derevni', *Sovetskoe kino*, 1925, no. 1 (January).

Katsigras, A. I. 'K voprosu o kino dlya derevni', *Pravda*, 10 August 1924.

Katsigras, A. I. 'K voprosu o kino dlya derevni', *Zhizn' iskusstva*, 19 August 1924, 18.

Katsigras, A. I. 'Kino i derevnya. Sovkino dlya derevni ili derevnya dlya Sovkino', *Sovetskoe kino*, 1926, no. 1 (February).

Kaufman, N. 'Kinoki', *Sovetskii ekran*, 18 January 1929, 8–9.

Kayurov, A. 'Politika prokata Sovkino', *Novyi zritel'*, 8 February 1927, 13.

Khanzhonkova, V. 'Iz vospominanii o dorevolyutsionnom kino', *Iz istorii kino*, 5 (1962), 120–30.

Khersonskii, Kh. 'Bor'ba faktov, vzglyadov, idei i sposobov vozdeistviya', *Kino-Front*, 1926, no. 9/10 (no date), 21–6.

Khersonskii, Kh. 'Dramaturgiya, kak metod kino-iskusstva', *Kinozhurnal A.R.K.*, 1925, no. 1 (January), 14–17.

Khersonskii, Kh. 'Kinointerventsiya', *Pravda*, 2 June 1926.

Khersonskii, Kh. 'O dramaturgicheskoi tekhnike amplua aktëra', *Kinozhurnal A.R.K.*, 1925, no. 2 (February), 19–22.

Khersonskii, Kh. 'Ot *Stachki* k *Potëmkinu*', *Kinozhurnal A.R.K.*, 1926, no. 2 (February), 3–5.

Khrenov, N. 'K probleme sotsiologii i psikhologii kino 20kh. godov', *Voprosy kinoiskusstva*, 17 (1976), 163–84.

'Kinofikatsiya derevni', *Zhizn' iskusstva*, 11 May 1926, 1.

'Kinofikatsiya Leningradskoi oblasti', *Zhizn' iskusstva*, 29 July 1928, 1.

'Kino-propaganda', *Zhizn' iskusstva*, 3 November 1925, 1.

Kirshon, V. 'Doloi obyvatel'skuyu fil'mu!', *Kino-Front*, 1926, no. 2/3 (no date), 17.

Kleiman, N. I. 'Tol'ko pyatnadtsat' kadrov', *Iskusstvo kino*, March 1976, 81–95.

Kogan, P. S. 'Kino i literatura', *Sovetskoe kino*, 1925, no. 4/5.

Kozintsev, G. M. 'Glubokii ekran. (Glavy iz knigi)', *Novyi mir*, 1961, no. 3, 141–72.

Kozlov, L. K. 'Metodologicheskie problemy istorii sovetskogo kino', *Iskusstvo kino*, June 1972, 122–4.

Krasovskii, Yu. 'Kak sozdalsya fil'm *Oktyabr'*', *Iz istorii kino*, 6. 1965), 40–62.

Kresin, M. L. 'Iz vospominanii starogo kinorabotnika', *Iz istorii kino*, 1 (1958), 92–6.

'Krizis nashego kinoproizvodstva', *Zhizn' iskusstva*, 10 August 1926, 1.
Krupskaya, N. K. 'O fil'me *Oktyabr'*', *Pravda*, 9 February 1928.
Krupskaya, N. K. 'Po gradam i vesyam sovetskoi respubliki', *Novyi mir*, 1960, no. 11, 113–30; republished in *Pedagogicheskie sochineniya*, vol. 11, 1963, 729–57.
Krupskaya, N. K. 'Rech' t. Krupskoi na Vseross. Konferentsii Obshchestva Druzei Sovetskoi Kinematografii', *Zhizn' iskusstva*, 31 January 1928, 7.
Kuleshov, L. V. 'Amerikanshchina', *Kino-Fot*, 25–31 August 1922, 14–15.
Kuleshov, L. V. 'Chto nado delat'?', *Kino-Gazeta*, 26 September 1923.
Kuleshov, L. V. 'Chto nado delat'', *Kino i kul'tura*, 1930, no. 11/12 (November/December), 8–15.
Kuleshov, L. V. 'Dvadtsat' let', *Iskusstvo kino*, March 1940, 47–8.
Kuleshov, L. V. 'Iskusstvo, sovremnnaya zhizn' i kinematografiya', *Kino-Fot*, 25–31 August 1922, 2.
Kuleshov, L. V. 'Iskusstvo svetotvorchestva', *Kino*, 1918, no. 12.
Kuleshov, L. V. 'Kamernaya kinematografiya', *Kino-Fot*, 8–15 September 1922, 3.
Kuleshov, L. V. '*Mister Vest*', *Zrelishcha*, 1924, no. 79, 14.
Kuleshov, L. V. 'Pryamoi put'', *Kino-Gazeta*, 25 November 1924.
Kuleshov, L. V. 'Souvenirs (1918–1920)', *Cahiers du cinéma*, 222 (July 1970), 20–5.
Kurs, A. 'Perspektivy kino', *Zhizn' iskusstva*, 7–10 November 1925, 14.
Lagorno, A. 'Meri Pikford i Duglas Ferbenks o *Potëmkine*', *Sovetskii ekran*, 8 June 1928, 7.
Latsis, A., and Keilin, L. 'Deti i kino', *Kommunisticheskaya revolyutsiya*, 1928, no. 5 (March), 76–82.
Lebedev, N. A. 'A.R.K.', *Pravda*, 3 October 1924.
Lebedev, N. A. 'Boevye dvadtsatye gody', *Iskusstvo kino*, December 1968, 85–99.
Lebedev, N. A. 'Da zdravstvuyet rabochii kino', *Pravda*, 6 December 1922.
Lebedev, N. A. 'Kino', *Pravda*, 3 January 1923.
Lebedev, N. A. 'Kino v provintsii', *Pravda*, 4 August 1923.
Lebedev, N. A. 'O kino-khronike', *Pravda*, 29 July 1923.
Lebedev, N. A. 'O kino-spetsialistakh', *Pravda*, 29 December 1922.
Lebedev, N. A. 'O Proletkino', *Pravda*, 8 May 1923.
Lebedev, N. A. 'Proletkino', *Pravda*, 27 December 1922.
Lebedev, N. A. 'Vnimanie kinematografu', *Pravda*, 14 July 1922.
Lemberg, A. G. 'Iz vospominanii starogo operatora', *Iz istorii kino*, 2 (1959), 117–31.
Leonidov, B. 'O stsenarnom golode', *Zhizn' iskusstva*, 19 August 1924, 8–9.
Levaco, R. 'Kuleshov', *Sight and Sound*, Spring 1971, 86–91, 109.
Likhachëv, B. S. 'Materialy k istorii kino v Rossii (1914–1916). (Publikatsiya S. S. Ginzburga)', *Iz istorii kino*, 3 (1960), 37–103.
Listov, V. 'Nachalo. Zametki o stanovlenii sotsialisticheskogo kino na sovetskom Vostoke', *Iskusstvo kino*, August 1970, 28–36.
Listov, V. 'O pis'me iz Petrograda, "Avtokino" i Vertove', *Iskusstvo kino*, January 1975, 109–18.
Listov, V. 'Propaganda on wheels', *Soviet Film*, no. 9 (148), September 1969.
Listov, V. 'U istokov sovetskogo kino', *Iskusstvo kino*, March 1969, 2–15.
Litvinov, A. 'Kino na Vostoke', *Kinonedelya*, 26 February 1924.
Lubitsch, E. (Lyubich, E.) 'Internatsional'nost' kino', *Kinonedelya*, 1924, no. 13, 3.

Lunacharskii, A. V. 'O revolyutsionnoi ideologii v kinodele', *Pravda*, 1 April 1924.
Lunacharskii, A. V. 'Pokhod protiv Charli Chaplina', *Vechernyaya Moskva*, 7 March 1927.
Lunacharskii, A. V. 'Produktsiya sovetskoi kinematografii s tochki zreniya eë ideinogo soderzhaniya', *Kommunisticheskaya revolyutsiya*, 1928, no. 4 (February), 46–54.
'Tov. Lunacharskii o kino', *Zhizn' iskusstva*, 24 January 1928, 2–3.
L'vov, A. 'Dokole zhe?', *Pravda*, 10 January 1924.
L'vunin, Yu., and Polyanskii, I. (eds.) 'Blagodarya lichnomu sodeistviyu V. I. Lenina. . .Novye dokumenty rasskazyvayut', *Iskusstvo kino*, January 1970, 3–16.
Lyubomirskii, O. 'Romantika kino', *Zhizn' iskusstva*, 26 August 1928, 4.
'Lyudi iskusstv o kinematografe', *Teatr*, 1915, no. 1755, 6.
Malevich, K. 'I likuyut liki na ekranakh', *Kinozhurnal A.R.K.*, 1925, no. 10 (October), 7–9.
Mallori, D. 'Krik "Beni Krika" ', *Sovetskii ekran*, 12 February 1927, 7.
Mal'tsev, K. 'K organizatsii Sovkino', *Kinozhurnal A.R.K.*, 1925, no. 1 (January), 2.
Mal'tsev, K. 'O sovetskom kino', *Kommunisticheskaya revolyutsiya*, 1928, no. 3 (February), 70–8.
Mamatova, L. 'A. V. Lunacharskii i razvitie sovetskogo kinoiskusstva,', *Iskusstvo kino*, November 1975, 72–88.
Mamatova, L. 'Protsess i skhema', *Iskusstvo kino*, January 1975, 118–38.
'Mastera o stsenarii (Nasha anketa)', *Kino-Front*, 1926, no. 9/10 (October), 12.
Mayakovskii, V. V. 'Kino i kiko', *Kino-Fot*, 5–12 October 1922, 5.
Mayakovskii, V. V. 'Otnoshenie segodnyashnego teatra i kinematografa k iskusstvu , *Kine-Zhurnal*, 1913, no. 17.
Mayakovskii, V. V. 'Teatr, kinematograf, futurizm', *Kine-Zhurnal*, 27 July 1913.
Meierkhol'd, V. E. 'O kinofikatsii teatra', *Zhizn' iskusstva*, 14 July 1929, 4–5.
Meshcheryakov, V. 'Kino v derevne', *Kommunisticheskaya revolyutsiya*, 1928, no. 4 (February), 55–62.
Messman, V. 'O zvukovoi fil'me', *Zhizn' iskusstva*, 30 September 1928, 4–5.
Michelson, A. '*The Man with the Movie Camera:* From magician to epistemologist', *Artforum*, March 1972, 63–72.
Milyavskii, B. L. 'Novoe o Mayakovskom', *Pamir*, 1973, no. 7 (July), 70–9.
Milyavskii, B. L. 'Pervyi stsenarii Mayakovskogo?!', *Literaturnaya gazeta*, 18 April 1973.
Molchanov, V. 'Kak rozhdalas' *Kinopravda*', *Pravda*, 7 November 1972.
Momus, 'Neobychainye pokhozhdeniya I. Erenburga', *Zrelishcha*, 1924, no. 77, 4–5.
Narboni, J. 'Le hors-cadre décide de tout', *Cahiers du cinéma*, 271 (November 1976), 14–21.
Nedobrovo, V. 'Devyatimesyachnyi balans kino-ekrana. Yazyk tsifr', *Zhizn' iskusstva*, 7 July 1925, 10–11.
Nedobrovo, V. 'K itogram kino-sezona', *Zhizn' iskusstva*, 15 June 1926, 19–20.
Nedobrovo, V. 'Kino pod znakom rekonstruktsii', *Zhizn' iskusstva*, 4 November 1929, 9–10.
Nedobrovo, V. 'Pochemu net geroya v sovetskom kino?', *Zhizn' iskusstva*, 16 August 1927, 8.

Nedobrovo, V. 'Romantika byta v kino', *Zhizn' iskusstva*, 14 December 1926, 5.
Nedobrovo, V. 'Samodeyatel'noe kino', *Zhizn' iskusstva*, 6 October 1929, 2.
'Novye vekhi', *Sovetskii ekran*, 21 June 1927, no p. nos.
'Novyi kurs Sovkino', *Sovetskii ekran*, 8 January 1929, 4–7.
'O *Kino-Pravde*. ("Vesennyi" vypusk i drugie)', *Pravda*, 25 May 1923.
'O kinostroitel'stve', *Pravda*, 22 August 1923.
'Octobre', *L'avant-scène du cinéma*, no. 74, October 1967, 1–54.
'*Oktyabr'*. (Itogi diskussii)', *Zhizn' iskusstva*, 27 May 1928, 8.
Oten, O. 'Kinokam', *Kino-Fot*, 19–25 September 1922, 9.
Ozerov, I. 'Pokushenie na ubiistvo kinematografii', *Vestnik kinematografii*, 1917, no. 123.
Padvo, M. 'Razmyshleniya u kino-pod"ezda', *Zhizn' iskusstva*, 18 May 1926, 7.
'Partiya i kino', *Kommunisticheskaya revolyutsiya*, 1928, no. 7 (April), 3–9.
Pavlov, G. 'Kino na okraine', *Sovetskii ekran*, 1 January 1927, 5.
Pertsov, V. '"Igra" i demonstratsiya', *Novyi Lef*, 1927, no. 11/12 (November/December), 35.
Pertsov, V. 'Literatura i kino', *Zhizn' iskusstva*, 12 July 1927, 10–11.
Pertsov, V. 'Sotsial'noe znachenie kartiny *Po zakonu*', *Kino-Front*, 1926, no. 9/10 (no date), 27–8.
Petrov-Bytov, P. 'U nas net sovetskoi kinematografii', *Zhizn' iskusstva*, 21 April 1929, 8.
Pikel', P. 'Ot khvostizma k chëtkoi klassovoi linii', *Zhizn' iskusstva*, 3 April 1928, 2–3.
Piotrovskii, A. 'Budem maksimalistami!', *Zhizn' iskusstva*, 13 December 1927, 4.
Piotrovskii, A. 'Detskoe kino pered novoi opasnost'yu', *Zhizn' iskusstva*, 14 October 1928, 6–7.
Piotrovskii, A. 'Dialekticheskaya forma v kino i front kino-reaktsii', *Zhizn' iskusstva*, 13 October 1929, 3.
Piotrovskii, A. 'Eshchë raz o "romantike"', *Zhizn' iskusstva*, 26 August 1928, 5.
Piotrovskii, A. 'Est' li krizis v sovetskoi kinematografii?', *Zhizn' iskusstva*, 25 November 1928, 6–7.
Piotrovskii, A. 'Kak zhe byt' s kul'turfil'mom?', *Zhizn' iskusstva*, 5 August 1928, 6–7.
Piotrovskii, A. 'Kinematografiya temy', *Zhizn' iskusstva*, 8 September 1929, 6.
Piotrovskii, A. 'Kino i pisateli', *Zhizn' iskusstva*, 17 January 1928, 6.
Piotrovskii, A. 'Kino romantiki i geroiki', *Zhizn' iskusstva*, 29 July 1928, 2.
Piotrovskii, A. 'Kino 1928 goda', *Zhizn' iskusstva*, 4 November 1928, 8–9.
Piotrovskii, A. 'Kinofikatsiya muzyki', *Zhizn' iskusstva*, 24 February 1929, 4.
Piotrovskii, A. 'Kinofikatsiya teatra. (Neskol'ko obobshchenii)', *Zhizn' iskusstva*, 22 November 1927, 4.
Piotrovskii, A. 'Kino-mul'tiplikatsiya', *Zhizn' iskusstva*, 21 April 1929, 9.
Piotrovskii, A. 'Ob "ideologii" i "kommertsii"', *Zhizn' iskusstva*, 27 December 1927, 5.
Piotrovskii, A. '*Oktyabr'* dolzhen byt' peremontirovan!', *Zhizn' iskusstva*, 27 March 1928, 12.
Piotrovskii, A. 'Platforma Petrova-Bytova i sovetskaya kinematografiya', *Zhizn' iskusstva*, 12 May 1929, 4.
Piotrovskii, A. 'Spornye mysli. Budem maksimalistami!', *Zhizn' iskusstva*, 13 December 1927, 4.

Piotrovskii, A. 'Zapadnichestvo v nashem kino', *Zhizn' iskusstva*, 30 June 1929, 7.
Plastinin, N. 'Chego zhdët sovetskaya kinematografiya?', *Pravda*, 16 March 1924.
Plastinin, N. 'Da dokole zhe?', *Pravda*, 16 February 1924.
Podol'skii, S. 'Puti sovetskogo kino', *Zhizn' iskusstva*, 19 May 1929, 2–3.
Poluyanov, P. 'Kino i teatr – vragi', *Novyi zritel'*, 19 February 1924, 9–10.
Popov, A. 'O vzaimootnosheniyakh kino i teatra', *Zhizn' iskusstva*, 28 February 1928, 7.
Potëmkin, I. 'O blizhaishchikh zadachakh O.D.S.K.', *Zhizn' iskusstva*, 6 April 1926, 5–6.
'Preduprezhdenie', *Kinozhurnal A.R.K.*, 1925, no. 10 (October), 1–2.
Preobrazhenskii, N. F. 'Vospominaniya o rabote V.F.K.O.', *Iz istorii kino*, 1 (1958), 85–91.
Pudovkin, V. I. 'K vosprosu zvukovogo nachala v fil'me', *Kino i kul'tura*, 1929, no. 5/6 (May/June), 3–5.
Pudovkin, V. I. 'Masterskaya Kuleshova', *Iskusstvo kino*, January/February 1940, 85–7.
Pudovkin, V. I. 'S. M. Eizenshtein. (Ot *Potëmkina* k *Oktyabryu*)', *Zhizn' iskusstva*, 14 February 1928, 2–3.
Radlov, S. 'Kino-drama ili kino-roman', *Kinonedelya*, 11 March 1924.
Radlov, S. 'Ugroza kinematografa', *Apollon*, 1917, no. 10, 46–8.
Rafes, M. 'O "kinoyazvakh"', *Pravda*, 16 March 1928.
Rakhmanova, O. 'O metode vospitaniya aktëra', *Kinozhurnal A.R.K.*, 1925, no. 6/7 (June/July), 11–12.
Rokotov, T. 'Pochemu malodostupen *Oktyabr'*?', *Zhizn' iskusstva*, 10 April 1928, 16–17.
Rokotov, T. 'Puti razvitiya sovetskogo kino', *Zhizn' iskusstva*, 2 August 1927, 3.
Room, A. 'Bytovaya i problemnaya fil'ma', *Zhizn' iskusstva*, 7 February 1928, 7.
Room, A. 'Kino i teatr', *Sovetskii ekran*, 19 May 1925, no p. nos.
Rovich, N. 'Bolezni kino', *Novyi zritel'*, 12 August 1924, 7–8.
Sadko, 'Kino-"teatr". V paroksizme kinoedstva', *Teatral'naya Moskva*, 13–18 June 1922, 7–8.
Sadoul, G. 'Actualité de Dziga Vertov', *Cahiers du cinéma*, 144 (June 1963), 23–31.
Sadoul, G. 'Entretien avec Frédéric Ermler', *Cahiers du cinéma*, 105 (March 1960), 1–11.
Sadoul, G. 'Progressivnye techeniya vo frantsuzskom kino (1900–1958)', *Voprosy kinoiskusstva*, 2 (1957), 358–418.
Samarin, K. 'Kino ne teatr', *Sovetskoe kino*, 1927, no. 2 (February).
Sats, N. 'Deti i kinematograf', *Novyi zritel'*, 14 October 1924, 6–8, and 4 November 1924, 8.
Sats, N. 'Deti zhdut svoyu fil'mu', *Zhizn' iskusstva*, 9 March 1926, 3.
Seleznëva, T. F. 'Teoreticheskoe nasledie S. M. Eizenshteina', *Iskusstvo kino*, October 1975, 110–23.
Serafimovich, A. 'Mashinnoe nadvigaetsya', *Cine-Fono*, 1911/12, no. 8.
Sergeev, B. (ed.), 'Agitpoezdki M. I. Kalinina v gody grazhdanskoi voiny', *Krasnyi arkhiv*, 1938, no. 1 (86), 93–165.
Serpukhovskii, V. 'Kino dlya detei', *Pravda*, 7 April 1923.
Shagin, V. 'Rabochii zritel' ob *Oktyabre*', *Zhizn' iskusstva*, 10 April 1928, 17.
Shapotnikov, V. 'Futurizm i teatr', *Maski*, 1912/13, no. 7/8, 29–33.

Shatov, L. 'Puti natsional'nogo kino-proizvodstva', *Zhizn' iskusstva,* 3 January 1928, 8.
Shentyapin, V. 'Kino-neuryaditsa i bor'ba s nei', *Pravda,* 29 June 1923.
Shentyapin, V. 'Moskovskaya kinokonferentsiya', *Pravda,* 14 July 1923.
Shentyapin, V. 'Nado pomoch' prodvinut' kartinu v massy', *Pravda,* 22 July 1923.
Shentyapin, V. 'Organizatsiya peredvizhnykh kino v derevne', *Kino,* 1923, no. 4 (June–September), 15–18.
Shentyapin, V. 'Peredvizhnye kino v derevne', *Pravda,* 12 June 1923.
Shershenevich, V. 'Boikot sovetskikh kompozitorov', *Sovetskii ekran,* 26 July 1927, 14.
Shershenevich, V. '"Kino"toe iskusstvo', *Zhizn' iskusstva,* 27 July 1926, 14–15.
Shklovskii, V. B. 'Dvorets, krepost' i kinematograf', *Zrelishcha,* 1924, no. 76, 14.
Shklovskii, V. B. 'Kinoki i nadpisi', *Kino,* 30 October 1926, 3.
Shklovskii, V. B. 'Kuda shagaet Dziga Vertov?', *Sovetskii ekran,* 10 August 1926, 4.
Shklovskii, V. B. 'Ob Esfiri Shub i eë kinematograficheskom opyte', *Iskusstvo kino,* May 1969, 109–16.
Shklovskii, V. B. 'Pis'mo k Charli Chaplinu', *Literaturnaya gazeta,* 1931, no. 12.
Shklovskii, V. B. 'Semantika kino', *Kinozhurnal A.R.K.,* 1925, no. 8 (August), 5.
Shklovskii, V. B. 'Sergei Eizenshtein i "neigrovaya fil'ma"', *Novyi Lef,* 1927, no. 4 (April), 34–5.
Shklovskii, V. B. 'Temperatura kino', *Sovetskii ekran,* 21 June 1927, 10.
Shub, E. I. 'Neigrovaya fil'ma', *Kino i kul'tura,* 1929, no. 5/6 (May/June), 6.
Skitalets, 'Zhizn' na polotne', *Gazeta-kopeika,* 26 November 1909.
Slivkin, A. 'Tov. Krasin i kino', *Zhizn' iskusstva,* 7 December 1926, 2–3.
Sokolov, I. V. 'Kuda idët sovetskoe kino?', *Sovetskii ekran,* 14 September 1926, 3.
Sokolov, I. V. 'Metody i forma', *Kino-Front,* 1926, no. 9/10 (no date), 15–17.
Sokolov, I. V. 'Metody igry pered kino-apparatom', *Kino-Front,* 1927, no. 5 (15 March), 10–14.
Sokolov, I. V. 'O postanovke stsenarnogo dela', *Kino-Front,* 1926, no. 1 (April), 5–8.
Sokolov, I. V. '*Shestaya chast' mira*', *Kino-Front,* 1927, no. 2 (1 February), 9–12.
Sokolov, I. V. 'Skrizhal' veka', *Kino-Fot,* 25–31 August 1922, 3.
Sokolov, I. V. 'Standartizatsiya kino-kritiki', *Kino-Front,* 1926, no. 2/3 (no date), 19–20.
Sollertinskii, I. 'Kino pod znakom rekonstruktsii', *Zhizn' iskusstva,* 4 November 1929, 9.
'Sovetskaya kinematografiya – edinyi organizm', *Sovetskii ekran,* 3 April 1928, 3.
Tanin, M. 'Daësh'. . .revolyutsionnyi "boevik"!', *Pravda,* 25 July 1923.
Timofeev, V. 'Kinofikatsiya derevni', *Zhizn' iskusstva,* 10 April 1928, 3.
Timofeev, V. 'Voprosy prokata', *Zhizn' iskusstva,* 10 January 1928, 7.
Timofeev, V. 'Za sovetskuyu kinoproektsionnuyu tekhniku', *Zhizn' iskusstva,* 14 October 1928, 1.
Tolkachëv, E. 'Vsyakii sam sebe Eizenshtein', *Sovetskii ekran,* 19 June 1928, 6–7.
Toporkov, A. '*Mister Vest*', *Zrelishcha,* 1924, no. 85, 10–11.

Toporkov, A. 'Sotsial'nyi stsenarii', *Kino,* 1923, no. 2 (6) (February/March), 5–7.
Trainin, I. 'Nuzhno peresmotret' vopros', *Pravda,* 11 March 1926.
Trainin, I. 'Voprosy kinostroitel'stva', *Zhizn' iskusstva,* 6 October 1925, 13–14.
Trainin, I. 'Zatrudnenie kino-promyshlennosti', *Zhizn' iskusstva,* 29 June 1926, 16.
Trauberg, L. 'Eksperiment, ponyatnyi millionam', *Zhizn' iskusstva,* 1 January 1929, 14.
Trauberg, L. 'Ryzhii – na pomoshch'!' *Kinonedelya,* 1924, no. 11/12, 5.
Trauberg, L. *et al.* 'Otkrytoe pis'mo kinorezhissërov', *Zhizn' iskusstva,* 27 May 1928, 9.
Tret'yakov, S. 'Fil'ma', *Kino-nedelya,* 1924, no. 13, 4.
Tret'yakov, S. 'Pobeda *Bronenostsa*', *Pravda,* 12 May 1926.
Tret'yakov, S. 'Stsenarnyi krizis', *Kino i kul'tura,* 1929, no. 3 (March), 6.
Trotskii, L. 'Vodka, tserkov' i kinematograf', *Pravda,* 12 July 1923.
Tynyanov, Yu. 'O FEKSakh', *Sovetskii ekran,* 2 April 1929, 10.
V.I., 'O nashem kinoprokate', *Pravda,* 11 September 1926.
Vainer, L. 'Kino-razgovory i kino-delo', *Pravda,* 29 September 1923.
Vainer, L. 'Nasha fil'ma i nash aktër', *Pravda,* 12 September 1923.
Vaks, L., and Yudin, N. 'V bor'be s vodkoi', *Novyi zritel',* 29 September 1929, 8–9.
Vertov, D. 'Fabrika faktov. (V poryadke predlozheniya)', *Pravda,* 24 July 1926.
Vertov, D. 'Kino-glaz', *Pravda,* 19 July 1924.
Vertov, D. 'Kinoki. Perevorot', *Lef,* 1923, no. 3 (June/July), 135–43.
Vertov, D. 'Kino-Pravda', *Kino-Fot,* 8 January 1923, 13.
Vertov, D. 'My. Variant manifesta', *Kino-Fot,* 25–31 August 1922, 11–12.
Vertov, D. 'Novoe techenie v kinematografii', *Pravda,* 15 July 1923.
Vertov, D. 'On i ya', *Kino-Fot,* 8–15 September 1922, 9–10.
Vertov, D. 'Otvet na pyat' voprosov', *Kino-Gazeta,* 21 October 1924.
'V.G.I.K. – 50. Tsifry i fakty', *Sovetskoe kino,* 1969, no. 41 (352).
Vil'ner, V. 'Vtoroe rozhdenie Beni Krika', *Sovetskii ekran,* 8 January 1927, 5.
Viner, A. 'O vliyanii kino na teatr', *Zhizn' iskusstva,* 27 March 1928, 8.
Vishnevskii, V. 'Fakty i daty iz istorii otechestvennoi kinematografii (mart 1917 – dekabr' 1920)', *Iz istorii kino,* 1 (1958), 38–81.
Vishnevskii, V. 'Fakty i daty iz istorii otechestvennoi kinematografii (1921–1924)', *Iz istorii kino,* 3 (1960), 125–53.
Vladimirov, M. 'O muzykal'noi illyustratsii v kino', *Zhizn' iskusstva,* 19 January 1926, 9–10.
Voevodin, P. 'Agitpoezd *Oktyabr'skaya revolyutsiya*', *Partiinaya zhizn',* 1957, no. 5 (May), 73–4.
Voznesenskii, A. 'Avtory dlya ekrana', *Ekran,* 14–21 February 1922, 12.
Voznesenskii, A. 'Otkrytoe pis'mo V. I. Nemirovich–Danchenko i K. S. Stanislavskomu', *Ekran,* 4 May 1922, 13.
Vul'fius, P. 'Kinofikatsiya muzyki', *Zhizn' iskusstva,* 3 March 1929, 4.
'Vysshaya kinoshkola strany. Beseda s A. N. Groshevym', *Iskusstvo kino,* October 1969, 41–4.
Vyvodtsov, S. 'Kino v Uzbekistane', *Sovetskii ekran,* 30 August 1927, 14.
Yakovlev, N. 'Kino dolzhno nakonets stat' nashim', *Proletarskoe kino,* 1 February 1925, 6.
Yakovlev, N. 'Nigilisty iz A.R.K.'a', *Sovetskii ekran,* 17 January 1928, 3.
Yakovlev, N. 'Sootnoshenie chastei', *Sovetskii ekran,* 12 February 1927, 3.

Yudin, N. 'Za derevenskii prokat "Sovkino" ', *Zhizn' iskusstva*, 27 July 1926, 14–15.

Yurenev, R. 'Teoriya intellektual'nogo kino S. M. Eizenshteina', *Voprosy kinoiskusstva*, 17 (1976), 185–225.

Yutkevich, S. I. 'V. E. Meierkhol'd i teoriya kinorezhissury', *Iskusstvo kino*, August 1975, 74–82.

'Za sovetskii stsenarii', *Zhizn' iskusstva*, 24 March 1929, 1.

Zil'bershtein, I. S. 'Nikolai II o kino: Po neopublikovannym materialam', *Sovetskii ekran*, 12 April 1927, 10.

Zinov'ev, A. 'Kino v derevne', *Pravda*, 9 August 1923.

Zlat, A. 'M. P. Efremov o zadachakh Sevzapkino', *Zhizn' iskusstva*, 11 September 1923, 23.

Zuvov, V. 'Puti kinematografa, kak iskusstva', *Zhizn' iskusstva*, 22 July 1924, 10–11.

INDEX

The system of transliteration used in this index is the same as that in the main text, except for the titles of newspapers, periodicals and films, which appear as in the Notes and Bibliography. There are separate entries for film directors and for their films, which are indexed under their translated title, the original Russian being given in parentheses. The Bolsheviks etc. appear under 'Party'.

The Adventures of Oktyabrina (*Pokhozhdeniya Oktyabriny*), 147–8
Aelita, 74
agit-trains, 48, 52–63 *passim*
agitation
  cinema and, 64
  propaganda and, 27–8
agitki, 28, 41, 48, 50, 51, 56, 57, 64, 80
agitpunkt, 52, 63
All-Russian Cinema Committee, 49
Andreev, Leonid, 14
The Anniversary of the Revolution (*Godovshchina revolyutsii*), 56
Anoshchenko, Alexander D., 133, 150
Antik, Pyotr, 17, 20
Arsenal, 97, 122
Arvatov, Boris I., 38
Association of Revolutionary Cinematography (A.R.K.), 115, 121, 150–1
Association of Workers of Revolutionary Cinematography (A.R.R.K.), 151
At the Red Front (*Na krasnom fronte*), 51, 55

Balázs, Béla, 140
Battleship Potemkin (*Bronenosets Potëmkin*), 28, 73, 94–6, 103, 116, 122, 138–42, 154, 174 n. 83
Bauer, Evgeny, 16, 23
Bay of Death (*Bukhta smerti*), 97
The Bear's Wedding (*Medvezh'ya svad'ba*), 95
Bed and Sofa (*Tret'ya Meshchanskaya*), 97, 110
Belenson, Alexander, 139
Benjamin, Walter, 37
The Big Wheel (*Chërtovo koleso*), 147, 149
blockade: Sovkino and V.U.F.K.U., 94, 117
Bogdanov, Pyotr A., 70
Boltyansky, Grigori, M., 25, 36–7, 130–1, 133
Bonch-Tomashevsky, M., 19
Brik, Osip, 34
Bukharin, Nikolai I., 93, 107
By the Law (*Po zakonu*), 135, 137–8, 149

Cabiria, 15
censorship, 4, 7–8, 21, 76, 112, 161 n. 123, 166 n. 28
Chaplin, Charles, 33, 65, 98, 148, 168 n. 7
Chardynin, Pyotr, 16
Chess Fever (*Shakhmatnaya goryachka*), 74
children, *see* juveniles
Chukovsky, Kornei, 6
Cibrario de Goden, Jacques Roberto, 72, 165 n. 14
Cine-Eye (group), *see* Vertov
Cine-Eye (*Kino-Glaz*) (film), 128
Cine-Fono, 18, 21
cinefication, 8, 87–8, 91, 101, 107, 120

cinema
  agitation and, 64
  agit-trains and, 52–63 *passim*
  alcoholism and, 9, 66, 79, 90, 105
  'Americanism', 38, 136, 147–8
  as art form, 1, 9, 14, 31–42, 124–51 *passim*
  countryside and, 31, 54, 68, 87–94, 100–1, 110–17, 172 n. 11, *see also* cinefication
  in the East, 68, 88
  economic propaganda and, 29
  effects on peasantry, 57–61, 68, 88, 90, 92, 130
  effects of sex and violence, 98–9
  February Revolution and, 15–25
  First World War and, 10–15
  fuel economy restrictions, 22, 24, 47
  government restrictions on, 6–7
  illiteracy and, 59, 87, 91
  literature and, 33–4, 39–40, 105, 125, 129
  machine and, 31, 35–9, 88, 91, 125–51 *passim*
  movement and, 31, 34, 124–51 *passim*
  nationalisation of, 43–50, 64–5
  and the new age, 32, 33, 35–40
  state monopoly of, 13–14, 44
  theatre and, 6–7, 17, 31–40 *passim*, 124–51 *passim*
  unionisation, 16–25
  universality of, 31–3, 35
  visual appeal of, 33, 35, 37–8, 118
  see also compilation film; documentary film; education; fiction film; film school; hoarding; juveniles; pornography; propaganda; taxation
compilation film, 134
congresses, *see* Party, Soviets
Constructivism, *see* Gan
Coogan, Jackie, 32
COQ, *see* KOK

Dementev, V. M., 13
The Devil's Wheel (*Chërtovo koleso*), see *The Big Wheel*
documentary film, 40–1, 124–34
Don Cossacks (*Donskie kazaki*), 5
Don Diego and Pelagea (*Don Diego i Pelageya*), 74
Dura Lex (*Po zakonu*), see *By the Law*
Dzerzhinsky, Felix, 99–100

Earth (*Zemlya*), 97
education: and cinema, 8, 10, 13, 14, 15, 18, 41–2, 159–60 nn. 54, 55
Eichenbaum, Boris M., 35
Eichenwald, Yuli I., 32
Eisenstein, Sergei M., 28, 33–4, 55, 56, 134–50
El Lissitsky, *see* Lisitsky
emigration, 16, 23, 46, 47, 51
The End of St Petersburg (*Konets Sankt-Peterburga*), 74, 97, 122, 142
entertainment film, 38, 68, *see also* fiction film
Ermolev, Iosif N., 11, 16, 20, 25
Erofeev, Vladimir, 77–8, 150
exports, 94, 106, 114, 170 n. 50, *see also* Germany

Factory of the Eccentric Actor (FEKS), 134, 144–51
Fairbanks, Douglas, 95, 98, 115, 174 n. 83, 183 n. 14
The Fall of the Romanov Dynasty (*Padenie dinastii Romanovykh*), 97, 113, 134
Fantômas, 15
FEKS, *see* Factory of the Eccentric Actor
Fevralsky, Alexander, 130
fiction film, 40–1, 124–51, *see also* entertainment film
film, *see* cinema
film school, 14, 51
'films without film', 51, 135–6
The Forty-First (*Sorok pervyi*), 74
Forward, Soviet! (*Shagai, Sovet!*) 96, 97, 174 n. 92
Fragment of Empire (*Oblomok imperii*), 97
Fritz Bauer, 97
Futurism: and cinema, 39, *see also* Brik, Mayakovsky, Meyerhold

Gan, Alexei, 39
Gardin, Vladimir R., 11, 16, 51
The General Line (*General'naya liniya*) see *The Old and the New*

Germany: reception of Soviet films, 94, 95
The Ghost that Never Returns (*Prividenie, kotoroe ne vozvrashchaetsya*), 97, 120
Glavkomtrud, 62
Glavpolitprosvet, 71, 111
Glavrepertkom, 112
Goldobin, A., 79, 80, 84–5, 88, 150
The Golem (*Der Golem*), 11
Gorbunov, Nikolai P., 70
Gorky, Maxim, 2, 57
Goskino, 71–87, 91
Goskinprom Gruzii, 73, 113
GOZ projector, 189
The Great Way (*Velikii put'*), 97, 134

The Happy Little Canary (*Vesëlaya kanareika*), 120
The Heir to Genghis Khan (*Potomok Chingis-khana*), see *Storm over Asia*
The History of the Civil War (*Istoriya Grazhdanskoi voiny*), 56
hoarding: of films, 23, 46, *see also* shortages
Hydro-Peat (*Gidrotorf*), 29, 56

Images of Red Russia (*Liki Krasnoi Rossii*), 94
'impeded form', 147
imports, 10–11, 15, 48, 65, 72, 74, 76, 95–6, 113, 118, 120, 122, 168 n. 8
  Lunacharsky on, 69, 80
  reduction by V.U.F.K.U., 94
  Sovkino and, 87
  state monopoly of, 46
  Vertov on, 127
  in workers' clubs, 92–3
'intellectual cinema', 140–1
International Workers' Aid, *see* Mezhrabpom

Judex, 23
juveniles: and cinema, 49, 78–9, 84, 88, 98–9, 120

Kadomtsev, Erazm S., 76
Kalinin, Mikhail I., 58
Keaton, Buster, 65, 95, 98
Kerzhentsev, Platon M. (*also* V.), 41–2, 111
Khanzhonkov, 5, 9–16 *passim*, 20, 25
Khapsaev, 16
Kharitonov, 11, 16, 23
Khersonsky, Khrisanf, 95, 141, 150
Khokhlova, Alexandra, 136–7
Kholodnaya, Vera, 16, 33, 161 n. 103
khozraschët, 69–70, 78
Kino, 36, 64, 116
Kino-Fot, 36, 38, 39, 130
Kino-Front, 40, 150
Kino-Gazeta, 39, 95
Kino i kul'tura, 121
Kino-Moskva, 71, 75, 79, 84
Kinonedelya (newsreels), 56
Kinonedelya (periodical), 44, 133
Kino-Pravda (newsreel), 130
Kino-Sever, 71
Kinozhurnal A.R.K., 141, 150
The Kiss from Mary Pickford (*Potselui Meri Pikford*), 74 168 n. 6
KOK (COQ) projector, 9, 89, 172 n. 17
Komarov, Sergei, 74
Komissarzhevsky, Fyodor, 23
Kommunisticheskaya revolyutsiya, 119
Komsomol'skaya pravda, 110
Kosior, S. V., 107, 109
Kozintsev, Grigori M., 15, 55, 144–50 *passim*
Krasin, Leonid B., 81, 82
Krinitsky, A. I., 107–9, 111–12, 117, 119
Krupskaya, Nadezhda K., 44, 46, 49, 59–60, 88, 141
Krylov, S. N., 110
Kuleshov, Lev V., 36, 51, 55, 134–8, 150
Kuleshov Workshop, 51, 56

Lace (*Kruzheva*), 97, 149
Lenin, Vladimir I., 50, 59, 65, 70, 131, 162 n. 1, 169 n. 23
  on agitation and propaganda, 27–8
  on cinema, 26, 29
  on consciousness, 26
  directive to Litkens, 41, 68, 70, 88
  funeral, filming of, 83
  as gradualist, 44

Lenin, Vladimir I. – *cont.*
on illiteracy, 27
and newsreels, 24, 54, 124
on revolution, 43
on Taylorism, 29
'Lenin' agit-train, 53
Leningrad, *see* Petrograd
Leshchenko, Dmitri I., 48, 49, 50
Lev Tolstoy and the Russia of Nicholas II (*Rossiya Nikolaya II i Lev Tolstoi*), 134
Lezhava, A. M., 70, 81
Liberman, L. A., 73, 76
Libken, Grigori, M., 6
Lisitsky, Lazar M. (*known as* El Lissitsky), 55
Litkens, E. A., 68, 70
Little Brother (*Bratishka*), 149
The Little Red Devils (*Krasnye d'yavolyata*), 39
Litvinov, Maxim, 62
The Living Corpse (*Zhivoi trup*), 159 n. 31
Lloyd, Harold, 148
Lumière, Louis, 1–4
Lunacharsky, Anatoly V., 40–51 *passim*, 68–9, 74, 77, 80, 82, 84, 95, 105–6, 110–11, 123, 131, 168 n. 7
Luré, S., 21
Lvov, A., 83

Maciste, 15, 16
Maltsev, Konstantin A., 114–15, 116, 117
The Man with the Movie Camera (*Chelovek s kinoapparatom*), 129
Mantsev, V. N., 77–82, 84, 85, 86, 90
Mayakovsky, Vladimir V.
and agit-trains, 55
on cinema as art form, 9, 14, 39
on *October*, 141
on Sovkino, 91
The Mechanics of the Brain (*Mekhanika golovnogo mozga*), 142
Meshcheryakov, Vladimir, 111, 112–13, 117, 119
Meyerhold, Vsevolod E., 14, 49
Mezhrabpom (*including* Mezhrabpomfilm *and* Mezhrabpom-Rus), 72, 73, 74, 82
Minervin, N. A., 48
Ministry of the Interior (before 1917): and cinema, 9, 13
Mir ekrana, 44, 46, 165 n. 13
mobile projectors, 88–9, 92, 94, 115, *see also* agit-trains, GOZ, KOK
Molodaya gvardiya, 130
Molotov, Vyacheslav, I., 59
montage, 34–5, 90, 126–51 *passim*
'montage of attractions', 138
Moscow Cinema Committee, 48, 49, 50
Moscow City Soviet, 17–18, 24, 25, 45–6, 48, 50, 72, 82
Mosjoukine, Ivan, 16, 23, 39
Mother (*Mat'*), 74, 97, 122, 142
movies, *see* cinema

Narkomfin, 84
Narkompros, 62, 77, 82, 89, 113
agitprop work, 54
All-Russian Photographic and Cinematographic Section (V.F.K.O.), 49–50, 51, 62, 64, 69–70, 71
cataloguing of films, 68
control over cinema, 45, 49, 65, 68
Extra-Mural Section, 43–4, 46, 48
Narkomvneshtorg, 70–1, 79, 82
naturshchiki, 51, 136–7
Nedobrovo, Vladimir, 96–7, 146–7
New Babylon (*Novyi Vavilon*), 97, 120, 122, 149, 151
newsreels, 80, 85, 131–4
before 1917, 4–5, 13
centralised control of, 78
February Revolution, 18, 21–4
Lenin on, 124
production of, 64
reception of in Central Asia, 92
Nicholas II, 1, 2, 10, 22
Nielsen, Asta, 32
N.K.V.D., 44, 99
Novoe vremya, 13
Novyi zritel', 38, 103, 104, 129

October (*Oktyabr'*), 73, 96, 111, 113, 122, 141, 142, 176 n. 51
'October Revolution' agit-train, 58–9
O.D.S.K., *see* Society of Friends of the Soviet Cinema

O.K.O., *see* United Society of Film Producers
The Old and the New (*Staroe i novoe*), 97, 138, 142
Olkhovy, B. S., 111
Our Hospitality, 95
The Overcoat (*Shinel'*), 149

Party
7th Congress, 67
8th Congress, 49, 67
9th Congress, 62, 67
10th Congress, 67
11th Congress, 67
13th Congress, 81–2, 84, 106, 117
15th Congress, 105, 106, 109
1928 Conference, 102–23
1929 resolution, 121
and Goskino resources, 75
on literature, 102
on propaganda, 67
rôle in cinema, 107, 109, 115, 116
V.Ts.I.K. and cinema, 53–5, 58, 61, 71, 77
Pathé, 4–16 *passim*, *see also* KOK
People's Commissariat for Enlightenment, *see* Narkompros
People's Commissariat for Finance, *see* Narkomfin
People's Commissariat for Foreign Trade, *see* Narkomvneshtorg
People's Commissariat for Internal Affairs, *see* N.K.V.D.
Perestiani, Ivan, 18
Petrograd Cinema Committee (P.O.F.K.O.), 45, 48–9, 50, 64, 69, *see also* Sevzapkino
Petrograd (later Leningrad) Soviet, 25, 45–6, 82
Petrov-Bytov, Pavel, 122
Pickford, Mary, 33, 65, 98, 115, 174 n. 83, 183 n. 14
Pikel, R., 118–19
Pionerskaya pravda, 114
Piotrovsky, Adrian, 104–5, 120–1, 122
Plastinin, N., 79, 150
Plekhanov, Georgi V., 27–8
P.O.F.K.O., *see* Petrograd Cinema Committee, Sevzapkino
politdom, 52
Poluyanov, Pavel, 32–3, 37
pornography: and cinema, 8, 13, 18, 22
poster: as propaganda weapon, 30–1
Pravda, 29, 40, 68, 74, 75, 77, 83, 84, 95, 150, 168 n. 4, 169 n. 22, 174 n. 90
Preobrazhensky, N. F., 49
private enterprise, 20–4, 46–8, 76, 83–4
Proektor, 16, 20, 25, 44
projectors, *see* GOZ, KOK, mobile projectors, shortages
Proletarskoe kino (periodical), 93
Proletkino, 72, 82, 84, 93
propaganda
and agitation, 27–8
and cinema, 30–1, 40–1, 65–9, 88, 100, 102–23 *passim*, 130
Protazanov, Yakov, 16, 23, 74, 161 n. 133
Pudovkin, Vsevolod I., 51, 56, 74, 134–5, 141–4
on sound, 35
Purishkevich, Vladimir M., 13

Rabkrin, 71, 77
Red Army cinemas, 71, 82, 87
'Red Star' agit-steamer, 57, 59–61
Robin Hood, 95
Room, Abram, 141
ROSTA, 31, 55

'screenplay crises', *see* shortages
Sevzapkino, 64, 71, 75, 76, 84, 91, *see also* Petrograd Cinema Committee
Shklovsky, Viktor B., 3, 39–40, 103, 131–2, 137, 144, 148
shortages
film stock and equipment, 10–11, 15, 46, 50, 64, 80, 104
'screenplay crises', 9, 34, 105, 118, 121
spare parts, 89
see also hoarding, 'films without film'
Shostakovich, Dmitri D., 149
Shub, Esfir I., 55, 56, 133–4
Shvedchikov, Konstantin, 110, 112, 117
A Sixth Part of the World (*Shestaya chast' mira*), 97, 128
Skobelev Committee, 12, 21–2, 25, 46, 48
Smirnov, N. I., 111, 114, 115–18, 120

Society of Friends of the Soviet Cinema (O.D.S.K.), 99–101, 114, 115, 150
Sokolov, Ippolit, 36, 128
sound film, 35, 143
Sovetskii ekran, 102–3, 116, 120, 121, 130
Sovetskoe kino, 41
Soviets
10th All-Russian Congress, 68–9
14th All-Russian Congress, 123
Sovkino, 74, 82–123 *passim*
Sovnarkom, 46, 70–1, 75, 76, 77, 78, 82, 90
Stalin, Joseph V., 64, 81, 105, 109
Stenka Razin (*Ponizovaya volnitsa*), 5
Storm over Asia (*Potomok Chingis-khana*), 74, 97, 120, 142
Stride, Soviet! (*Shagai, Sovet!*), see *Forward, Soviet!*
Strike (*Stachka*), 122, 141, 149
S.V.D., 97, 149
Svobodnaya Rossiya newsreel, 21–2

Tatlin, Vladimir E., 49
taxation: and cinema, 65, 76, 78, 79, 82, 84, 90–1, 105, 109, 112, 119
Ten Days that Shook the World, see *October*
Tenth Muse café, 19, 21
theatre
and cinema, 6–7, 17, 31–40 *passim*, 124–51 *passim*
as propaganda weapon, 30
Thiemann and Reinhardt, 10, 11, 15, 16
Third Meshchanskaya (*Tret'ya Meshchanskaya*), see *Bed and Sofa*
Tisse, Edward, 51, 56
Tolstoy, Lev N., 5–6, 159 n. 31
Trainin, Ilya P., 110, 151
Transatlantic, 16, *see also* Cibrario de Goden
Trotsky, Lev D., 53, 65–6
Tsyurupa, Alexander D., 78
Turkin, Nikandr, 19, 21
Turksib, 97
Tynanov, Yuri, 138

The Union for the Great Cause, see *S.V.D.*
Union of Cinema Mechanics, 20
Union of Employees in Cinema Theatres, Offices and Studios, 20
Union of Patriotic Cinematography, 18, 20, 24
Union of Piano Accompanists, 20
Union of Workers of the Fictional Cinema (S.R.Kh.K.), 19, 20, 21
Union of Workers in Cinema Enterprises, 20
United Society of Film Producers (O.K.O.), 20, 21, 23, 24, 43, 47
The Unusual Adventures of Mr West in the Land of the Bolsheviks (*Neobychainye priklyucheniya Mistera Vesta v strane Bol'shevikov*), 136–7

V.A.P.P., 115, 121
Vengerov and Gardin, 11, 14
Vertov, Dziga, 55–7, 124–34
Vesenkha, 49, 62, 70–1, 82, 99, 112
Vestnik kinematografii, 19
V.F.K.O., *see* Narkompros: All-Russian Photographic and Cinematographic Section
Voevodin, P., 70, 150
V.O.K.S., 114
Voznesensky, A., 33, 35
Vserabis, 47
V.Ts.I.K., *see* Party
V.U.F.K.U., 73, 92, 117, *see also* blockade

The White Eagle (*Belyi orël*), 97
Workers' and Peasants' Inspectorate, *see* Rabkrin
workers' clubs, 71, 72, 82, 87, 92–4, 100

Yutkevich, Sergei I., 144–50 *passim*

Zhizn' iskusstva, 77, 84, 94, 103–5, 118–22
Zvenigora, 113, 122